THE HATE GAME

THE HATE GAME
SCREAMING IN THE SILENCE

GARY TREW

Copyright and Disclaimer

Copyright © 2024 by Gary Trew

All rights reserved.

No portion of this book may be reproduced in any form without written permission from the publisher or author, except as permitted by Canadian copyright law.

Registration Number: 1214394

This memoir is a work of creative non-fiction. It reflects the author's recollections, interpretations, and opinions of events. All persons within are actual individuals; there are no composite characters. The names of some individuals have been changed to respect their privacy unless the matter was of public record. The author would like to acknowledge and thank those who have consented to be represented in this memoir. While the author has made every effort to provide an accurate account of events, certain facts and details may be subject to the limitations of memory. The views expressed in this memoir are solely those of the author and do not necessarily reflect the views or opinions of any individuals or organisations mentioned.

This memoir addresses sensitive topics such as sexual assault, the loss of a loved one, suicidal thoughts, verbal and physical abuse, and mention of the Holocaust. While the author has taken great lengths to ensure the subject matter is dealt with respectfully, it may be troubling for some readers. Discretion is advised.

Book Cover by Papillon Creative

Photographs are from the author's personal collection. Photo of the Knoll School/Business Park courtesy of Derek Mann (P.16)

First edition, 2024

*This memoir is dedicated to Denis, Gwen and Trevor.
Much loved; never forgotten.*

FOREWORD

I was honoured and excited when Gary asked me to write the foreword to his upcoming memoir. I wanted to write something that gave the reader an idea of who Gary is and what he means to those of us who have the pleasure of calling him our friend. Gary and I first met when I had the chance to mentor him through our work as social workers. Gary has also mentored me, though he may not have always known it. Most people know I have a bit of a twisted sense of humour, but I often wonder if Gary understands it even today. The first time I talked to Gary, he called me by my last name. I couldn't let it go and still enjoy calling him "Trew" occasionally.

Gary and I hit it off and I saw how he brought his past life experience to the job and how people connected quickly with him. His co-workers loved him too, and Gary brought heart, warmth, and a fun sense of humour to our office that was much needed.

Gary also has a way of building you up and helping others see their potential. I was applying for a leadership position and Gary played a big part in my success. He helped me prepare and didn't allow me to doubt myself. Gary has done that a few times over the years with me and others—another one of his many gifts.

I enjoyed working with Gary and hearing the stories from his past

FOREWORD

life growing up in England. Whether facing adversity as a child, surviving a helicopter accident in the navy, or making arrests as a bobby, you were always in for something interesting. Some stories are hilarious, while others will break your heart. What Gary's experiences offer more than anything, is a sense of hope.

Regarding his own family, Gary is a proud dad and now grandpa. Gary is all about his children and he often brought his experience of raising four girls to his work, making him relatable with clients.

I had a lot of laughs with Gary and also teased him any chance I got. Whenever I told Gary to speak English, he said I was not pronouncing things correctly. We still debate if it's "water" or "wataar." I once described Gary as being "passionate" about something, and he thought using the word passionate in the context I used it was a bit odd.

All teasing aside, I can't say enough how much I have appreciated Gary's support and friendship. He is a natural helper and caregiver. He always found a way (sometimes I don't know how) to support families and protect children with minimal legal process. I can't wait to read more about Gary's life. I know his story will make you bust a gut, shed a tear, and teach you a thing or two. So, sit back in your favourite cosy chair with your favourite drink and enjoy the adventure you are about to embark on about a man named Trew, I mean Gary...

Daryl Marceau (Acting Director/Team Leader,
Children & Family Services, British Columbia.)

I have known and been friends with Gary for nearly 30 years. He really is a special guy with a big heart who leaves a lasting impression with everyone he meets. In my years of working with Gary I was always amazed by how he could just connect with people from all ages, cultures, and backgrounds. My kids grew up playing with his kids and we spent many happy years doing fun and crazy stuff as families. Gary is especially gifted at connecting with young people, and has always been able to engage with those who have had troubled and painful backgrounds. I can honestly say that knowing Gary changed my life,

FOREWORD

and the work I do today has been largely shaped by his influence on my life.

REV. WYATT, CHELTENHAM, ENGLAND.

Through his humour and genuine compassion, Gary left an indelible mark on the young people in his care. His belief in them drew out strengths and abilities they didn't know they had and gave them the courage to keep going. He saw their resistance for what it was, and his patience and resolve allowed them to trust again. He transformed their lives from one of pain and confusion to one of hope. Working with Gary was a reminder that what's needed most is love, understanding, mercy, hope and forgiveness—these were never in short supply when he was around.

ANNE HAZELTON, SUPERVISOR OF CHILD AND YOUTH CARE,
HEBRON CENTRE, GOV'T OF NOVA SCOTIA.

We have been good friends with Gary for many years. He has a heart for youth and the hurting. He has a gift for relating to all ages, using his disarming sense of humour to break down walls and connect heart to heart. He has lived through some very difficult life situations over the years and has come through with even more insight into others' trauma and pain which has enabled him to relate to and counsel throughout his life. Gary can see the lighter side of things and continues to have the ability to bring humour and God's love as he touches and deals with hurting people and painful situations.

BILL & SUE, SINGING WATERS MINISTRIES, TORONTO.

I first met Gary when I was 18 years old and continue to be a friend of his family, I even considered myself a part of his family for many years because Gary made me feel so welcome. He was like that with children and young people—he has a big heart and always roots for the underdog

FOREWORD

and anyone who needs encouragement and support. He believes in you and gives you the courage you need to draw out your strengths. He is funny, and kids love to be around him, so much so that you could describe him as a kid magnet. And now that I am many years older, I know that Gary has been through a lot in his life, but he has never let that take away from his ability to be a fun and safe person to be around. It's amazing how much love and support he has to give to others when he has been through so much himself. But maybe it is precisely because of what he has been through that he cares so much for those who are hurting and need love the most. I am forever thankful for Gary and his family for the years I got to spend with them both in England and Canada.

Ms. Ash Admassu, Youth Worker/Teacher, London.

PREFACE

COMMENTS FROM EX-PUPILS OF THE KNOLL SCHOOL FOR BOYS

> I had many bad memories of the place, and I wish I had more happy ones. I hope I learned something from my time there, but I can only think of survival. (Anon.)

> In my first three days, I was picked on twice and had to fight to protect myself in a hallway and in the playground. Just after the second fight—I should say it was more like an ambush—I was singularly blamed by a random passing teacher for starting the fight. The b*****d didn't even ask for my side of the story. (C.)

> P.E. teachers were special sadists at "Knollditz." Certain kids really suffered at their hands. I remember one instance when a rotund lad called B struggled to vault over the horse. Mr "Marine" made him keep trying in front of the whole class, ritually humiliating him in the process. The poor kid was in tears at the end of the lesson. (Anon.)

PREFACE

> Hippo was a dead shot with a piece of chalk; he could bounce it off your forehead from the other side of a classroom. (D.)

> Hippo was a sadistic bastard. (R.)

> In my last year (1974), I was lined up outside a classroom, and out of the blue, a guy, who I think was named "R," appeared right in front of me and thumped me hard squarely in the face. I fell to the floor—the punch was unexpected and hard. I had absolutely no idea why he did this. None. He was a big lad and whenever I recall the incident, I still wish horrible things on him. (C.)

> The metalwork teacher. He used a metal ruler and thwacked the palms of both my hands for talking in class. As I recall, it was one almighty thwack to each palm and eff me, did it sting. The pain was so bad I may have wished him dead—maybe he is now. (C.)

> I was in the lunch line and there was a small boy in the front of the line. Someone shouted, 'Let's kick him,' so the pupils played "kick the dog," a game played often: a circle of boys would kick the victim who was in the centre. (W.)

> I don't particularly have fond memories of the Knoll. (M.)

> I was bullied mercilessly and became very depressed at times. (B.)

> I hated pretty much all my time at the Knoll. Not a single teacher seemed to have the special ability required to inspire me or, as I recall, none of my classmates. (M.C.)

PREFACE

Sadly, my friend, took his own life a few years after we had all left the Knoll. (D.C.)

> At ten past three, I remember feeling a tangible sense of relief. (Anon.)

I remember after an art class "B" kicked the s**t out of me. I remember his boot in my ribs – it really hurt! (W.)

> On the day of one of my GCSE exams, a group of bullies stared and threatened me through the exam room window; it was my favourite subject, and I ended up with a D grade (fail). I retook it at BHASVIC a few months later and got an A grade–which I should have got at the Knoll. (G.)

There were some sadistic teachers at that school. Do you remember the art teacher, Mr Ramsey? He enjoyed cracking people on the head. I think in our addled minds, we affectionately named it a "head-onesie." These bastards would not survive in teaching these days—some of them would be doing time for assault. (M.)

> I wore a thick parka even in the summer because you never knew who had an air gun and could shoot you. (W.)

A kid screamed at me that I had better be at the school gates at five past three and be ready for a scrap; the teacher that marched me to the headmaster completely ignored this threat. (C.)

> While queuing up outside a classroom, a thug just appeared in front of me and for no apparent reason, punched me hard, smack in the side of my face. I went down like the proverbial sack of potatoes. (D.)

INTRODUCTION

Colditz Castle, near Leipzig in Germany, became notorious as Oflag IV-C, a high-security prisoner-of-war camp for Allied officers who had repeatedly escaped from other camps. Labelled "incorrigible," these POWs were considered beyond reform. The Nazis made Colditz a *Sonderlager* (high-security prison camp)—the only one in Germany. It was deemed escape proof.

Similarly, children aged 11 to 16 at the Knoll School for Boys in Hove, Sussex, often referred to their school as "Knollditz" or "Knollditz-by-the-Sea," reflecting their perception of the school as a place they could not escape from. The five years of mandatory attendance felt like a prison sentence to many, and school staff often labelled pupils as "incorrigible."

The Hate Game provides readers with a glimpse into the hazing and initiation rituals that took place at the school from 1972 to 1977. Older students subjected first-year pupils to sadistic games, often with themes linked to the Holocaust or World War II. The school's bleak and unostentatious appearance, built with dark red bricks and concrete, resembled the notorious H-Block prison in Northern Ireland. Moreover, with a bit of imagination, the view of Knoll School from Old Shoreham Road

INTRODUCTION

also bore a resemblance to the building at the end of the Auschwitz II Birkenau concentration camp railway line.

While Auschwitz and Knoll School served vastly different purposes, both had mottos that reflected their underlying ideologies.

Auschwitz's well-known sign bore the slogan *"Arbeit macht frei"* (Work sets you free), while Knoll School's blazer featured the motto *"Laborando Vincamus"* (We conquer through labour). A more fitting motto for Knoll School could have been *"Vincimus spiritu tuo opprimendo"* (We win by crushing your spirit).

My experience at Knoll School was marked by bullying, erratic teacher behaviour, and a pervasive sense of hopelessness.

Like many others, I learned to navigate the harsh environment despite these challenges. While some former students have fond memories of Knoll School, unfortunately, many others found their experience detrimental to their education and mental well-being. Moreover, many pupils attended the school in the 1950s and 1960s. Although it was still a demanding environment, the lack of care and the abuse inflicted upon pupils (in the name of discipline) by several of its staff may not have been as evident.

In this memoir, I aim to explore a coming-of-age narrative that reveals resilience and laughter amidst some of the darker moments I experienced. For many years, I screamed in the silence of my mind, feeling too ashamed and embarrassed to share my story.

The Knoll School closed in 1979 and merged with other schools to form Blatchington Mill Comprehensive School. The dark and gloomy building, which retains its foreboding appearance, now serves as a business park.

CHAPTER 1
RITE OF PASSAGE
AUGUST, 1972

Before starting at the Knoll School, I tried to enjoy the summer holiday. I rode around the streets on my new bike. For the first time, I ventured up to Hove Park alone. I pedalled under the railway bridge on Fonthill Road, up the steep hill, passed by the Goldstone Ground, the home of Brighton & Hove Albion Football Club, and then rode across the busy Old Shoreham Road to Hove Park. While on my bike, I daydreamed about many different things. As I rode around the park's perimeter, up and down the hills, I imagined being a fighter pilot engaged in a dogfight with an enemy aircraft. I was James Hunt in a Formula One racing car and a British Cavalry officer in the Light Brigade charging at the Turks. In these moments, I was free. I had no friends; I was "Norman No-Mates," but I had my imagination and daydreams.

I heard a rumour an initiation event occurred for all the new kids on the first day of term. This event was called "D-Day." I'd met a couple of boys in the neighbourhood who were in their second and third years at the school. Among these guys was one named Pete, who lived on the street next to mine. I'd seen him a few times while testing my new bike. Pete, exuding confidence with his long, mousy blond hair and mischievous hazel eyes, struck up a conversation and complimented my "cool" bike. This surprised me as I half expected him to ask, "Seriously, mate, what's the deal with the girl's bike? It's got tiny wheels, sparkles, and is a shitty-brown colour."

Pete seemed like a convivial kind of guy. Despite my dad giving me threats of death if I let anyone else play on the bike, I occasionally allowed Pete to ride it. I walked my bike along the pavement—Pete walked alongside me. Having found out I'd start my new school within a few weeks, he smirked and informed me my first day at Knoll School would be "a bit of a nightmare."

His comment stopped me in my tracks. "Why?" I asked, staring at his face to see if he was winding me up.

His lips curled up in a smile, "D-Day."

My brow furrowed, "D-Day. What, like June 6th—the Normandy landings?"

"No, you effing idiot. D-Day is d-for-ducking day. D-Day—Ducking Day."

"Oh, Ducking Day!" I parroted. *What on earth was Ducking Day?*

Pete nodded as he guffawed. Then, baring his teeth with a wolf-like snarl, he explained, "The new boys turn up on the first day in their new school blazers, shirts and ties, and their school caps on their cute little first-year heads. The older kids grab these new kids, drag them to the toilets, and steal their precious new caps—like taking a scalp. The caps become trophies, one for each ducking."

I felt a fluttery, nervous tummy feeling. *Oh my God!*

Not satisfied that I had understood my future first-day fate, Pete added, "Once in the bogs, we grab hold of the newbie, turn him upside down, put his head down the toilet bowl, and flush his little first-year head. That's 'D-Day!'"

"No way," I spluttered.

"Yes, way. It's like a real-life, effing baptism. It's a 'welcome to our school.' It will all be over in a few minutes. Don't worry."

Don't worry? I was speechless; I could hear my heart pounding in my ears.

"Just make sure you ain't a wuss. Some kids want their mums and bawl their eyes out. Pathetic!"

Yep, that's probably going to be me.

Pete's smile became broader. "Some of these wussy kids get pissed on while their heads are down the toilet. The chain gets pulled, and the water washes away the piss from the kid's bonce."

"What about the teachers?" I gulped. "Surely, they'd stop it?"

"Oh, they turn a blind eye. It's tradition—it's 'D-Day!' The teachers don't give a shit."

I must have turned as pale as a ghost. I sighed and walked my bike with Pete at my side. I'd read about schools like this in Dad's Frank Richards's books about older school kids bullying the younger ones and making their lives a misery, abusing them, and calling them "fags," an English private-school boy who acts as a servant to an older schoolmate. The Knoll wasn't a fancy-dancy school; it was situated in the slummiest area of town.

He's trying to wind me up. Keep a brave face, and don't show him I'm terrified. I felt like crapping my pants.

Despite what he had shared with me that day, Pete and I developed a quasi-camaraderie in the ensuing week before the start of school. The truth was that we were utterly dissimilar people from poles apart backgrounds. It highlighted the gap between Pete, a local guy and an amiable kid, and me, a gullible and naïve lad with almost zero understanding of life. He was shrewd, street-smart, and sceptical of authority. I was clueless, trusted adults and had been living under the protection of my parents. Although I had a brother and sister, they were a decade older than me, and I rarely saw them. I was the annoying, spoilt little brother.

One weekend, when I returned home on the bus from the Top

Rank disco that Mum and Dad had, surprisingly, allowed me to attend, Pete informed me he had been hanging out with his girlfriend. We sat on the double-decker bus, chatting casually. I took the window seat, and he sat next to the aisle. I asked Pete what he had been up to, as I hadn't seen much of him at the disco. Pete grinned like a Cheshire cat, shoved his fingers in my face, and told me to smell whatever was on his fingers.

My head shot back in response—as if he was infecting me with the Black Death. My head was glued to the bus window; I was unable to avoid his fingers pushing into my nostrils. I wrinkled my nose at the unfamiliar, musky scent.

"That's my girlfriend's pussy," he said matter-of-factly. I didn't know why he wanted me to smell his girlfriend's cat. Sure, he wouldn't be aware I struggled with cat allergies, but it was a weird request for me to process—not that I had the time to do so.

"Do ya want another sniff?" he said, holding his hand close to my nose, "Lovely pussy smell."

"No, Pete. Stop it," I said, batting his hand away from my face, "I don't like pussies, I'm allergic to them!"

"I never took you for a homo!" He put his fingers to his nose and sniffed like a sommelier smelling a vintage claret. He took long, deep whiffs, making strange "mmmm," "oh," and "ahh" sounds.

A few months earlier, at Middle Street Primary, I had sat the eleven-plus exam—a rite of passage into the next stage of a child's life. My dad used a motivational pep talk to help me understand the importance of passing the exam. Pass, and a grammar school education awaited me, with entry into university and career opportunities in medicine, law, or becoming a fighter pilot in the RAF. Fail, and the future was much bleaker—mandatory attendance at a secondary or technical school. Dad informed me this would, inevitably, lead to me working in hairdressing or cleaning toilets. More likely, I'd end up in prison, where I'd be licking toilet bowls for my prison husband. I didn't know what my dad meant by this, but it sounded as desirous to me as embalming the dead. So, I had to pass the damned exam. Dad tutored me, and I took the exam full of confident cockiness. One of the questions asked was:

The black cat confidently perched on the black mat, while the ginger cat boldly occupied the blue mat adjacent to the green sofa. What colour cat sat on the mat?

A) Green B) Ginger C) Blue with Pink and White Polka Dots D) Black.

When the results were posted, shockingly, I had failed the exam. I was such a thicko that I must have answered the easy 11-plus question, "A polka dot-coloured cat sat on the black mat," rather than a black one. Dad demanded a recount as he was so surprised at the results. Yes, they had made an error; I had passed, but my score was not high enough to get me into the grammar school of my choice. I was offered Varndean Grammar in Brighton. I had come to terms with a commute to my new school, as I had done so to get to Middle Street in Brighton. Unfortunately, Dad's modus operandi was to make abysmal, non-collaborative decisions that had terrible ramifications for our family. He continued to do this for his favourite child (me) and decided to send me to the infamous Knoll School for Boys in Hove.

Everyone in the area knew the school had a gnarly reputation. However, Dad talked with Knoll's headmaster, who convinced him the Knoll School was the non-fee-paying equivalent of Eton, Harrow, or Cheltenham College. Dad had made up his mind—Gary was going to the "excellent" Knoll School.

Anyway, back to my bus journey with my new, but coarse friend, Pete. Having gone on about his girlfriend's "pussy" and me being a "homo," I was utterly confused. Not wanting to ask him what a homo was, I thought it best to impress him, as he was one of the few kids I knew that went to Knoll School.

"Was it a black pussycat?" I asked him, still feeling the sting of misunderstanding the 11-plus-question about black cats and mats. He responded by laughing, "Mate, you're such a perv!"

Two worldviews were colliding. It had only taken a few minutes for Pete, a current student at Knoll School, to expose me to a new normal that included crudity, inappropriate behaviour, and foul language. Pete was a friendly kid who had vaguely promised to keep an eye on me on "D-Day," which meant he'd make sure someone didn't either urinate or defecate on my head while being "ducked" in the filthy school toilet.

The idiocy of failing the 11-plus exam dawned on me, and I was filled with regret. However, in the back of my mind, I felt resentment that my dad had taken another non-collaborative decision that may have had a massive impact on my life.

Gary Trew, 11 Years of age.

CHAPTER 2
"D-DAY"
SEPTEMBER 5TH, 1972

Anxious soldiers waited their turn on the deck. The storm caused the ship to sway and lurch wildly. The soldiers enjoyed an extravagant meal the previous evening, and now the remains of the steak and potatoes were strewn about the floor. They leaned on the railing, smoking cigarettes while they observed the shoreline. With a tap on the back, the sergeant gestured for them to proceed. As the troops climbed into the small Higgins boat, the motor roared to life, drowning out the distant sounds of battle. Vomit covered the floors of the crafts; puke stained the soldiers' backsides from the soldiers behind them. The Germans opened fire, the sound of machine guns filling the air as they showered the invading troops with bullets. The level of tension was off the charts. Dread filled the air as soldiers' bladders and bowels betrayed them, a stark reminder of the impending horror.

JUNE 6TH, 1944, NORMANDY: THE NARRATIVE ABOVE IS DERIVED FROM VARIOUS DOCUMENTARIES AND THE AUTHOR'S PERSONAL CONVERSATIONS WITH VETERANS.

THERE WAS A SMALL HOPE PETE AND THE OTHER KIDS HAD BEEN winding me up about "D-Day." A week before school started, my dad took me to Broadley Brothers on George Street to get measured for my first-ever school uniform. We got the mandatory list from the school, which included a black blazer or jacket, black or dark grey slacks, a grey sweater, black shoes, a maroon and yellow tie, and a maroon cap. The school blazer and cap had the Knoll School crest. The Knoll School motto emblazoned on the school badge was *Laborando Vincamus*. Mum was so proud of me as I dressed up for her. She painstakingly taught me how to put on my tie as a single or Oxford knot and gave me a refresher course on tying a double knot with my shoelaces.

The morning of that first day of school in September was the longest for this naïve, 11-year-old, sheltered little boy. I felt sick to the stomach as I sat down for breakfast. Mum made bacon, eggs, sausage, and beans with toast, and a massive piping hot mug of tea. Dad prepared my lunch: a bag of crisps, a Mars bar, an apple, and a juice box—my parents knew I would not eat school dinners. Seeing my parents in the kitchen together was unusual, especially as Mum had the radio blaring out *Sugar Me* by Lynsey de Paul. Dad abhorred pop music.

I felt a gentle pat on my shoulder. Mum pointed at a gargantuan plate of fried food. "Eat up, Gary. This should fill you up until lunchtime."

It looked delicious; the smoky smell of fried bacon and charred sausage was an aroma to die for. Despite the flutter of butterflies in my stomach, I couldn't resist picking up the knife and fork, taking a bite, and tucking in. I savoured every delicious morsel.

Mum's voice broke through the music. "Hurry up, lad. You don't want to miss the bus and be late on your first day."

I scoffed down the leftovers, stood up with cup in hand, blew furiously on the hot tea, took a few gulps, and slurped down the rest. I grabbed my brand-new black briefcase and headed out through the basement door. Mum followed me up the concrete stairs and stood by the entrance. I walked ahead and glanced back at my big-hearted mother, who hated goodbyes. A big smile spread across her lips as tears flowed down her face. I turned down a last-minute hug. I fought tears, frightened her kindness would upset me. Her mantra was "big boys don't cry" and "warriors don't blubber," and I aimed to be a tough, secondary school soldier. As I stole one final glance, Mum's hands waved at me; she gradually shrank into the distance.

Put her out of your mind. Grow up, Gary! Crying is a weakness. Focus on getting through the day. I felt like I'd rather cut off my own head with a breadknife than go to this new school. My heart pounding, I walked along Livingstone Road towards the nearby bus stop on Sackville Road.

Breathe, Gary, and take deep breaths, I reminded myself. Mum advised me to do this if I ever felt overwhelmed. I reached the road's end and saw the bus stop 50 yards away. Quite a few boys stood there, waiting. I crossed the road and approached the queue, noticing several lads dressed like me—blazers and caps, holding smart, new briefcases. Other older students wore grey jumpers, black trousers, shirts, and ties loosely knotted around their necks.

Dad would disapprove—scruffy buggers.

I avoided making eye contact with anyone and waited for the number five bus to pick me up and drop me right in front of the Knoll School. *So far, so good. I wished my tummy would stop gurgling.*

Suddenly, acid reflux hit the back of my throat, and I tasted regurgitated bacon, sausage, and baked beans. *Please, don't be sick.* In my morning panic, I'd forgotten to brush my teeth. *Try not to breathe on anyone.*

I don't mean to downplay the bravery of the soldiers who stormed the beaches of Normandy three decades before my experience at Knoll School's D-Day. Their feelings and sacrifices are incomparable. At the tender age of 11, I'd never felt my stomach churn with such intensity—the fear of what I didn't know overwhelmed me. The memories of what I encountered on my own D-Day have remained with me for a long time.

The bus arrived. I paid my fare and sat on the lower deck with other new kids and older adults who appeared to be heading to work.

As I travelled on the bus to school, my guts didn't stop moving—I wished I had stayed on the toilet longer. I desperately wanted to release my bowels.

Idiot! Why did I have bacon and eggs this morning and not a bowl of cereal? I was breathing heavily, and my heart was racing.

Deep breaths; stay calm—it's no big deal. Don't be such a baby.

I wanted to stay composed, calm my nerves, and breathe through my nose. I was failing epically. I'd never felt fear like this before, and I didn't want to appear scared to the other school kids on the bus. It was hard to swallow; my mouth was bone dry. I held my hand to my mouth and burped. *Gross.*

Pete's words had taken root in my imagination, *"We grab hold of the newbie, turn him upside down, put his head down the toilet bowl, and flush his little first-year head. D-Day!"*

I was halfway to the school. I glanced at the boy sitting next to me. He, too, held on to a shiny, new briefcase. He also wore a school cap with light brown curly hair underneath it, and his big, bright eyes were open wide.

I bet he's as terrified as me.

He had a friendly, innocent face. "Do you think they'll duck us in the toilets on our first day?" I asked him.

"I bloody hope not. I've heard about D-Day," he said. Frown lines formed on his brow. "My dad will go apeshit if I mess up my school uniform."

I looked away from him and gazed at the grubby floor of the bus. *Crap, he'd heard about D-Day, too!*

"Here goes—we've arrived!" the boy said, alighting from his seat. I tried to follow him, but I lost my curly-haired neighbour as other lads aggressively bundled past me to make their own exit from the bus.

An elderly lady pushed past me, eager to get off the bus and not miss her stop. For some bizarre reason, the *Hell's Grannies* sketch by Monty Python came to mind, where gangs of old ladies terrorised neighbourhoods, vandalising property and blowing their old age pension on milk, tea, and Jammy Dodger biscuits.

I bet the Hell's Grannies are the ones who will grab us and ram our heads down the toilets.

I giggled to myself. I loved watching *Monty Python's Flying Circus* with my dad—we'd both cry with laughter. The sillier the sketch, the harder we'd laugh. Tears would flow down Mum's cheeks, watching Dad and me busting a gut. Laughing has always helped me deal with stressful situations. Dealing with the darker side of life, police work and child protection, when given the choice of grief and horror, laughter helps me to forget about sadness. It's hard to be sad when I laugh as an escape.

I stepped from the bus and beheld the austere-looking Knoll School in all its gloomy glory. I'd not seen the school before. Pete, and his friend Ronnie, nicknamed the school "Knollditz" after the Nazi prison camp. My body and brain were no longer in sync.

It won't be that bad. Grow a pair. My legs protested as they trudged to school through an imaginary quagmire. *Pete or the teachers might rescue me.* I was at the gates.

Gary, get your arse moving!

Any vaguely positive thoughts were short-lived. I was to experience the scariest moment of my life. Now, the brain and its body have achieved complete synchronisation. A distressing scene played in my mind—my head submerged in a basin of cold water. I wished my imagination would stop.

I was taken aback by the turmoil that greeted me. A gang of larger, taller boys were causing bedlam. I heard ear-piercing screams as kids were dragged away from the entrance by a glom of senior pupils.

Oh no. Refrain from making eye contact; walk quickly and head to the classrooms. There was no evidence of teachers in the vicinity. *Where were the classrooms? Where were the damn teachers?*

I was suddenly seized from behind by large hands, causing me to struggle for breath. My chest felt utterly hollow. I was punched in the back—a low blow to the kidneys—I gasped. My school cap was snatched from my head, pulling my hair at the roots. "I've got another scalp!" someone cheered, holding my cap triumphantly in the air.

There was a lot of noise and laughter. I was unable to see individual faces—everything was a blur. I was trapped in a headlock by a shadowy figure. I felt a sharp pain in my leg, like being kicked by a horse. "Take the bastard to the bogs!"

Terrified, I wriggled and squirmed, trying to pull the boa constrictor from my head with my right hand. Clinging tightly to the handle of my briefcase, my fingers refused to release their grip. I was desperately trying to escape—my head and neck were squeezed tighter.

With my head in a vice-like grip, an angry voice boomed, "Stop moving, you little c**t, or I'll choke you out!"

"Duck him! Duck him!" voices chanted ahead and behind me. Their feverish laughter pissed me off. I ceased resisting. My compliance eased the choke hold. I could finally breathe again. I was helpless—I hated myself for surrendering. I was jolted and shoved into the junior toilets. As I was manhandled into a small toilet cubicle, I saw dark figures crammed into another booth—a boy's head was being forced into a toilet bowl. Older boys held his feet and legs—coins spilt from his pockets. He cried out for his mum: "Help me! Please help me! I beg you, please don't do it! Mum! Mum!"

Then it was my turn. Three big kids flipped me over. I panicked and thrashed like a bucking horse. The pressure of gravity forced blood to rush into my eye sockets, disorienting me further as I took in the sight of the large black shoes on the toilet floor. My head spun like a carnival ride gone haywire.

My head was plunged down the toilet. The shock of icy water on my face left me breathless—these few seconds felt like they'd never end. My eyes burned as I caught a whiff of the astringent pine of the cheap disinfectant puck deposited in the cistern. I closed my eyes and held my breath, but not before the water travelled up my nostrils. I opened my stinging eyes and blinked feverishly. I gagged, coughed, then heaved at the idea that my face might have been washed in urine or something even worse. I glared at the grimy green and yellow watermark stain on the white porcelain bowl as I heard the flushing sound of the long chain pulled from the cistern.

The water cascaded around the bowl, splashing onto my face and further drenching my hair as it hung limply in the toilet. The boys rendered my arms unable to move. I resigned myself to my inevitable fate and held my breath. I was held upside-down like a rag-doll amidst hooting and jeering. In the grim, dirty washrooms, I recalled the echoes of boys' screams and their attackers' maniacal laughter. The sounds and smells were a living hell for me, but things were going to get a lot worse. "Piss on him," I heard one voice say.

Once again, I found myself in a desperate frenzy to break free. I squirmed and writhed like a worm on crack cocaine, fuelled by an insatiable desire to escape. In my upside-down world, I saw one of the boys holding onto my right leg. My flailing left foot connected with his chest. The enraged boy regained control of my rebellious limb, deadened my leg with a fierce blow, and called out to one of his pals to piss on me.

No, no. Not that. Please not that.

I heard a zipper being undone. "Sod off," I screamed, "Get off me, you bastard." I had no more fight left in me. I was desperately tired as cortisol released from my brain mopped up the saturated adrenaline levels in my blood.

"Golden shower for you, boy!"

I gasped for air, my heart exploding from my chest. *I will kill each one of you bastards one day.* I needed to know who they were—but how?

A vaguely recognisable voice broke through the pandemonium. "That's enough, lads. He's a good kid. He's all right, leave him be." I was unsure, but it sounded like Pete's voice—the Pete who lived around the corner and sometimes rode on my bicycle.

Dizzy and bewildered, I was promptly turned around in midair and dropped back onto my feet, then shoved away, stumbling over my numb legs away from the stalls. Water dripped into my eyes, and I wiped my face with my blazer sleeve. The cacophony of noise continued with the other victims' screams and shouts, mixed with the howls of their tormentors' laughter. I saw and heard boys snivelling.

I ran and exited the toilet area with wet hair trickling into my ears and neck. *Well, that was fun—not!* I was unsure if I'd soiled myself—I was past caring anyway. I trembled like a leaf as I followed the arrows on the walls directing pupils to various classrooms. My class was the first on my right. I'd finally escaped. *Thank God I got away.*

I saw a notice: *1W, Mr McNeil's class.* I heard many voices in the classroom—loud, excited, high-pitched murmurs mixed with raucous laughter. I stumbled through the open door, and a slim, middle-aged man with dark hair made eye contact with me. He told me to hurry up and find an empty desk and chair to sit at.

"1W, settle down. Shh." Mr McNeil held his index finger up to his mouth. "Quiet, settle down." Safety enveloped me like a soft blanket. *Settle down?* I thought, incredulously.

If this were your first day at school and you had just experienced the humiliation of having your head forced into a filthy toilet bowl, you might be feeling a bit emotional.

It crossed my mind Mum and Dad may kill me when I turned

up after school, *sans* my new school cap on my very first day. I sat at the desk. I was utterly shattered and had used up so much energy trying to resist, but was too small and weak to defend myself. My hair was wet, my tie bedraggled—I looked and felt like a drowned rat.

While McNeil talked, I felt my pockets for the few coins Dad had given me for bus fare, which were still there. I wanted to leave and go home. McNeil's mouth moved, but I couldn't focus on what he was saying. I stared at the blackboard. My hand robotically copied a timetable into a maroon exercise book left by McNeil. I wrote my name on the cover. The school crest featured a shield with the words *Laborando Vincamus* underneath.

Two conflicting voices battled in my mind.

Just go home.

Stay. The worst is over.

It will get worse.

No, don't be a coward. McNeil's mouth continued to open and close.

I hate this place.

So does everyone else. Where else are you going to go?

Before I knew it, the bell sounded for the first break. I peered out of a large, old window onto the concrete playground. I sighed, desperately wanting to stay in the classroom, but we were not allowed. I saw several large kids loitering, waiting for our reappearance. It dawned on me that not only did I have to possibly survive another D-Day experience, I also had a long lunch break to contend with.

Teachers will be in the playground—get a grip.

They weren't, and they were also absent during the lunch hour. Thankfully, Pete was there and advised me to walk around with him. I felt for the other kids who had to run the D-Day gauntlet repeatedly that day without a long, mousy-haired guardian angel like mine by their side.

The chaos didn't end when the final bell sounded that school was over for the day. Gloms of boys waited outside the school gates. Fights broke out. The bus stop area looked like a combat zone, with big kids surrounding smaller kids and shoving and hitting each other.

Nope—I'm walking home.

So, I sauntered the 40-minute journey back to Livingstone Road, past Hove Cemetery, a poignant reminder of how I felt, deep inside—dead, like a corpse. That was the longest day of my short life. Unfortunately, it wasn't to be the cruellest.

Entrance to Knoll School on D-Day. Knoll School closed in 1979. The premises are now used as a Business Park (Image used Courtesy of Mr Derek Mann, Oct. 2023).

CHAPTER 3
LABORANDO VINCAMUS
1972-73

THE SCHOOL ORGANISED THE KNOLL PUPILS INTO FOUR CLASSES—W, X, Y, and Z—based on their academic level. The school motto, *We Win by Working Hard*, made me realise I had to be prepared to put in a lot of effort to achieve victory, even if the meaning of "win" was unclear. However, it was a challenge because working hard usually goes hand in hand with a harmonious and peaceful environment, unless it pertains to working hard in a war zone.

The classroom ambience and setting at the Knoll were unlike anything I had encountered before. Mr Boycott, the geography teacher, bore a striking resemblance to the Mad Professor, complete with a bald head and a wild mane of greying hair. Like stalks of wheat, hairs sprouted out of his ear regions.

Boycott could easily be mistaken for Zebedee, the beloved character from *The Magic Roundabout* cartoon that played before the BBC's six o'clock news broadcast on TV. Zebedee was a bizarre jack-in-the-box character with a metallic spring instead of legs who'd disappear from the set with a loud boing.

Every time Boycott looked at the chalkboard, a couple of mischievous classmates would shout "BOING," causing the classroom to burst into laughter. The instant Boycott heard the sound, he responded by flinging his board rubber towards the source, even if he couldn't pinpoint its exact location. The vein on Boycott's forehead bulged and throbbed, warning the class that the Deputy Headmaster's cane would be the consequence of any further foolish noises. I was constantly on edge, never knowing when his missile would come hurtling towards me.

Aside from the "BOING" noises, the teacher always demanded the pupils' attention. The slightest whisper during his class would set him off, causing him to erupt angrily and scream at my classmates. Boycott's shriek was so mighty that it caused his mouth to froth, resembling a vigorously shaken soda can. The pupils sitting nearby at the front of the class shrank back in fear as he screeched and sprayed spittle. The front-row boys were confronted with an unpleasant dilemma—stay seated and face the possibility of being covered in saliva or attempt to dodge it and potentially face detention. Boycott resorted to throwing objects to get his pupils' attention—board rubber, chalk, and sometimes textbooks flew from his hand.

With his thick Yorkshire accent already tricky to understand, his penchant for keeping us on edge made for an unpleasant classroom environment. While sitting in a geography lesson, I couldn't shake the feeling I had accidentally stumbled into a linguistics class. Great Britain is renowned for its rich tapestry of dialects and accents, each with unique charm. With his Yorkshire upbringing, Mr Boycott spoke with a one-of-a-kind Yorkshire brogue and peppered his speech with the vernacular.

With a slurp, he sipped from a steaming, piping hot mug of Tetley tea on his desk and declared, "Eee, that's a reet good brew tha'." Translated, it would mean, "Ah, that's a proper tasty cup of tea, that is!"

His classroom emphasised maintaining order through fear rather than promoting educational growth. The chalk or board rubber frequently glided through the air, dancing from his hands as if guided by an invisible supernatural force. Despite amusement at certain pupils' occasional "BOING" noises, I sat in Boycott's lesson with apprehension and unease. Witnessing angry teachers hurling objects at the class was a new and unsettling experience. I learned little because I was too busy trying to avoid getting hit by the board rubber and desperately avoiding being caught laughing—a response more based on nerves rather than disrespect.

The lesson concluded, and a feeling of unease settled over the classroom. Anxious glances were exchanged among the pupils as we prepared to navigate the narrow and crowded corridors, wary of encountering the older troublemakers who took pleasure in making our lives miserable. The constant jostling and rough play made it nearly impossible to navigate the area without being bumped, hit, or sucker-punched by the other boys.

On the other hand, a handful of teachers at the Knoll were exceptional in their ability to inspire and educate. A teacher named Mr "Jock" McNeil deserves an honourable mention. His English classes were a breath of fresh air during my junior years, providing a welcome respite from the oppressive atmosphere in other classes. Despite the chaos outside his classroom, his lessons provided a peaceful haven, enabling him to captivate the entire class without resorting to threats of punishment and violence.

Amid a challenging zoo-like setting, McNeil stood out for his eagerness to spread his passion for the English language. Instead of focusing on grammar fundamentals, he captivated us with creative writing exercises that provided a welcome distraction from all the commotion elsewhere. By tapping into daydreams and imagination, I was able to thrive in his class. With his amiable and introverted disposition, McNeil gave off a genuine sense of being a kind-hearted individual. The experience of escaping into a realm of creativity through the power of words was something I absolutely adored. "Jock" McNeil's lessons ignited our imaginations, urging us to delve into an alternate realm. Amidst an environment of brutal harshness and savage discipline, his classroom and my imagination became my sanctuary.

"Jock's" encouragement to express ourselves in word form was bliss. I love to write and create. This also led to a passion for reading, which helped save my life through some tumultuous years—from the whacky and hilarious Joseph Heller to the brutalities in the Gulags described graphically by Solzhenitsyn. I am forever thankful to Mr McNeil for opening my mind when everything around me demanded that I shut off my feelings and emotions to survive. "Jock" McNeil was so gifted that his class took the English "O" Level a year early, with a staggering pass rate. An incredible achievement with the "incorrigibles" attending "Knollditz."

CHAPTER 4
PLAYGROUND HOLOCAUST
1973

THE SOUND OF THE BELL FILLED THE AIR, INDICATING IT WAS TIME for morning break, or as some prefer to call it, recess. For most 11-year-olds, the best sound of the day is the end of lessons—time to play! It wasn't for me or many other new kids at Knoll School for Boys. Senior and junior boys had separate play areas called quadrangles; classrooms and corridors flanked the two playgrounds. The school's student body was about 600 pupils, with 30 to 40 teachers.

The dimly lit corridor gave off a pungent, musky smell of sickly-sweet throw-up and sweaty bodies mixed with the faint whiff of recently laid floor polish. The strange, noisy, reverberating school hallway sounds made me uneasy. My tummy grumbled loudly, and reminded me I urgently needed to find the toilets—the same ones that had caused me so much embarrassment on my first day. There was a feeling of dissociation between me and my body. My throat tightened as I swallowed hard, determined to not appear like a scared rabbit.

As I joined the masses of other kids leaving their classrooms, I felt lost in the crowd. The overwhelming hullabaloo of the boys' laughter and excited yells filled my senses, leaving me no choice but to keep going straight, trying to find my way through the chaos. I was unable to stop or change direction, so I couldn't reach the toilets—maybe I could go to them during the break.

In the nick of time, I sidestepped a repulsive puddle of vomit that the janitor had treated with sawdust. The smell of puke made me nauseous. I desperately wanted to reach the double doors to the junior quadrangle—an asphalt playground, shaped like a rectangle. No trees, monkey bars, or climbing apparatus were present in the quadrangle, only a rock-hard surface with two doors on either side.

The autumn sky was a serene blue, dotted with fluffy cumulus clouds. With the sun shining brightly overhead, I longed to inhale the crisp, fresh air and rejuvenate my body, mind, and spirit.

My social circle was still small at my new school, as I had only made a few friends. Well, my "few" actually meant none at all. I missed the familiar sights of my primary school, the laughter of my friends, and the nostalgic memories of Brighton. Sadly, none of my old school chums lived in Hove. Knoll Boys predominantly drew students from the nearby catchment area, with many that came from the rough, working-class council estates that lined the school's perimeter. Numerous pupils had relatives, including brothers and cousins, who were either currently attending or had attended the school in the past. The non-grammar school girls attended the Knoll School for Girls in Hangleton, a nicer part of town. I lived quite far from my secondary school, so every morning I had to catch a bus to make it there by 8.45am. Only a handful of new boys boarded the morning number 5 or 5B bus, which conveniently stopped right outside or near the school. Two boys in my class, Billy and Angus, caught the bus with me, but I'd not come to know either of them.

I wanted to see if I could join a game with someone I recognised. While being pushed through the hallway towards the playground, I had a weird thought I could've been a cow in a past life, going through the same chaos at a slaughterhouse. I went

THE HATE GAME

along with the flow of bodies towards the exit that led to the concrete playground.

By sheer force of momentum, I was spat out into the playground through the double doors like water fired from a water cannon—similar to those used to control feisty protestors. I lost my balance and fell. I rested my knees on the concrete surface, but only momentarily. Not wanting to be pushed onto my face, I stood up quickly and followed the rest of the 11-year-old boys into the centre of the junior play area.

What was going on? Why was I being corralled into an area with the other boys?

I shielded my eyes from the dazzling rays of sunshine. My heart felt like it would explode in my chest. A sense of dread washed over me as I anticipated what was about to happen.

When I look back now, the memories come flooding back, vivid with sights, sounds, and even smells—trauma has a way of etching them into your mind. For *The Hunger Games* fans, I felt like Katniss "May the odds be ever in your favour" Everdeen, as she was dropped into the competitive kill zone with her peers. However, unlike the hero of Suzanne Collins's book, I certainly didn't volunteer to attend The Knoll. I had no prior training, no provision of weapons, and no warning of what I was about to experience. There was no chance to form alliances—we were all new, fresh, first-year students. I hadn't seen or talked to guardian angel Pete since D-Day. I had no siblings or other neighbourhood friends to protect me. I felt like a stranger in a foreign land.

I soon discovered the tall shadowy figures surrounding us were the brutal, arrogant, tough, and merciless older pupils. The odds would never be in our favour! This was not *The Hunger Games's* 'reckoning,' where cunning teens competed against other teens until the strongest and wisest individual triumphed over the rest. This situation was more like William Golding's fictional *Lord of the Flies*, and my years at the Knoll were true tales of innocence lost. I was one of the weak, vulnerable, frightened kids pushed out to the middle of the school courtyard to face tall, formidable-looking shadows.

Were we herded there by the prefects or the teachers for a special announcement? Why weren't the kids with me scared? Why were we in a circle, surrounded by bigger kids?

Adrenaline kicked in. Freeze, fight, or flight alarm bells urged me to make a split-second decision. I scoped out possible escape routes. There were none. Bigger kids, like sentinels, guarded the two quadrangle exit doors. Commands were barked at us by a large, older youth with a big mouth, called Mitch Skinner. As my eyes became more accustomed to the light, I saw he had dirty blond, unkempt hair, a prominent nose, and piggy eyes. He was strutting around with a strange gait, as if he had some weird, twisted thing going on with the top of his spine.

I stood in the sunshine, struggling to keep my hands from shaking, but my body betrayed me as I shivered with fear. This felt wrong. I'd been brutally "baptised" into the Knoll School on "D-Day" on the first day of school, so this current situation didn't look at all promising. A short, stocky kid called Arnold Fickle stood next to Skinner and ordered the encircled boys to shut their mouths, stand to attention, and listen.

I looked upward, rolled my eyes, and sighed. *What the heck was going on? Are we in the army or something?* Skinner, the despot I endured for the next half-decade, was the central figure, barking orders and spewing vitriol at us.

"Swine! Ugly pigs! You are now going to take part in some—" he paused, a wide grin spreading across his face, "Holocaust games."

Holocaust . . . what?

With a snarl, Skinner declared the brutal and merciless "rules" of his game. "Listen here, you first-year shits—this game will be fun. Consider this our history lesson to you."

Fun? History lesson? This must be some kind of prank.

"It's all part of your introduction to our school. If I were you, I wouldn't resist. If some of you obey my orders and aren't stinking Jew boys, you may be lucky—I might invite you to join my elite, *Waffen SS*."

I quietly sniggered. *This guy was nuttier than a bar of Cadbury's whole nut.*

"But . . . and this is a BIG BUT, if you are a cowardly *undermenchen*, a faggoty Jew—then welcome to MY world. If we have any doubts about your ethnicity, we can always find the truth. You can't hide your circumcised pricks from us." Skinner held up his hand and wiggled his pinky finger at us. The other youths surrounding us nodded in agreement.

There's no way they're pulling my pants down.

I couldn't believe what I was hearing. I knew quite a bit about the Nazis' rise to power in the '30s, Hitler seizing power, *Kristallnacht*, and the invasion of Austria, Czechoslovakia, and Poland. Dad encouraged me to learn from history and the war he fought in as he detested what had transpired. I also knew about the concentration camps, many of their names and locations, internment, gas chambers, Zyklon-B, and the Final Solution. Dad felt it was important that the younger generation be reminded of what he and his generation fought and died for. It was shocking and horrific. Good prevailed over evil, thanks to the Yanks and the rest of the Commonwealth. The Second World War ended, and the Nazi party was defeated. Unfortunately, the fascist hatred of the Jews lived on; Dad said there will always be those who use power to oppress the vulnerable and helpless. However, I was not in Berlin, Warsaw, or Paris back in the day. I was in a school quadrangle in a trendy seaside community on the south coast of England in the 1970s, an hour away from London.

Skinner interrupted my thoughts as he screamed, "Are you ready, Jews?"

Jews? What the—

I found my voice, but it came out as a squeak, "Um, hello. I'm not Jewish," I murmured in protest. One or two brave boys were more vocal and cried out, "Leave us alone" and "piss off, you knob!"

I giggled nervously. I couldn't believe what was happening, standing like a statue, in shock and total compliance.

"Shut the fuck up, you dirty *schweinehund!* You're getting punished for being the new kids in our school. Some of you resisted your mandatory D-Day baptisms—how dare you?" He wiped spit from his lip with his sleeve. In the days, months, and years to come, he produced an excessive amount of spit, enough to fill a large kitchen sink.

"This game will be fun, you shits," he said as he looked at his buddy, Fickle, the beefy, gormless-looking guy beside him, "Shall we play?" he asked rhetorically.

Did he mean play or pray?

Skinner's sidekick returned a grin. Turning his head towards me and the confused huddle of first-year boys, Skinner barked, "I'll ask again—would you like to play a little game?"

"No," I said, clearing my dry throat.

"Is that a yes?" he sneered, "How about we play Jews versus Nazis?"

Jews versus Nazis? Wait, what did he just say? Play? I wasn't in the mood to "play" anything. I wanted to go back to Mr McNeil's safe and peaceful classroom. Bile rose from my tummy. Remembering my sodden wet hair on the D-Day initiation "game," I anticipated the worst and hoped for a timely intervention from a teacher.

In a dreadful German accent, Skinner screeched, "Only ze strongest vill survive!" He and his buddies roared with laughter. "*Achtung!* When you get caught—" The brute pointed at a small area to the rear of the quadrangle. "See the alcove over there—that will be your personal Belsen, your Auschwitz, and your very own Treblinka! We will throw you dirty Jews into the gates of hell, and you will be beaten and gassed until you are broken and compliant."

I took a deep breath and exhaled through my nose. The circle containing Skinner's henchmen nodded their heads in unison, hooting and howling like hyenas. A few hefty kids guarded the entrance to the far alcove, parallel to the corridors adjacent to the main hall. These "sentries" may have looked thick as shit, but they were big and intimidating—and rubbed their hands together in anticipation.

"They look more like *dummkopfs* than elite German guards," I said to the kids nearby me, neither of whom I knew. As usual, my way of dealing with fear, discomfort, or awkwardness was to use stupid humour. One or two of the kids sniggered at my witticism.

"You there." Skinner pointed at me. "What the fuck are you laughing at? This is not a joke." He held a marker pen in the air and waved it around. "When we catch you filthy pigs, you will be tattooed with your Star of David or our swastika."

No way.

Finally, Skinner gave a smirk, his piggy eyes glinting with mischief as he barked out, "Welcome to Knollditz-by-the-Sea."

Utterly disgusted by what was transpiring, a brave kid tried to walk away, determined to distance himself from the scene. He shook his head, refusing to play Skinner's game. Three burly "guards" pounced on him. I watched as they dragged him towards the alcove—the entry point of "internment."

Skinner yelled, "Get the rest of the dirty Jews!" Pandemonium broke out. I froze and hid behind the other kids before me. As Skinner's lackeys charged, I made a break for freedom, and ran for my life towards the south side of the concrete jungle. It was mayhem. I was petrified.

Surely, a teacher will come and stop this absurdity.

Some kids flew and were immediately caught and dragged away. Others dodged, ran, and side-stepped some more. It was over in a flash. I was caught. My heart skipped a beat; my breath momentarily trapped in my throat. The sharp pain of my hair being yanked, the intense pressure of a headlock, and the many blows to my head are sensations I can still feel today, as if it happened a short time ago.

Complex Post Traumatic Stress can present itself in different forms and levels of severity. Even now, my body responds to the lingering sensations of fear, anger, anxiety, and helplessness that I experienced. At that instant, my brain seemed to dismiss the importance of processing and comprehending the present as if it didn't matter. *Legs, it's time to spring into action*, I probably thought, feeling a surge of adrenaline as I prepared for the need for speed. *Heart rate, crank up. Yo, arms! Brace yourself for the danger ahead. Why? Well, this is what's important right now. But I need to process this—Hey, brain, chill the feck out—we'll get back to the processing part later.*

Only after many years did I finally find the strength to confront and truly feel what had happened. Initially, these feelings were like releasing Norma Bates from Hitchcock's Psycho into my mind, causing unease. The presence of my inner social worker provided a comforting reminder of my safety, teaching me how to stay grounded in the present.

We were packed like sardines into the nook of the playground concentration camp. I was scared, bewildered, and disorientated. My hair was sore at the roots—my head ached.

Who punched me?

This was beyond a sick joke, but it became sicker as someone shouted, "Bundle!" It was an instruction for the big kids to dive upon us, like they were in a rugby scrum. Skinner's voice, "Gas them! Gas the Jews!" and "Gas! Gas! Gas!" still echo in my ears, decades after the event.

The bullies charged at us. I was at the front, near the entrance. Suddenly, a fist collided with my face, causing a sharp pain to surge through my cheekbone. The next thing I knew, I was hurled onto the unforgiving concrete floor. I found myself trapped beneath a pile of bodies as the bigger kids, the "Nazi guards," heartlessly leapt onto the heap, inflicting pain on everyone beneath them. I was filled with panic, but there was no place to flee, no means of escape.

The dull ache on my face ceased momentarily as I was desperate to breathe. Gasping for air, I was at the point of blackout, as the mass of kids weighing down upon me made it almost impossible to inhale. The metallic taste of blood trickled from my nose and the cut on my upper lip.

I heard laughter, cries for help, grunts, and moans, followed by loud, wet-sounding, stinking farts.

The crazy bastards are farting on us to simulate Zyklon-B gas.

One boy's head was forced into the backside of a "guard," who promptly broke wind in the poor boy's face. It stank so bad even the thug holding onto the boy had to let the lad go, as he gagged and waved his hands to dissipate the rotten egg smell.

"Pure, Knoll School Fart Gas," yelled Skinner, standing nearby and laughing hysterically. My new school had taught me my first life-lesson: I realised I didn't want to be associated with any group, be it Jewish or Nazi, if a similar situation were to occur again. Though I was just 11-years old, my heart ached for my mum's presence, and I wished for the security of a big brother to shield me at school.

The weight from the bodies above me gradually lessened, and I could breathe freely again. The bigger kids on the top of the scrum started to get off the smaller kids below them. Once released, I dusted the playground dirt from my once-smart, spanking-new school uniform, straightened my tie, and listened to the beautiful sound of the bell, reminding kids to return to class. Wiping blood from my mouth, I looked into the eyes of another boy who also picked himself up from the ground and said, "Well, that was fun!" I don't know who the kid was, but we both laughed.

The question that kept bothering me was—where were the teachers? What about protection from the staff? They were not visible at all. It went without saying that the teachers, for the most part, were probably sipping tea in the staffroom, either unaware or deliberately ignoring the events unfolding around them.

In the five seemingly endless years I had to endure this school's insanity, not once did I witness a teacher take action to address the pupil's quandary. Whether heads were submerged in the toilet basins or boys being mercilessly sucker-punched in the face during a lesson—the teachers remained silent. Shamefully, I felt like no teacher took any action to address our predicament. Not only did the bullies at Knoll School mistreat gay pupils, disabled children, and passive boys, but I suspect that unspeakable acts took place in the vandalised school toilets. The cherry on the Knoll School cake when all is said and done is that several of its teachers were also guilty of physical, verbal, and mental abuse and, at times, violent assaults on children— seemingly without fear of consequences.

CHAPTER 5
TATTOO YOU—NAZI OR JEW?
1973-1974

I KNEW THE SO-CALLED "GAME" WOULD HAPPEN AGAIN THE NEXT day and the next, and it was far from the only torment Skinner thought to visit on us. Who on earth would devise such a game? It was terrible enough to participate in this hate game of Jews versus Nazis, but the honest "reckoning," the saddest of truths, was the realisation that there were no adults present to protect us. Like many kids in the 1970s going through traumatic childhood events—I had to suck it up and scream to myself in the silence. This became a pattern for the next few years.

After herding the pupils into the centre of the quadrangle—the obligatory "escape and evasion" part of the game, then being roughly thrown into the "gas chamber," Skinner and his cronies spiced up the entertainment and marked us with a black felt marker pen.

"Nazi or Jew?" he yelled, pressing his face within a few inches of mine. His breath was stale; spittle landed on my face. I turned my head, and shut my eyes to avoid eye contact.

"Leave me alone. I want to be neither."

"Then you'll be a Jewboy." His sidekick held my head in a vice-like grip, facing Skinner.

"Pig boy, choose—Jew or Nazi?"

I looked away, avoiding his maniacal face. My stomach churned. My heart was thumping so rapidly, I was sure Skinner heard the panic scream within me. I almost capitulated.

If I choose a swastika—he'll leave me alone.

At that point, I didn't care if he victimised other kids. It was pure survival. I remained silent. He crudely drew a Star of David on my forehead. "Now, you ugly shit, fuck off."

I felt Fickle release his grip slightly, so I yanked myself free before Skinner could spew more abuse at me; I ran like the clappers.

Great, I was now marked as a Jew. I bet the knob couldn't draw a proper star, and I was marked with Satan's pentagram.

Now free from the bully's grasp, I stopped in my tracks as I approached the double playground doors that led to either the toilet area or the classroom sanctuary. The loos were not a safe area—"D-Day" had taught me as much. I looked behind me one more time to make sure my tormentors were not in hot pursuit of me, then took a cotton handkerchief from my blazer pocket with my free hand and spat on it. I covered my forehead with my spittle and then feverishly tried to remove what had been daubed onto it. The black marker left its print on the soft cotton cloth.

Mum will go nuts when she sees her spotlessly clean hanky covered in black felt pen.

When Skinner and his sidekicks waved their marker pens in the air, every young pupil knew what was coming: the hate game, and they would quasi-brand many kids during morning or lunch breaks. I wanted a third option. Jew? Nazi? Neutral? I desperately wanted to be like Sweden or Switzerland during World War II. My war hero dad considered these nations as cowards, but I didn't care. I now adore Switzerland and cherish Sweden. I didn't want Skinner to draw either a swastika or the Star of David on my arm or, worse still, my forehead, as I'd have to visit the menacing school toilets. If I braved the loos, I could wash off the marker scribble. However, the toilet areas were scary, and I didn't want to meet more bullies who patrolled the area and then risk being late for class. The consequences of being tardy depended on the teacher's mood—if, say, the out-of-breath pupil burst into their classroom and announced the following:

Sorry, I'm late.

Why are you late, boy? Why do you have marker pen on your forehead? Class laughs.

I'm a Jew, sir.

A Jew? Wear your damn Star of David around your neck or at the synagogue, not on your forehead. You have a sixty-minute detention here after school.

Or...

Sorry, I'm late.

Why are you late, boy? Why do you have marker pen on your forehead?

I'm a Nazi, sir. Class gasps.

Get out of my class, you little racist bastard! Report to Mr Oxford for a savage caning!

Whatever I chose would result in a grumpy response, detention, or Gary, the miscreant, being sent to the headmaster to receive "six of the best" from his cane. There was another alternative, one that I wished I dared to do at the time. I walk into class with a swastika drawn on my forehead, get yelled at by the teacher, and be sent to the headmaster for supporting Hitler or mocking the Holocaust. I'd get lashed with the cane, run home, tell Mum. Then, I'd sit back, buy some popcorn, and watch her storm the head's office to give him a taste of his own medicine. Mum had done this once during my brother Paul's time at school when he was (in her mind) unjustly caned.

I wanted to lie low, be the grey man, even a chameleon, and not be noticed by anyone. I really didn't want to explain to a teacher why I venerated either fascism or Judaism. Snitching wasn't an option. Teachers were turning a blind eye to the "D-

Day" and current playground savagery. I couldn't tell Mum or Dad what had transpired, and my siblings were not around. I had to survive five more years of this crap on my own, suffering in silence.

    Keeping these experiences to myself was non-negotiable. Dad had condemned me to The Knoll. In my mind, he didn't care. I assumed he'd tell me to "grow a pair," as he believed the headmaster's soundbite of "It's an excellent school." Mum would have either fallen behind Dad or would have stormed the Bastille. In any case, I didn't feel my parents were safe people to share my feelings with. Many baby boomers and ex-pupils still believe "what doesn't kill you makes you stronger." Thanks (not), Friedrich Nietzsche, for your "suck it up, buttercup" philosophy.

CHAPTER 6
PHYS ED - STICKS AND STONES
1972-1974

MONTHS WENT BY AND THINGS DIDN'T GET ANY BETTER. WITH THE toilet duckings that occurred, the constant verbal abuse and the ludicrous "Holocaust games," I can't say the first few months at school were fun. When I moved to my new school, I couldn't believe how much I disliked gym class, especially as I loved sports at Middle Street Primary. We were a group of skinny, runtish 11-year-olds, each with unique shapes and sizes. However, one or two boys were large for their age. These days, adults are sensitive about childhood obesity and bend over backwards to not body-shame anyone, especially children. At Knoll School, Mr Marine, dressed like an SAS drill instructor, would not give anyone a sympathy card, overweight or underweight. I was terrified of that man. All he did was yell and mock the pupils. If you did everything he demanded, his anger focussed on the less fit members of his class.

"Hey, don't tell me your name," he yelled at a pupil called Maddocks. Marine appeared deep in thought—his angry eyes looking up at the tall gymnasium ceiling as his hand rested on his chin like the philosopher Aristotle. "Umm, this is an easy one for me—" We stood in a line, paying attention like we were on a parade ground. The teacher suddenly nodded like he'd discovered some profound quantum physics dilemma. "It's Billy Bunter!" The class laughed in unity at Marine's body-shaming joke.

"No, it's Maddocks, sir," his face bright red, head bowed down.

He stared at the boy. "Oh, so it's Maddocks?"

"Sir, yes, sir."

"Are you stupid? Do you have a brain to go with all those doughnuts you ate this morning?" Once again, Maddocks looked at the ground. The entire class laughed out loud.

"You, Mr Maddocks, will have a tough time in my class. This is Physical Education, not a 'Save the Whale' rally."

I felt for the kid—I really did. However, Marine wasn't taking the piss out of me. Rotund boys were referred to by the P.E. staff as "lard arse" and "porker." Sometimes, they'd yell at them when they tried to climb the 20-foot ropes attached to the enormous wooden apparatus that swung out when it was time to display our climbing skills.

"Hey, fatty! Your muddy plimsolls look like you've spent the weekend on the family farm. Did you eat the entire herd of cows, perchance?" I got off easily being called "runt," "streak of piss," and "faggot-arse."

During the unforgettable shaming incident, Mr Marine had us do circuits around the gym. One obstacle he included was the pommel horse, which we had to jump over or navigate. Maddocks made every effort to conquer this piece of gym kit. He tried to leap over it, climb onto it, and hoist himself up and over it. Each time he attempted to pull himself up onto the gym apparatus, his heavy breathing and frustrated groans filled the air. No matter how hard Maddocks tried, Marine refused to let him skip the pommel horse.

"You will get over this piece of kit. We will all wait and watch you climb over it, and if it takes you all week, we will be here to see you get your fat-arse over it." He folded his arms, stood back, and watched as Maddocks failed time and time again. Eventually, the boy burst into tears and sobbed uncontrollably, shoulders slumped and moving up and down. There was a deathly silence. He seemed helpless. I rubbed my temples. *What was he supposed to do now?*

Marine shook his head repeatedly. "Maddocks, get out of my sight!" he yelled. I don't remember seeing the boy again. Maybe he switched classes, or his mum or doctor wrote him a sick note. Not being able to yell, "Leave him alone," I screamed in silence for the lad. *Thank God I wasn't overweight, but I wished I wasn't so skinny.*

Thankfully, one of the other P.E. teachers, Mr McDougall, wasn't as verbally abusive as Mr Marine. Unfortunately, he lacked any kind of empathy for the pupils in his care. He was an unpleasant man with an angry "don't mess with me" demeanour and savage temperament. McDougall barked orders at us and handed out punishments like a man possessed. He delighted in taking the class on long runs in the cold and rain, leaving us little time to shower and change before the next class. I detested the forced runs but sucked them up, as I was neither the fastest nor slowest—doing the bare minimum to run with the last third of runners to give me enough time to have a shower and not be late for class.

There were the extracurricular physical activities. Despite enduring lengthy cross-country runs in the English rain, my dislike for running persisted, especially with the discomfort of wearing low-quality plimsols. The rugby and football try-outs occurred on a muddy, quagmire pitch resembling the infamous Battle of the Somme at Greenleas Recreation Park. This area was where dog owners could let their pets relieve themselves. As a football fanatic and dedicated athlete, my desire to play sports quickly vanished. The idea of getting my knees or arms dirty with mud and dog shit after playing a game of football or rugby was far from motivating.

So, during the first year, I despised most sports—not because of the sports themselves (although they were terrible) or the subpar conditions (except for summer), but because I wanted to avoid the school's grimy shower area. The facility had showers. Nonetheless, the water was often cold unless you were fortunate to be among the first to shower, typically reserved for the more accomplished and physically fit runners. There were no lockers, so I placed my gear on a wooden bench with coat hooks. Following my P.E. activities, I was forced to endure icy cold showers, only to discover some moron had thrown my or my classmate's clothes into the showers when we returned to the changing room.

Several boys returned from their activity, unable to find their uniforms. Bigger boys were standing by the changing room door, smirking. Shirts, ties, vests, and trousers had been thrown into the wet showers and soaked with water. Mr McDougall, present in his office adjacent to the shower area, did not appear to be aware of what was going on, despite victims yelling and freaking out when their kit was eventually discovered. He just stood by the door to his office and yelled at stragglers putting on their soaking wet clothes.

The deed was often done by older thugs who didn't appear interested in learning. They were given way too much free time by a school system that cared little about them and didn't know what else to do to maintain order. It felt like the teachers could terrorise and abuse the compliant ones—the ones who wanted to learn—but gave the bigger, more troublesome pupils a free pass.

One day, after a mind-numbing time spent in a French language lab listening to pop music instead of basic French in our headsets, I had to attend Mr McDougall's P.E. class. Once again, the class was forced to run for half an hour in the cold and rain. I left my dry clothes in the changing rooms, but on returning to the changing area and having little time to transition between classes, I realised my clothes had disappeared. When I looked into the showers, my heart sank as I saw both my own and my classmates' gear scattered across the drenched floor. Everything was soddened, and the donkey of a sports master had done nothing to stop this mindless practice.

After retrieving my dripping-wet underwear, shirt, trousers, tie, and socks from the shower, I wrung water from them as best I could by hand. I put them on to avoid being late for the next class and receiving detention or a couple of lashes with the headmaster's cane. I sat in the remaining classes shivering and feeling extremely uncomfortable with two or three of the other victims—our clothes soaked to varying degrees.

The bell for the end of school finally rang, and I walked home at double time in the drizzle to avoid the daily commotion near the bus stop or on the bus itself. Despite the urgency to reach home, staying off the bus kept me safe from the older hooligans.

Once home, Mum saw my wet clothes hanging out to dry on the kitchen chairs. She was initially angry at my stupidity for wetting my uniform until I told her some idiot played a prank and threw my clothes into the shower. Mum, being Mum, phoned the school and freaked out at whoever had the misfortune to answer the call. I gave Mum no names, as it was generally the same idiots that made other kids' lives miserable. Although bigger in stature, these same louts were often useless at sports or wanted to avoid attending lessons. Hence, they either hung around the corridors, created mischief, used the loos, or loafed around the school enjoying a smoke.

I informed my mum it was my fault for being careless so she wouldn't take matters into her own hands by going to the sports teacher in person. Although it would be satisfying, it wouldn't be helpful if Mum went berserk and threw McDougall's gear into the shower—which she was more than capable of doing. Mum was fearless, but didn't consider the ramifications for her children, including being on the receiving end of more beasting, abuse, and teasing. So, I said as little as possible to avoid the bullies and the teachers putting a big target on my back.

Despite her call ruffling a few teachers' feathers, I didn't get into trouble on my return to school. Mr McDougall, for example, gave me a death stare as a greeting, and as usual, I shivered in fear —he was one scary dude in my eyes. McDougall then made super-aggressive comments to the class that anyone misusing the showers would be severely dealt with.

I hid my smirk well. However, the shower-bullies had the last laugh at my expense. After these negative experiences, I decided not to shower, choosing to wash myself when I returned home. I ensured I had a deodorant stick at hand and tried not to walk around the school like a smelly cat.

A few days later, however, I started to sniffle. My nose was runny, and an annoying cough soon developed. Within 24 hours, I had a raging fever, and I was soon gasping for air.

I can't definitively say wearing soaking-wet clothing for a few hours nearly cost me my life. However, Mum was convinced that was the case. For once, she wasn't blaming my poor diet or perceived misbehaviour as a catalyst for the wrath of God on my affliction. I had never felt so ill in my life.

My head pounded, and my temperature rose above 104 degrees, but the worst thing was I could barely breathe. It felt like my chest area was being held in a vice—I could only take in minuscule breaths—it felt like I was drowning. Mum and Dad made me put my head over a bowl of boiling water containing menthol crystals for relief. I remember hallucinating and having horrible visions of being held under the water in a school toilet, gasping for air, and my lungs filling with revolting toilet water.

"How did your son die, Mrs Trew?" asked the headmaster.

"He drowned in a school toilet, Mr Oxford."

"Tut-tut, oh dear. I guess it's far better to die instantly from *drowning than suffer the ignominy of typhoid, dysentery, or cholera,"* replied the uncaring headmaster.

One delirious nightmare was memorable. My parents were negligent, allowing me to wander off unsupervised into King Alfred swimming baths. A dark figure grabbed me from behind and carried me to an empty pool, throwing me in feet first. The pool filled up, not with water, but sewage. The pool walls were deep, and there appeared to be no way of escaping it.

"Dad, Dad," I cried. *"Mum, help me, please help me."*

My voice echoed around the pool. Skinner, the school bully, stood at the side of the pool, looking down at me. He wore devil horns and swished his tail as he began to prowl around the pool, laughing and yelling, *"Poor, dirty Jew boy!"* and *"Drown in Jew shit!"*

The stinking effluent had reached my neck—the smell was intolerable. The excrement now touched my mouth, I wretched and cried out, "Help me. Help me. Please, I'm not Jewish!" Skinner guffawed, and his eyes glowed red. I made a blood-curdling scream and realised that someone was putting cold flannels on my brow to cool me down. No sooner did I choke down another scream than relief came like an injured soldier given battlefield morphine—Dad was there, mopping the sweat from my forehead.

"It's okay, son. You were having a bad dream. I know you're not Jewish—what were you dreaming?" I was too parched to tell him anything. He put a glass to my lips, and I sipped some water.

Mum was also in the room. My eyes couldn't focus, but I could hear them talking. "Lou, I'm worried. He's getting worse. I'm not sure his fever will break."

The next thing I knew, our family doctor, Dr Harris, arrived. Dad sat me up from a prone position. The doctor took out his stethoscope and placed it on my heart and chest area, reading the thermometer he'd popped into my mouth. He stepped away.

"I'm afraid the pneumonia has got into both lungs. I'm of two minds; we call an ambulance and get him to the hospital, or I can give the boy a large shot of penicillin. In the latter case, you'll have to ensure he is given a double dose of antibiotics every four hours."

My parents knew the practicalities of not having a vehicle to go back and forth to the Royal Sussex Hospital in Brighton, so the doctor gave me a shot of antibiotics in the bum. Dr Harris warned my parents that if I became worse, they needed to call for an ambulance to rush me to the hospital.

Later, Mum told me the doctor had said to her if Dad hadn't called him when he did, I would be dead. The pneumonia was bad—both lungs were infected. Dad carried me in his arms to the spare room, made a fresh bed, and bought me a giant teddy bear to keep me company. He checked in every hour. Mum returned to work full-time.

I fought for each breath, feeling like the air was being squeezed out of me. Fluid had filled up my lungs, and I experienced pulmonary oedema. It was like dying the death of a thousand cuts. I tried to draw in air, and hardly anything entered my lungs. It was exhausting.

"Dad," I gasped, "I'll never take breathing—" more short breaths, "for granted—" final breath, "again."

"Shush, son. Rest now. I'll be next door. I'll check on you again in a minute." Dad may have a cold exterior to many folks, but he was a wonderful caregiver. Thankfully, the pink liquid wonder drug kicked in within a few days. My breathing became more manageable, my fever broke, and things improved.

Nevertheless, I refrained from eating—I had little appetite for food and I couldn't even eat my favourite treat of char-fried liver strips and Heinz baked beans. I drank orange squash (water mixed with orange concentrate) and occasionally a cup of soup. I recall my sister Carole's head appearing at the door.

"Oh my God, you look like a living skeleton."

Sweet—just what I want to hear.

"You're as pale as a ghost."

Always nice to be told how horrible I look.
"Have you escaped from Belsen?"
Funny, not funny—I'll fit in nicely when I'm forced to play Jews versus Nazis again.
"See you later, Skelly Boy."
I can't wait to hear how ugly I look.

After a month passed, I found I could finally take normal breaths, but I was still fragile and didn't want to return to that hell hole of a school. Eventually, much to my chagrin, Dad told me I must return or they may back-class me. I couldn't cope with adding another year to my ordeal, so I faked feeling better and returned to classes. No one asked me why I'd been away; the teachers acted like I'd not missed a day. I returned to "Knolldtiz" but only for a brief spell.

The craziness of hateful school playground activities hadn't abated, and I was weaker than ever. To be excused from P.E. (thank God), Mum had written notes for me, much to the disgust of Mr McDougall, who was initially shocked at my appearance. "You don't look well, Trew. Some fresh air might help build your immunity."

Pretty soon, his compassion ran out, and as I produced sick note after sick note, he began to mock me, calling me a "shirker," a "little faggot," and a "wimp." Classy.

Unfortunately, having returned to school too soon, I fell ill once again with similar fever and breathing issues. The high temperature and shortness of breath returned. The doctor arrived at Livingstone Road and advised my parents to keep me home until I fully recovered, as I had a second pneumonia attack. The doctor switched the antibiotics to streptomycin. I developed colossal mouth and throat ulcers within a few hours of taking the medicine; I couldn't swallow and struggled to breathe again. The family doctor returned to see me the following day and told Dad I had an allergic reaction to the meds. So, he reluctantly put me back on penicillin.

Dad was kind and encouraged me to read some of his schoolboy favourites, like Enid Blyton's *Famous Five* books and Frank Richards's classic writings. I loved reading about Billy Bunter and the bullies at Greyfriars School as I could relate to Bunter on many levels—apart from our weight differences. He was huge, and I was like the Walking Dead. I read many different books to help with the boredom and returned to school for the last few weeks of the term.

Back at school, I had lost so much weight to my already slim body that I looked pale and gaunt; pejorative names flowed from Skinner's mouth. Malnourishment caused my face to become emaciated, but my eyes stayed the same size, giving me a strange appearance, like a fluffy-tailed lemur. Skinner and others seemed to love my new demeanour. "Froggy, you are *definitely* a Jew. Did you go on holiday to Dachau or Treblinka?"

I silently agreed with him. I not only looked like someone who'd just been released from a concentration camp—I resembled a startled frog. His names for me were beginning to make my blood boil. I wanted to punch him so badly.

The bully and his cronies had a penchant for finding demeaning names to torment me further. Even Mum, Carole and Dad started to tease me—this felt like a dagger through my heart. I started to despise myself and the way I looked.

"Gary, sticks and stones will break your bones, but words will never hurt you!" smiled Mum, one of her favourite sayings.

"That's bullshit," I told her. "The worst Mum-made proverb ever."

"Watch your mouth. You may have the appearance of—"

"Don't you dare even say it," I hissed, with a face like thunder.

"—a—a—cornered, wild animal." Carole giggled.

"More like a startled fish," added Mum.

Carole and Mum cackled at each other's comments. "Gary, just grow a pair," Mum waded in, "Don't take words to heart. Sticks and stones may break—"

Putting my "that's a bullshit proverb" theory to the test, I interrupted Mum in full flow. "Shut up, you stupid Welsh witch," and to my sister, "You useless, ignorant Irish slut."

Carole smirked, but looked shocked. Mum stared me down like a prize fighter sizing up his opponent. Like a cobra striking its prey, Mum lashed out at me but lost her balance as she didn't see the vacuum cleaner on the floor between us. I guffawed, turned towards the doorway, and ran up the stairs to my bedroom. Now armed with a broomstick and a face the colour of puce, Mum chased after me, repeatedly hitting me on my retreating back until I managed to reach the bedroom, shut the door on her and flip the flimsy internal bolt.

"You ever talk like that again, and I'll tan your hide," she yelled.

From behind the safety of a heavy, wooden door, out of breath, I replied, "Sticks and stones will break your bones, but words will never hurt you."

Mum slowly retreated down the stairs, broom in hand. "How dare you, you stupid boy—they are just words!"

Neither Carole nor my mum ever called me a name again—well, not to my face. What really sucked was I had missed a lot of schoolwork because of illness, putting me well behind the class. However, I didn't realise I was destined to skip even more school the following year.

CHAPTER 7
HIPPOPOTAMATHS
1972-1974

I KNOW I'M NOT BAD AT MATHS; HOWEVER, WHEN I LOOK BACK TO my Knoll School days, I really sucked at the subject. At Middle Street, I found mathematics easy-peasy, lemon squeezy and had no issues. I also had my dad help me with basic algebra and geometry. Mum also chipped in, assisting with solving simple fractions. Thanks to Mum, I had learned my twelve times tables off by heart by the time I was eight.

When I hit secondary school, Dad had given up on me—probably for failing my 11-plus. I was so lost in maths class that I plucked up the courage to ask him if he would help me figure out algebra. I needed courage as Dad looked increasingly irritated by any interruption that interfered with his recording of jazz and swing albums on his HiFi system.

I had butterflies, and my throat was dry. I was unsure if it was due to the algebra or the look on my dad's face when I asked for help. He drummed his fingers on his leather chair as I tried to find the correct page of the exercise book.

I showed him the algebra questions and circled the numbers that I wanted him to work through with me. Dad was a maths and physics whizz from his Air Force Days. His cold-as-ice blue eyes looked into my big, greeny-blue peepers.

"Well, get your bloody pencil and write out what you think the answer is, *explaining* each part of your answer."

I gulped. My "bloody" pencil was shaking in my hand. I stared at the blank page of my book and gingerly wrote down the question.

"Yes, brain of Britain—that's *the question*."

"Dad, I don't know how to start it."

"Start it? Start it? Start the car? Start the clock? Start the bloody what?"

This is worse than maths class.

"Start solving the equation," I squeaked.

"Well, duh. I guess that's why we're here."

No, this was worse than being in the crosshairs of the Knoll School maths teacher.

Dad snatched the pencil from my hand and scribbled down the answer quickly and neatly. "See?"

"Oh, yes," I lied, staring at his scribble. I shook my head and looked up at his face. "Actually, no, I don't 'see.' You went too fast."

"I'll do one more. These are easy, lad. Don't be the village idiot of the Trew family."

Village idiot? Music to my ears—was it that obvious?

He scrawled down another question. He was looking at me with his death ray stare even though he was looking at the crown of my head, or maybe he was penetrating my amygdala.

"Well?"

I cleared my throat, "You, you take x and, and multiply it by 2y—"

"And?"

I stared at the sum.

"And?" he growled.

I still didn't look at him; I imagined his nostrils flaring and the vein in his temple pulsating as his blood pressure hit four figures. Silence, apart from the thudding of my heart.

I've disappointed him again. He's so mad at me. I can't—I just can't—I've gotta get out before I cry.

In adrenaline-flight mode, I snatched the pencil from his hand, grabbed my books, jumped up from the floor, and stomped out of the room, slamming the door behind me in Denis Trew fashion.

Mum met me at the bottom of the stairs. I teared up, feeling like my spirit had been crushed. Mum had been listening at the foot of the stairs and was worried about the tuition lesson. "I'm sorry, Ga. I've never been any good at algebra. We can try to figure it out together," she pointed to the kitchen table. Looking at my inflamed and sore eyes, she said, "Come on, he doesn't mean to snap. He has no patience if you don't get something the first time. It was the same with Carole."

Mum made me a cup of tea, and we sat together at the kitchen table, trying to figure out how to do the algebra questions. The problem was, apart from Mum having as much clue how to tackle algebra as I had, the textbook questions didn't contain any answers, so we never knew if our trial-and-error attempts were correct.

I wish I could say that doing maths (or 'math' in Canada and the USA) at the Knoll was an experience that piqued my curiosity and sparked intellectual engagement. It did the opposite, and I dreaded each time I had to walk into the prefab buildings at the rear of the school.

The students jokingly called their teacher "Hippo" Grippo, not because of the play-on-words similarity to the longest side of a right-angled triangle—the hypotenuse. No, it was due to the times in class when he bore an uncanny resemblance to an enraged hippopotamus. The sight of Mr Grippo, a short and corpulent fifty-something individual wearing a tightly buttoned jacket, sent shivers down the spines of the front-row students, as the solitary button was under so much pressure due to his increasingly bulging girth. Hippo's solitary button on his buttoned-up jacket defied the laws of physics—a true freak of nature. I swear the button's thread must have been made with titanium and welded onto a titanium plate, with the buttonhole lined with diamonds for added strength. As I was so lost during Mr Grippo's algebra lessons, I amused myself by trying to calculate the speed at which his button would fly off at any given moment, using the equation, pressure equals force divided by area. With my ability to daydream, I also imagined the potential carnage to the pupil on the receiving end of said button.

Having missed a load of classes, I was always playing catch up. I dreaded him calling me out to the front—to walk the walk of shame in front of everyone—only to fail to complete the maths problem he set on the blackboard. Thankfully, Grippo never knew my actual name. When my luck was in, he called me "You Boy." However, I believe he also referred to me as "moron," "idiot," "numbskull," or when my luck was really in, as "you useless retard." Nothing beats the feeling when an important and influential adult remembers your name.

Once singled out, I left my uncomfortable wooden chair and heavily graffitied desk, slowly walked to the front of the class, and stared blankly at the blackboard. I was frozen in my adrenaline-induced fight-or-flight body. I gaped at the blackboard, doing my best to avoid eye contact with him. I stood at the front of the class like a deer caught in headlights. To this day, I hate being called out by instructors or facilitators to answer their questions. I put it down to a kind of complex PTSD received from a couple of years of Grippo's maths lessons.

Another noteworthy phenomenon is he appeared to have eyes in the back of his head. Grippo once asked a boy sitting on the left of the class a question, and without moving his head, hurled a board rubber at an unsuspecting boy on the other side of the classroom with Pilbara Death Adder-striking speed. Forewarned by his sixth sense, the boy ducked his head as he saw the projectile heading towards him at the last minute. Unfortunately, the board rubber struck an even more unsuspecting boy sitting behind the original victim in the face. It happened to me twice, much to the merriment of the class.

On several other occasions, he struck me on the head with chalk as I was trying to copy my friend Billy's answer, or figure out the maths problem in my exercise book. Instead of apologising, he made out the missile had been aimed at me, and a double punishment would transpire as Grippo called me out to the front and scolded me for being an "imbecile."

Thankfully, many students, like Billy, were good at maths and keenly put their hands up to answer his questions by saying, "Sir, sir, please, please, sir!" When Mr Grippo did not select these keeners, the "Sir, please sir," turned into an "Ooh, ooh, sir," or the keener made sniffing sounds while standing up on their desks with a hand raised high in the air. This was great; however, it also drew attention to those of us who didn't know the answer to the question and didn't have our hands raised. Wise-old Grippo would select the non-keener that sat next to the super-keener. I figured out that, like playing Russian Roulette, if I held up my hand limply, with no enthusiasm whatsoever, he would rarely pick me to shout out the answer I didn't know. I also remember Grippo handing out detentions for not answering a question correctly. Oh, the fun of mathematics.

On a positive note, I'm forever grateful to Mr Grippo for his trigonometry formulas and mnemonics, which he drilled into our heads with threats of death. "Some Old Hulks Carry A Huge Tub Of Ale" still sticks with me after all these years. It goes without saying that this equation implied the sine of an angle was equal to the proportion of the length of the side opposite the angle to the size of the hypotenuse. Conversely, the cosine of the angle is the ratio of the adjacent side to the hypotenuse. This was a valuable life lesson for me, especially for a career in . . . *social work.*

Anyway, I'm more knowledgeable than you may think!

CHAPTER 8
LAST CHRISTMAS
DECEMBER, 1974

Dad was a handsome man. Piercing, grey-blue eyes, good teeth, a fine head of hair, and sharp features helped to make him so. I inherited his Kirk Douglas dimpled chin and his sardonic sense of humour. To those who didn't know him, he presented himself as an austere military man with an upright bearing, and was seldom seen without a collar and tie. Denis had a very dry wit and loved TV shows like Monty Python, The Goodies, and inappropriate slapstick comedies. I never witnessed an angry word to my mum. His signature sign of displeasure was to walk away from his wife, stomp upstairs, THUMP, THUMP, THUMP, and slam the living room door behind him. This area was his sanctuary. This was his room; he had his tan-coloured chair, a sofa and an old rocker, his pipe and tobacco, and his music system.

 The only time I ever saw Dad on the sofa was when he heard the news from his sister that his mother had died—he lay there and sobbed—a strange reaction from a son who had very little to do with his parents in adult life. What ghosts were there from the past were firmly locked up in the vault of his heart. An hour later, the altercation with Mum had been forgotten, and he was being playful and teasing with her again. Denis was a war hero who never bragged or shared too much about what he'd experienced.

Dad's nickname for me was "Doody." I cherished it when he called me that. I was very close to my dad, and although he loved Carole, I was definitely his favourite. He loved that I was fascinated by all things military, and I wanted to pursue a career in flying, just like he had done in the past.

Just as I found joy in my childhood pleasures—indulging in chocolate bars or exploring a Spitfire at an air show—my dad, too, found solace in the beauty of music and the peace of solitude.

Denis loved jazz, swing, and most of the big band sounds. He may have expressed being super-unhappy when his beloved Tottenham Hotspur lost their football game . . . or when Labour Party leader Harold Wilson was threatening to become the UK's new Prime Minister, but once the needle touched his Miff Mole and His Little Molers, Andrew Sisters, Crosby, or Sinatra records, he was as chilled as a "make love, not war" stoner smoking a huge doobie or spliff at the Woodstock festival.

Apart from having the nose or olfactory sharpness of an African bush elephant, Dad had an ear for musical sounds that would make the greater wax moth jealous. His ability to perceive pitch, timbre, harmony, and melody was remarkable. Yet, to my knowledge, he never played a musical instrument.

On one occasion, playing with my miniature plastic armies, I'd been simulating the epic battle of Tobruk with the Australian 9th Division, supported by British tanks and artillery resisting the attack from the 15th Panzer Division led by "Desert Rat" Erwin Rommel. Dad removed his headphones and interrupted me, "Doody, come and listen to this. Pure genius."

I slipped over to his chair, climbed onto his lap, dodged my head to avoid his pipe, and listened to the sound of *Java Jive* by the Ink Spots.

"Fantastic!" I said, not knowing what made the sound "pure genius."

"That's what perfect pitch sounds like, son."

"Yes, Dad."

"None of your brother's beatnik noise that he listens to." I scrunched up my face and frowned.

"Like the Beatles and the Beach Boys?"

"Yes. Their harmonies are good—top-notch. The sounds and weird arrangements are awful. I'm sure my ears bleed when I hear your brother's crap."

He took a puff of his aromatic Old Holborn tobacco, slipped his headphones back on, nodded his head, tapped the armrests of his chair, and sunk into the jazz euphoria once again. Who needs methamphetamine when you have the rush of the Ink Spots or Tommy Dorsey surging through your veins? I loved it when Dad was in his happy place. I loved my dad.

Unlike every middle-aged person on earth, Dad made out that he didn't have a past. Mum knew a bit about her husband, but he kept most of his family and their history at arm's length. He probably shared more about his life with me than other family members, especially his knowledge of the Royal Air Force. Mum was less secretive, but voiced her shame about her traumatic past. Mum and her 10 siblings had been abandoned by their mother, and she felt much shame. Dad was convinced that her past did not have to define her future, and he made a deliberate choice not to dwell on or revisit her pain. He had his own demons to fight with. Mum often told me that Dad wasn't interested in her former years, so she shouldn't be bothered about his. They were Yin and Yang, opposites in personalities, but they made it work without me witnessing them arguing.

Gwen resented what her mother had subjected her and her siblings to as children—terrible hardship, poverty, fear, hopelessness, and abandonment. She told story after story of her chagrin but was kind-hearted, softly spoken and loved being around people. Mum overcompensated and made her children feel that they should never have the need to leave the nest.

Mum was a social butterfly and struggled with her husband's reclusiveness and desire for solitude. At times, she was jealous of the relationship I had with Dad; this was a product of her own demons—insecurities, the fear of rejection and abandonment issues.

Carole was definitely a daddy's girl. During the autumn term at the Knoll School, my sister Carole returned home from Scotland, where she had served in the WRNS at Faslane, the Royal Navy's leading presence in Scotland, including the nation's nuclear deterrent. Mum and Dad were proud as peacocks that my sister had joined the ranks of family service members like them and Dad's dad and grandad before them. Carole met submariner Mike, fell in love, and became pregnant. Even though Dad didn't express his disappointment to me, I overheard Mum saying he was deeply saddened Carole had left the Navy. However, he soon became very excited about his first grandchildren.

Carole gave birth to identical twin boys, and I became an uncle at thirteen. The twins' dad, Mike, had met our family, and I liked him from the first day I met him. He quickly became like a caring brother to me. He was attentive and playful and always made me laugh. I adored him. In addition to displaying a silly sense of humour, he had a cool job working on one of our nuclear submarines. Although Dad didn't like many of Carole's boyfriends, he liked Mike.

My mum loved all her children; however, Paul was the first among equals in her eyes. Paul needed Mum's love more than Carole or I because he was always at odds with Dad—two worldviews collided, and it was never pleasant to experience. Paul, Carole, and I were like three different dogs, each with its unique bark and wagging tail but joined together by a deep mother's love. Thankfully, we all got along much better in later years.

Mum was doubly excited. Firstly, she LOVED babies. Secondly, we were approaching Christmas, her favourite time of year. Despite my mum's protestations, I refused to write a wish list for "*Siôn Corn*," as my mum would say in Welsh, or *Father Christmas*. Father Christmas was dead to me, so I asked my parents for a Thomas Salter Chemistry Lab set for my only present. Since Mum sensibly shopped for the following year's Christmas presents during the January sales, the chances of receiving something I wanted were remote.

One morning, while eavesdropping, I overheard Mum and Carole talking about my dad. I tended to be a stickybeak, playing in the background, but listening to everything the adults talked about. I heard them say something about Dad passing blood in his stools.

I blew my passive-listening super-spy cover and asked, "What's a stool?"

Mum became flustered and said, "A stool is your poop. Doody, why are you listening? Children should be seen and not heard." Mum cleared her throat, picked up a cloth, and busied herself by dusting the cupboards. Then, reluctantly, she shared that my dad had been bleeding from his bowels for quite a while.

Her words caused my chest to tighten. "Is passing blood a bad thing?"

It was clear that neither Mum, Dad, nor Carole wanted to tell anyone about this. Apparently, Dad got so concerned that he told his wife. Mum arranged for Dad to see the doctor, who referred him to a specialist.

Mum assured me there was nothing to worry about—he probably had bleeding internal piles. "Piles? What are piles?" I asked.

"Haemorrhoids," Carole added unhelpfully.

"What are haemorrhoids?"

Mum and Carole told me to go upstairs and mind my business. They didn't seem concerned. I'd seen my dad sick with colds, and Mum told me he was the worst patient in the world. He also struggled with gout, a weird-sounding condition that caused him great pain—his feet would be jutting out on a pouffe—he couldn't lay a sheet on them due to the pain. "Big baby," Mum would mutter to me out of Dad's earshot, and Carole would snigger.

December came, and Mum told me Dad had to go to the hospital to have an operation; she instructed me to not annoy him or get on his nerves. She said an x-ray had shown he had some problem in his tummy and the surgeon would fix it. Dad had refused to have the operation immediately, as the medics had suggested; he wanted to have Christmas at home and enjoy it with his family. He was due to be admitted into Hove General Hospital soon after Christmas.

I was glad to have my dad at home for Christmas Day. Everything was very low-key, and Dad wasn't making it a big deal, although he wasn't his usual happy self in the run-up to Christmas. Ordinarily, my dad would prattle on about football or he'd engage in playful antics such as tickling or chasing me, and we'd share laughter and engage in mock battles. However, he became quiet and serious around me.

Dad took whatever diagnosis he'd been given very seriously. He started to eat All Bran and tripled the roughage he'd typically eat. I didn't see him smoking his pipe with the regularity I'd witnessed in the past. Dad was doing his best to get better, and whatever was troubling his tummy, having a new eating regimen should work its magic and do the trick. He sat at the kitchen table, stirring the brown gruel-like mush in a cereal bowl.

"Are you going to be okay, Daddy?" I asked.

"Of course, son. You have nothing to worry about," Dad reassured me. If Denis Trew said there was nothing to worry about, there was nothing to worry about.

Christmas came, and Dad appeared in better spirits, ensuring he had his once-a-year drink of Bacardi and Coke. I was thrilled and shocked to receive the Thomas Salter chemistry set as one of my Christmas presents. Unfortunately, other household members were less pleased with the gift as the smell of rotten eggs permeated the living room area. Sulphur dioxide stunk out the entire home as one of my chemistry experiments went pear-shaped. "Stupid boy," commented Carole, and Dad thought it was hilarious—it was good to see him laugh.

Dad was admitted to the hospital and had an operation to fix his bleeding "stools." A few days later, the test cricket was on Down Under. England and Australia were contesting the classic Ashes series. Where cricket was concerned, it became my favourite pastime.

CHAPTER 9
ASHES TO ASHES: SHORT STUFF DOWN UNDER
JANUARY, 1975

DAD WAS RECOVERING POST-OP IN HOSPITAL; MUM WAS AT WORK, and England was defending the Ashes from our arch-enemies, Australia. The cricket series was taking place Down Under—the "Poms" were getting a hammering due to the Aussie fast-bowling combination of Jeff Thompson and Dennis Lillie. Never in the history of test cricket had the English batters received so many injuries through fast, short-pitched deliveries. Although I disliked Lillie, I also idolised him and was in awe of his aggressive bowling action and handlebar moustache. While it would probably have taken me 108 years to grow a "mo" like his, I was mesmerised by this Aussie. His bowling companion, Jeff Thompson, had a weird throw-the-javelin type action, which generated considerable pace and intimidated the English batsmen.

Mum had warned me time and time again not to play cricket in the kitchen as something would break, and I would be "in for it." She threatened me with everything from a good hiding to the Bubonic Plague, courtesy of God Himself, as everything in the kitchen was considered sacred. Mum's pride and joy was her

Welsh Dresser. This was a piece of wooden furniture with sliding glass in the upper part, shelves, and a small cupboard underneath. Mum loved to display her Welsh crockery and precious ornaments. The Welsh dresser also acted as a perfect set of cricket stumps that I'd prop against the cupboard.

However, Mum's threats were often hot air, and the little Doody mouse would play while the Mumma cat was away. So, I did. I simulated the short-pitched bowling of the Aussies by throwing a tennis ball as hard as I could against the kitchen ceiling. Using trigonometry, I hurled the ball at such speed and angle it bounced from the ceiling onto the wall and floor to the waiting English batsman (aka Doody), who was holding his cricket bat and "hooking" the fast, short delivery onto another wall for four or six runs—a difficult skill to perfect in one's cramped kitchen.

I managed it like so: my left hand held the batting handle. With my right hand, I hurled the ball fast against the ceiling and quickly placed my right hand under the left hand on the bat handle to hold the cricket bat correctly. I watched the ball closely as it was about to hit my head. I quickly raised the bat and "hooked" the ball into the side wall with the bat; I scored an imaginary four or six runs, and all would be okay. If Doody missed the ball, the ball would hit Doody in the face, and it would hurt, and Doody would cry like a baby—like Brian Luckhurst and Mike Denness, the English batsmen. These two clowns kept getting struck with the ball in the game. I would show those damned Aussies a bit of true (Trew) British grit and skill.

I daydreamed away to my little heart's content. The England team needed Doody, and when Doody simulated the conditions Down Under in his kitchen, he would always come out on top. He'd be hailed as "the Pom who helped England beat the ex-convict Aussies." So, in my fantasy world, I was holding the England cricket team together, and I did this regularly while Mum and Dad were out of the house.

I prepared to bat. Doody Trew walked to the batting crease. I imagined being taunted ("sledged" or "chirped") by Aussie bowler Max Walker and wicket-keeper Rodney Marsh, "Here comes another whinging Pom—the ball will hit his shiny sunburned bonce, Rod!"

I let out my best Western Australian voice, "Yeh, Max, these Pommie bastards are a little fragile!"

I looked up at my imaginary adversaries and shook my head in disdain at their comments.

"Yer. Has this chicken-shit Pommie bastard grown out of his diapers, Rod?"

"Nah, he's still wearing them, Max—he's about to shit himself!"

I'd had a fair dinkum Aussie accent and talked out loud without fear of discovery. The house was empty, and I had an Ashes series to win. However, had I been busted talking to myself in various accents—I was fair game to end up on a shrink's sofa.

I took guard. "Leg stump, please, Umpire," I called out to the imaginary official. I went through this strange routine of touching my imaginary cap, shaking my shoulders, and readying myself for imaginary Dennis K. Lillie to run in like thunder to bowl.

Ritchie Benaud, the gnarly-faced Aussie commentator, had a distinctive Sydney accent, "In comes Lillie; he's growling and snorting. He approaches the bowling crease and delivers the hard, new ball. Wow—incredible—at one hundred m.p.h!"

The ball was thrown against the ceiling, and I watched it rise towards my face. My bat was ready and waiting, eyes level, head not moving. Suddenly, I made a "hook shot," but the ball travelled faster than I'd expected this time, so I had to compensate by reacting with a faster follow-through. *Houston, there might be a problem.*

My momentum continued, and my cricket bat crashed through Mum's glass cabinet immediately behind me. Glass exploded from the impact of the three-pound willow cricket bat. Not only were the glass cabinet doors no more, many of Mum's Welsh china and porcelain ornaments had been smashed to smithereens. I'd obliterated half of Mum's precious Welsh dresser. It was a great shot, though. However, the consequences would now be severe.

"Oh, no! No, no, no . . . oh shit!" *How am I going to explain this disaster?* I had an idea. Back in the day, my two budgies had "disappeared," and my mum claimed they had "escaped" their cage and flown to their freedom. I never believed her. I could suggest the two budgies had returned, flown back into the kitchen, and gone nuclear on Mum's cabinet—as payback for her letting them escape the house three years prior.

Mum's words played back in my mind, "Two wrongs don't make a right." I sighed. Nope, there was no way out of it; England had lost the Ashes, and Mum's homecoming would turn Doody into "ashes" as she would surely go ballistic.

I cleared up the mess, cutting my fingers several times on shards of glass. I vacuumed, tidied up, and waited like I was on death row for her to return home and pronounce the death sentence verdict. No stay of appeal by Dad, as he was still recovering in the hospital from his bleeding piles.

Two hours later, Mum arrived. She had finished work and popped into the hospital to visit Dad. I intercepted her in the hallway before she caught sight of the mess in the kitchen. Her complexion was pale, and she seemed unhappy. Mum rarely greeted me without a smile on her face. I can't have looked any paler. "Dad sends his love. He doesn't want you to see him in the hospital—he'll be home soon."

"That's good news," I wasn't that bothered when Dad was coming home as I wanted to navigate the wrath of the Mumma Bear before dealing with Dad. "Mum, you're going to kill me."

Mum raised her eyebrows and continued to struggle to take off her coat. "Why, son?" My eyes welled up with tears.

"I broke your glass cabinet. I'm sorry."

No, be honest—I demolished it.

Mum took a deep breath and sighed. "Playing cricket?"

I gulped. "Yes, Mum." She hung up her coat and shook her head. To help her understand why I disobeyed her, I said, "It was England versus Australia." (This would not have mattered to Mum, as she hated cricket—but it mattered to me and my believable defence narrative.)

She walked past me and entered the kitchen to view the damage. I walked past her and stood with my back to the sink, and what she was looking at filled me with feelings of shame and sadness. Mum loved that piece of furniture. Her light green eyes gazed at what used to be her Welsh dresser.

"I'll get it fixed before your father gets home. He doesn't need to know," she said.

I waited for the salvo of anger to be fired in my direction. Mum used to threaten me with Mr Smack, a wooden spoon with a sad, non-smiley face drawn on the flip side of the ladle; my stupidity deserved a whack on the bum. *He doesn't need to know.* What the heck? I expected the worst and hoped for the not-so-bad. I had told her the truth, which was difficult, and there were no consequences.

Tears welled up in her eyes. She must have really loved that dresser. I moved across to her and gave her a hug. Mum's shoulders jigged up and down as I felt her sobbing.

"Sorry, Mum," I said and skulked up the stairs to my bedroom.

I didn't realise at the time that Mum was in shock. She was coming to terms with the news from the hospital surgeons—Dad had his entire lower bowel and intestines removed, and her life, and our lives, would never be the same again. Cancer of the colon sounded a little more serious than bleeding piles. However, the C-word was not mentioned by Mum—it was Carole who bluntly told me to start behaving more appropriately, as Mum would need all the help and support she could get.

England lost the actual "Ashes" series 4-1 to the Aussies, and yes, as I lay on my bed, I daydreamed, not about Mum, her dresser, or even my dad. England should have sent for the 13-year-old wonderkid Gary "Doody" Trew to sort out the Aussie fast bowlers, but they didn't—their loss.

CHAPTER 10
THE POLICY OF TRUTH
FEBRUARY, 1975

Eventually, before his release in the New Year, Mum hinted that things might change for my dad and our home life when he finally returned from the hospital. I wasn't too concerned about this, as my family had kept the details of my dad's surgery to themselves. They wanted to keep me in the dark about anything that might upset me. However, curiosity killed the cat.

"Mum, Carole said that Dad's condition was worse than expected. What's going on. Please be honest with me?"

Mum sighed. "Your dad has had his bowels removed. The cancer was in a tricky spot in his tummy; to make sure it was all gone, they took everything out."

"What? Why?" I was utterly shocked. It was one thing to take what Carole said with a pinch of salt—she was always trying to wind me up. A few years back, my sister told me to always check the toilet bowl as reticulated pythons sometimes lurked beneath the water line. The snake might put its fangs into my bum and pull me back into the sewers. Far-fetched, yes. But to a very gullible kid who believed everything his family told him—the trusting teenager was beginning to doubt her truth. However, if

Mum confirmed what her daughter said without smirking or laughing, it was something I'd believe.

With a serious expression, Mum looked directly at me. "Your dad has, or had, cancer of the colon—that's why he was bleeding. The good news is that the surgeon has managed to cut all of it out. Your dad now has a bag on his tummy to collect his food, and instead of pooping, it goes into a bag."

I felt nauseous. I couldn't imagine anyone having to wear a bag and poop into it. "What about his bum?"

Mum said they had to stitch it up so he no longer had a bum. "Your dad joked he was glad he wasn't a gay guy—or it would have been awful for him."

I had no idea what my mum was talking about. "What's a gay guy?" Mum's cheeks reddened, and she told me to not ask so many stupid questions.

"Anyway," said Mum, "his diet will be very different now. No more fried food, and no more of his frigging pipe!"

I drove everyone nuts with my incessant questions. I constantly broke Mum and Carole's rule that children should be seen and not heard. However, the thoughts of Dad wearing a bag, like a huge Tesco shopping bag, to collect his poop and him being glad that he wasn't a gay guy didn't show any signs of relenting. I followed Mum around the house; she couldn't shake me off.

"What kind of bag?" "How big is the bag?" "Is the bag inside or outside of him?" "Do gay guys have bags?" I wouldn't stop. Carole wasn't her usual self since having the twin boys. Usually, she was super-tolerant of her annoying little brother. Now, Carole was super-snappy with me.

"Gay men like it up the arse. If their arses were sewn up, they would have to have it shoved in their ears. Dad's bag is called a colostomy bag, you silly boy—it's attached by a rubber ring below his stomach. Now go away and stop annoying Mum."

Not having siblings closer in age to me or many friends did not help me understand basic anatomy or anything to do with the birds and the bees. Boys at school were crude, and I had learned pupils call each other faggot, poof and queer, and I laughed along with them. I was trying desperately hard to avoid any attention, and the last thing I wanted was for Skinner or other kids to think I was a dum dum. Carole once told me that some boys and girls fall in love with their own sex. I thought nothing of it. I liked girls and had crushes on girls at Middle Street. Surviving Knolditz was my priority; girls were not on the agenda for me at my all-boys school.

Looking back, despite Dad's military background and conservative values, I never heard him or Mum say anything derogatory towards same-sex couples. The one exception would be that Mum believed actor Rock Hudson was "living a lie." She thought he was a very handsome man, but would laugh when he was in an embrace with an actress in a movie. She commented to Carole, cackling, "What a waste," and, "I bet he wishes she was a he!" At the time, I hadn't a clue what she was suggesting. Mum was "in the know" about something—but would never let on what it was. At school, nobody wanted to be called "queer" or "a bender," as the bullies would be merciless. Skinner would pin pink triangles on your uniform instead of the Stars of David.

Ultimately, I wanted my family to be honest with me. I was a terribly naïve but curious kid, who had become fed up with my mum's yarns and Carole's sarcasm. They appeared to be addicted to keeping me in the dark.

Dad finally came home—he looked pale and had lost a great deal of weight. He wasn't unrecognisable, but had a grey complexion and darkish rings under his eyes. Mum had divided the front room into two. Dad now spent much of his time in the rear annexe. One of Dad's favourite songs was Al Bowlly's, *My Canary Has Circles Under His Eyes*. He sang the song or whistled the tune when he thought I looked tired and wanted me to go to bed. I smiled and sang it to Dad. He looked at me blankly, not realising I was referring to his new, haggard look.

The upstairs area took on new odours and sounds. Mum closed the door to his room when she changed his colostomy bag.

"Lou, I'm not going to be able to live with this," he whimpered, "I hate this, Lou. Look what I've become." Dad was well-known for his sense of smell. The changing of the bags caused him to wretch and gag. I turned up the volume of the telly as I didn't want to hear Dad's voice.

"Denny, don't be such a baby; if it doesn't bother me, then it shouldn't bother you!" Each time the bag had to be changed, Dad sounded distressed, yet Mum had been a nurse and had lived in a barn full of animal smells for most of her childhood. Hearing Dad crying made me want to cry, too.

Later, when alone with my mum, I asked, "Why is Dad sobbing? Why is he so upset?"

"Don't worry, Gary, he'll get used to it. You know your dad—he's just a bit of a big baby. Like most men, your dad is a terrible patient," said Mum, matter-of-factly.

I scowled back at her with indignation. *Why can't you leave him alone?*

"You know what it's like when your dad catches a slight head cold? It's like he has caught the Black Death or malaria. He'll be fine, and adjusting to his new situation will take time." Mum showed me the bag and explained what she did when she changed it for him.

I shuddered and shook my head, "The smell isn't nice—the entire house smells of Dettol and sickly-sweet diarrhoea. I feel like gagging when I smell it."

Mum nodded. "I told you things were going to be a bit different when your dad got back from the hospital. You'll get used to it. I used to have to sleep in a barn with cow and pig poo next to my straw pillow." Mum never ceased to tell us stories from her childhood. At the time, I had no idea how much trauma she had experienced when her mother abandoned her and her siblings.

Unlike fussy me, she ate everything, and ensured that we all had food on the table. Mum had milked cows, fed pigs, slaughtered chickens, cared for the farm horses, and was made to speak in a foreign language. She lived in utter poverty and would never let me forget how she loved her children and how much of a bitch her mother was to her and her siblings. The problem was I'd heard her stories so often that I was emotionally immune to them.

A few weeks later, thanks to Mum's care and positivity, my dad felt a bit better, so he started to go out for walks on his own and sometimes got on a bus and went to town. Dad took me out for a walk to the George Street shops—the only time he did so post-surgery. I held his hand tightly, as he seemed frail, and I didn't want him to fall. "I'm sorry, son," he said. "I'm sorry for all the bloody nonsense!" His eyes welled up with tears.

Umm—you said the "b" word. "Dad, what nonsense?"

He was referring to the noises coming out of his colostomy bag, as he couldn't control them, which happened often and unexpectedly. He added, "I was on the bus the other day, and the bloody bag made a loud farting noise. The other passengers looked at me like I was rude and disgusting."

"Dad, I've never noticed any sounds," I lied. "If people knew about your colostomy and what you've been through, they would understand."

However, Dad no longer wanted to take me to watch Brighton & Hove Albion play football, as he was too embarrassed by the fart noises. He wasn't strong enough to lift me to sit on the metal terrace crash bar. I told him I was getting bigger, and it didn't bother me. I just wanted to hang out with him like we used to.

One day, I returned from school and was met with a sight that became etched in my mind and has been hard to erase after many years. I opened the basement door and dumped my school bag in the corridor leading to a downstairs bedroom to my immediate left. Dad was on his hands and knees and had crawled halfway up the stairs. He groaned and was spluttering, "Oh, my God," and "Jesus Christ," as he navigated each stair. I felt sick inside.

I heard laughter coming from the kitchen; it was Mum and Carole. I called up to Dad, "Are you okay?" It's as if he ignored my question, trying to reach the first floor and his sanctuary. "Oh God. Oh God," he whimpered.

I stared at my mum and sister, cracking up at each other—clearly mocking Dad with, "Ooh, ooh, ooh . . . it hurts so bad."

"What's going on. Why are you laughing at Dad?"

"It's your dad . . . he's such an actor, he should get an Oscar for his performance; he's not that sick. The doctors said a lot of his pain was in his head. They took every bit of cancer out of him. He just wants attention."

My blood boiled—I told them I was appalled at them both. They then mocked me for being a daddy's boy and suggested I change his colostomy bag in the future.

I'd never seen my dad behave like that. Mum often dismissed his gout pain and tended to ignore his moans and groans, like when she changed his bag. Dad was groaning and crawling on all fours, trying to climb the stairs. I was nearly 14—yet I knew this was no act. I was disgusted with them both. Something started to change in my heart's attitude towards them. My dad was my everything, and in his time of need, he was met with giggling, mocking and laughter.

I deeply resented Mum and Carole for behaving that way and did not forgive them for many years. Unknown to me, Carole had been grappling with her own internal struggles—fear, irritability, mood swings—as she was overwhelmed by postpartum depression. Despite her husband's illness, Mum maintained a stoic, stiff upper lip attitude, never showing any outward signs of worry or weakness.

The intergenerational trauma of abandonment in our family, along with our coping mechanisms for loss and death, began to manifest. I was too young and delicate to comprehend these matters, only realising them later. I chose to channel my anger towards others to avoid self-reflection and judgment. Nobody had my dad's back.

Unfortunately, neither sister nor mother comprehended how gravely ill Dad had become. They both had their own stuff going on and were hushed about it. I had my school nightmares to deal with, so I guess we all suffered in silence.

On one occasion, I plucked up the courage to share I was struggling at school, especially with the name-calling. I daren't mention the playground hate games for fear that Mum would exacerbate the situation, or they would tell me to suck it up and be a man. I'd had years of Mum telling me to not complain or show emotion when I hurt myself—as "real men" don't cry.

"Son, can you imagine being a soldier and letting a tiny bump or bruise get under your skin? What if your enemy started calling you names? Would you throw down your weapon and surrender? Your bones are shattered by bullets and bombs, not by the names people call you. You're nearly 14; it's time to man up!"

This was Mum's mantra, even if my leg had been blown off. If upset, she'd sing, "The more you cry, the less you pee," and add, with a frown and a shake of her head, "If you can't pee—you'll die of blood poisoning."

A few days later, as I watched the telly alone, I heard Dad cry out once again. I came out of the front room and looked over the bannister. He was climbing the stairs, huffing and puffing, his grey face wincing as he muttered, "Oh Jesus," with every stair climbed. I wanted to help him up the narrow stairs. He snapped at me and told me to go away—he didn't want me to see him like that. I didn't want to see him like that either. A cloud of gloom hung around me for the rest of the day.

What are they not telling me?

Mum and Carole keep repeating, "He's fine. The pain is in his head." "He feels sorry for himself. There's nothing wrong with him—the cancer has been removed." "Gary, he'll adjust—give him time." "Maybe the best place for him is to go back to the hospital, to give *us* a break—he's exhausting us all."

Livingstone Road used to be a sanctuary for me. It was where I fled from the horrors of school—my refuge. Lately, it had become a place I did not want to be. The smells. Dad's groans. Mum's exhaustion and intolerance. Carole's personality changes. I had no one to share my worries with. The only escape was to retreat to my bedroom, read a book, lie on my bed, and daydream.

CHAPTER 11
DON'T CRY—DAD'S GOING TO DIE
MARCH, 1975

As my 14th birthday rolled around, Dad's health took a turn for the worse, sending him back to the hospital. He begged Mum to call out the doctor to visit as he was in so much pain. He took paracetamol (Tylenol) and aspirin to control the pain—very different from the oxycodone and fentanyl of today. Dr Harris took one look at him and called for an ambulance to take him back to the Hove General Hospital at the end of Livingstone Road. Concerned about his health, Mum thought that his colostomy might be infected, and she trusted that the doctors and nurses would be better equipped to provide the necessary care.

I daydreamed about my dad watching me play cricket for Sussex and England—how I'd make him proud one day. I'd recently been chosen to represent the best young cricketers across the country, an elite one-week intensive academy that Dad insisted I attend—despite my fear of the food, the other attendees, and that I'd be the youngest player there. Dad purchased a new Gray-Nicolls Scoop cricket bat and a set of batting pads and gloves for me. Finally, he'd come and watch me compete, and I could make him proud. I'd spent hours seasoning the bat with linseed oil and repeatedly banging a cricket ball covered with a thick sock against it. This was the bat that had been bloodied in the war against the Aussies in my kitchen a couple of months earlier when I demolished Mum's Welsh dresser.

Despite the potential crime of the century of using my dad's record player and HiFi system, I cranked up Elton John's *Don't Shoot Me I'm Only the Piano Player* album. The speaker's sound quality was divine. As the stylus rode over *Elderberry Wine* and led into *Texan Love Song* with its "Ky-Aye-Yippee-Yi-Aye" chant, I somehow heard the door noisily open in the basement—they were back. Flip, maybe Dad is back too? I reached over to the stylus, lifted it, and removed the album, quickly shoving the record into its sleeve.

Silence—then the blood-curdling scream. I froze. It was Carole; it sounded like a shriek I'd heard on Hammer House of Horror movies I'd sneakily watch on the telly. Maybe she's had another row with Mum?

THUMP! THUMP! THUMP! Somebody was charging up the stairs; their footsteps were faster than when Dad angrily storms to his room from the kitchen. It's never Mum that makes a noise. It was Carole, for sure. She was wailing and crying at the same time. I stared, wide-eyed, at the closed front room door. My heart beat out of my chest as I braced myself for Carole to push the door open. Maybe she'd carry on upstairs and avoid me altogether.

Please, God, don't let her come in.

My sister burst through the door. Black make-up ran down in streaks from her red-raw eyes. Her nose glistened with snot. Without taking a breath, she yelled, "He's dying. Dad's dying. He's got two days to live—my God, Gary, we won't have a dad!"

I stared at her like a zombie; she turned on her heels and headed back down the stairs—wailing and crying and moaning.

Then silence—shattered only by the relentless thump of my

heart. Its thunderous beats reverberated from the depths of my ears: *Lub dub, Lub dub, Lub dub.*

I sat in Dad's chair. I gripped the armrests so tightly that my nail marks were on the tan surface. *Lub dub.* "Dad is dying!" "Dead in two days!" I muttered to myself—it was impossible to process the news. *Lub dub.*

Mum stood at the entrance of the living room door. Her mouth moved, but all I could hear were my shallow breaths and the sound of my heart thumping out of my chest.

So, this is what it felt like for my friend at primary school when she witnessed her dad die in front of the family on Christmas Eve a couple of years ago.

"Gary! Gary! Son, I'm sorry." It was Mum. My catatonic stare focused on her gaunt, tortured face. No streaks ran down her cheeks like Carole, who looked like Boris Karloff's double, but dark smears of mascara smudged around her eyes.

"I asked the doctor if there was anything they could do. They had removed the cancer; the surgeon had promised. It was too late—he has it in his lungs. It's everywhere. He hardly knew who we were when we saw him."

Her lips kept moving as I looked away, lost in a trance-like daydream. Of course, I remembered that I dreamt he would die. I saw it and screamed out in the middle of the night. Mum and Dad rushed into the bedroom, and when I stopped screaming, I burst into deep sobs. I lied to them and told them a creature was in the room. Carole found out and teased me. A few weeks later, I totally lost it when I saw Dumbo being taken away from his mother. Carole mocked me once again—she didn't know I'd seen Dad die in the dream. The stupid Disney cartoon triggered some profound visceral reaction to what was about to come my way. I had cursed him. I lied, and Mum made me swear on my dad's life. I tried to escape the big, fibbing hole I had dug. No, it was Mum's fault. She insisted on me swearing on *his* life, not hers or Paul's.

We are both responsible. I killed my dad. I'm taking ownership. I looked up at Mum.

"You did it, too. It's your fault," I yelled at her. She stepped back, and her face looked like she'd seen a ghost.

"What? What do you mean?"

I left the chair, stormed past her, and headed upstairs to my bedroom.

She called after me, "Why are you blaming me?"

I yelled back at her, "You and your stupid God—and your stupid religion."

Mum had no idea what triggered me: the lie, the curse, and the dream. That's all in the past. I'll only think about this if he dies. But he's not dead yet—where there's life, there's hope.

Now, the chickens had come home to roost. Mum's "loving" and "kind" God wanted payback for my swearing on Dad's life. Mum constantly drilled into my mind, "What goes around, comes around," and she firmly believed it was the law of sowing and reaping—the immutable law of the universe. Engage in wrongdoing and face divine retribution. Show disrespect and incur the wrath of God. Pull a face at her—God will strike me with palsy. "God rains upon the just and the unjust," she'd say, "but pours His wrath upon those who break his commandments."

I was terrified of *her* God—little wonder Dad never let her talk about religion in front of their children. She constantly did so behind his back. I slammed the bedroom door so hard it almost came off its hinges. I dived upon my bed, face down, head deeply smothered by the pillow. *If only my heart would stop the pounding.* Boom, boom, boom. It was deafening. I turned over to lay on my back, gazing at the anaglypta cream ceiling, waiting for my tears to dry and my heart to calm. I made images up in my mind with the textures and patterns. Finally, I made a face from the weird pattern—the side portrait face of a man.

Could it be God? Hang on—if God can kill my dad because I broke a commandment, maybe he can reverse cancer if I please him and make a sacrifice like Abraham did in Mrs Stanger's lesson.

"God giveth," Mum often said, "and he taketh away." I started to pray the most heartfelt prayer I could pray. I held my hands together, like in the books they'd make us read at Middle Street Primary—the one about Abraham and Isaac and Daniel and the Lion's Den. I prayed—asking God to keep my daddy alive. I begged and pleaded and said the *Lord's Prayer* repeatedly. With tears running down the side of my face, drenching an already soaked pillow, my sore throat croaked, *Morning has Broken*, the song we used to sing at Middle Street during assembly.

The next thing I knew, it was morning. *Maybe it was all a dream?* My dreams were always so vivid and colourful. *Maybe everything was okay?* That would be God's best birthday present for me.

CHAPTER 12
SECRETS REVEALED; A WISH FULFILLED

MARCH 26TH - APRIL 1975

PAUL VISITED DAD AND WAS SHOCKED TO SEE HOW THIN HE WAS. The nurses had taped his wristwatch to his arm to keep it from falling off.

"When is the lad coming to see me?" Dad asked.

"He has been busy, Denny. I'm sure he'll come soon," Mum lied.

"I'd love to see the lad; I love the little bugger."

"I know you do. This is all very overwhelming for him. He loves you too—you are his world."

I couldn't bring myself to visit my dad. To this day, I deeply regret this and several other choices I made at the time. His estranged little sister, Mona, and other sibling, Rene, were with him for his final few hours on earth. He had previously shunned Mona because she had married a German, even though Dad had fought in the war against the Nazis.

Dad clung to life until Mum arrived by his side. A tear rolled down his face as he passed away in her arms, her husband of twenty-five years.

The loss of my father brought on sleepless nights as my mind raced with thoughts and emotions I couldn't quiet. The swearing on his life? The dream? The curse? Years before, I had broken a window and lied to cover up my culpability; Mum didn't believe me and made me swear on Dad's life. Two years later, I had a graphic dream, or rather, a nightmare, and saw my dad's death. A big, black locomotive of cancer was chasing him down; he couldn't run away from it. He died. Later, and for the only time in my life, Dad spanked me for my poor attitude, and I yelled at him, "I hate you—I wish you were dead!"

My damn dreams, they always came to pass. The picture of the sinister-looking train chasing Dad in my childhood dream reared up behind my closed eyes. The sound of a steam train echoed in my ears, its low chug-a-chugger getting closer with each passing second. With his dark raincoat flapping in the wind, Dad sprinted, his trilby hat barely staying on his head. A look of pure terror was etched on his face.

"Faster, Daddy, faster!" I urged, my young heart pounding in my chest. The train, shrouded in shadows, rapidly approached him. It was unrelenting. And then the sound of a loud, squishy "Splat." I stared in horror, my eyes wide open, my face reflecting my fear.

The voice of the accuser was like a worm in my brain: *It was you who did that to him. You killed your daddy. Your mum did, too. Then, God did the rest.* Gary, Gwen, and God—the unholy Trinity.

In their mixed-faith marriage, it was poignant that my dad requested a priest before his death. His sister Mona had thoughtfully given him a crucifix, further highlighting the significance of his final wishes. This had upset Mum, according to my brother Paul. Religious tension, even before the passing away of his spirit. Religion . . . didn't I just love it! It wasn't until many years later that I discovered this from one of my cousins. I had no involvement in the funeral and didn't even go. Still, I think he should have been buried in accordance with his faith, despite his deep-rooted distrust of priests and nuns from his childhood experiences.

I didn't have much to say to Mum when she returned home from the funeral. I'd mentally and emotionally checked out.

If he never existed, he can't ever cause you pain. Erase him from your thoughts. Act as if you never had a father. If he did exist, then you've just had your heart crushed. You'll want to join him; you'll want to die.

On the day of the cremation, after my car ride with a family friend, I arrived home first and retired to my bedroom to take my mind off events. I was so angry at myself for allowing my heart to be so open and vulnerable to a human being. I was furious with Dad. How dare he go and die on me, especially when I loved and needed him the most. I loved my mum, but my relationship with Dad was very special. I thought about the saying, "It is far better to have loved than to have not loved at all." What kind of idiot would even suggest that?

Damn love; damn Dad and his stupid cancer-giving pipe and tobacco; damn his exposure to atomic radiation in the States. Yep, damn him travelling overseas; damn Australia for breaking his heart, hopes, and dreams.* Yep, just damn everything! More than anything, damn Mum for making me swear on his life. Most importantly, I damn myself for cursing him to his face, wishing he was dead. The reality for me was I thought I'd killed my dad.

Suddenly, there was a knock on the door, and red-eyed Mum walked in to see if I was okay.

"Yeah! Best day ever!" I snarled.

"Dad's funeral was very interesting, Ga. It's a shame you couldn't be there."

"Okay, I've changed my mind. I'll go!" I responded, flippantly.

Mum sat down at the end of my bed, uninvited. "It was a bit of a shocker," she said.

"Why?"

---

* The Trew family emigrated to Australia in 1966 as "Ten Pound Poms." It was a disaster—this is covered in the second memoir: "I Think I Killed My Dad."

"I think I saw a ghost. We saw you."

"Well, that's awkward. I was in a car with your work buddy, Roy Whitbread, listening to George Harrison's Dark Horse on a very dark and gloomy day. Perfect."

"No, Ga. We saw *you* walk into the church—your *doppelganger*."

I stared blankly at her. I wanted her to leave my bedroom. Talking about Dad's death caused a lump to form in my throat. I fought against tears.

Just go. Please go away.

"A group of people appeared at the chapel with your auntie Rene and Mona. One of them was your double. Perhaps this guy was a few years older, but he looked like an older version of you."

She'd sparked my curiosity. "Who were they?"

"They were Dad's German relatives."

Mum said the group of people attending Dad's funeral came over from Germany. One of whom was Dad's little sister, Mona. Mum didn't share that Mona was with my dad when he died.

Mum looked catatonically at my bedroom wall as she rambled on. I wanted her to leave but listened to her chattering away into space. Mum said she knew nothing about Dad's life before their marriage. She understood he had four sisters and a brother, Uncle Patrick, who died at a young age with a swollen head that 'exploded' in his mother's kitchen.

Nice visual, Mum.

The German relatives shared Dad's antics and his rebelliousness as a teenager with Mum. He'd falsified his birth certificate to join the RAF in the early days of the war. Dad was also shocked when his once-favourite little sister married "the enemy" and he found out about his new brother-in-law, Rudi, a German art dealer who had connections with the Third Reich—maybe even Hitler himself. I was sure Mum added the Hitler part to see if I was listening to her as her gaze left the wall and fixed itself upon me.

Mona married an art-dealing Nazi?
Mum said that Rudi, according to Dad, had affairs. Now, she had found out from the relatives that Uncle Rudi had a relationship with the killer of Rasputin, the mad Russian monk. Mum said she wasn't sure about the Hitler connection. Yes, Rudi was an art dealer and may have done some business with the crazed Austrian psychopath, but he had left Germany with Mona in fear of the Gestapo to find sanctuary in neutral Ireland. My brow furrowed.

If he was running away, it's hardly likely he was pro-Nazi.

Mum was happy knowing she had made new connections with Dad's estranged family. She'd been married for over twenty-five years, and this was the first she'd heard of her husband's background. Mum learned more about her husband during that time than throughout her entire married life. She was also touched his relatives had taken the time to visit England and pay their last respects to a man who had ghosted them for years. These sure were some kind-hearted and very thoughtful relatives.

I wish I had asked Dad about his past. Back then, there was no internet, Facebook, or even email to communicate with people. Mum would have maintained the connection if social media had been available. Mum kept in touch with Auntie Rene and her husband Leslie, and Paul had links to our cousins, Mike and Anthony. I'd met my other cousin, Dominic, several times. As Dad was so reclusive, it wasn't possible to build a relationship with anyone outside our family unit. Another of Dad's sisters had settled in Canada, married a guy, and lived in British Columbia, ironically, which is a short ferry journey from where I'm currently living. Yet another auntie lived most of her adult life in the USA. I only met Auntie Rene.

I've worked with children and families for most of my life; I've come to understand not only was my own family screwed up, but most families are. Each has secrets and things they'd rather keep in darkness than bring to the light. This is one of the initial reasons I put pen to paper and documented my family's life. If my grandchildren and great-grandchildren are curious about their past, at least they have something to refer to. Even the families that presented as perfect, regular, and not screwed up were most probably deceiving themselves.

AFTER MY DAD'S DEATH, I stayed in my bedroom, consumed by grief, with a decision to make. At 13, I had been selected to attend an elite cricket academy in southern England a couple of months before he passed away. The coaches invited young guys who could become pro cricketers to come together and receive specialised coaching. It had thrilled me to accept the invitation, but the in-house academy was due to start a few days after Dad's funeral. The offer included room and board for a week and a unique opportunity to receive coaching from the top professionals in the field. I wasn't in the right frame of mind to attend the academy, especially as I felt so raw and vulnerable. Dad was a very competent cricketer and had trials to play for the County of Surrey as a spin bowler; his buddies at the time were the famous Bedser twins, who played for England back in the day.

Dad had little spare cash, yet he purchased an entire cricket kit for me. He knew about the invite from the academy. He wanted the other kids and coaches not to look down on me because I didn't have an expensive fancy-dancy kit like them. Cricket was a snobby game played at all the best private and grammar schools. The county and national selectors were also of a different class of person, often posh, and had well-to-do backgrounds. Back then, players representing England rarely emanated from a secondary school stream of education. Dad hadn't wanted his son to stand out for the wrong reasons. He had received reports from coaches and scouts that I had a lot of potential for a 13-year-old kid. Although relatively small and scrawny, I bowled the ball with a velocity like many pacey adult bowlers. Sure, I would mature, bulk up, and develop muscle mass. My shoulders would widen and toughen—a significant physical trait in quick bowling. However, at 13, having gone through bouts of pneumonia, I wasn't the stockiest kid in the world. That said, one of the academy coaches would play a decisive role in determining my cricket future.

So, staring at the ceiling in my bedroom, I had a conundrum: did I or didn't I attend the academy? When I crossed paths with Mum, she brought up the subject of the cricket academy, and felt I should attend, as it was what my dad would have wanted. Mum's brother, Eric, and his wife, Margaret, visited us from Wales to support her at the funeral. Both were lovely, kind, and empathic people. Eric took me to a sports shop and bought me my first brand-new cricket ball. It was expensive, and Eric insisted I use it at the academy, saying, "Use the ball to bowl your heart out! Gary *bachgen*! (boy)" My time with Eric helped me make the decision. I was going to suck up my grief for a week and not miss the opportunity, as I would surely regret it.

I took the train to the academy, carrying a big bag of kit and clothes. Once there, I realised I was one of the youngest. I certainly didn't socialise with anyone. I didn't want anyone to talk about their parents or ask about mine. Just one mention of my dad, and I would emotionally lose it. Each night after coaching and net practice, I returned to my private room and stared at the ceiling; tears running down my cheeks and soaking my pillow. My dad had never witnessed me play and never would.

Stop it. Don't think about him. He's gone. Look angry. Scowl. Bowl fast—no one will want to talk to you.

THE HATE GAME

One coach, Herb Barker, took a particular shine to me because of my batting ability. I'm told I was a highly technical player for my age. I used a very "straight bat" and played the hook shot against fast, short-pitched deliveries (remember Mum's Welsh dresser). The coaches hurled the ball down at me as fast as possible. Gary, the young, skinny kid, smashed the ball away into the surrounding nets with a snarl; I was plain angry about life. The deliveries bowled to me got faster and faster; each time, I hit the ball more and more aggressively. I pissed off some older players as they tried desperately hard to impress the coaches; they bowled fast and short. I responded by hooking the ball into the net and making the bowler look like an arse. A couple of coaches focused on me. They gave me individual attention and valuable batting coaching. I appreciated this. However, I was at the academy as a bowler, yet the coaches were fixated on my batting prowess.

The final event at the academy was a fiercely competitive indoor game. Once more, I did not bowl. I was frustrated because I knew I could do better than the older bunch, yet the coaches did not allow me to demonstrate my greatest strength.

Your loss, losers.

It was my turn to shine—I batted well, and scored the winning runs. I smashed a short ball for six runs with a hook shot. Overwhelmed by excitement, the team gathered around me, hoisting me up onto their shoulders. I felt a mix of elation and discomfort, like a bittersweet symphony playing in my heart. Just a few weeks after their dad's death it's hard for someone to bask in the celebration and be treated like a hero. Barker, the coach, praised my skills and promised to stay in touch during the school cricket season. He hugged me.

Leave me alone. Go away. It's not gonna happen; I won't be going back to school anytime soon.

On the train back to Hove, I breathed a deep sigh of relief. It was nice not to think about death, and the experience had been a

positive one. I was transfixed by the picturesque scenery passing by. The vibrant green fields of Sussex were a sight to behold.
Maybe I'll get through this nightmare after all.

Denis Paul Trew (1923-1974)

CHAPTER 13
DARK DAYS AND LONG NIGHTS
SUMMER, 1975

THROUGHOUT A LONG SEASON, A HEAVY SENSE OF MELANCHOLY weighed upon me. Mum left me alone and didn't force me to return to school. I had no intention of speaking or engaging with others. Throughout the spring-to-summer transition, a feeling of discontent haunted me. The weight of death in my family was overwhelming, and I was unsure how to cope. The sense of being abandoned engulfed me, but at the same time, I craved solitude. It was ironic—go figure.

A wave of sympathy washed over me as I witnessed my mum's suffering. Our relationship was marked by constant ups and downs. Yet, she always displayed a heart full of kindness and unwavering generosity. Throughout the years, she consistently expressed her dissatisfaction with my dad while embracing the freedom granted to her in their non-traditional dynamic. Now he was dead and no longer in her life—she seemed lost. Despite the circumstances, my dad's death unexpectedly deepened the bond between my mum and me. Paul, her beloved blue-eyed son, had lost his position as the favoured man-child, and I had seamlessly slid into the role. I was still a little brat, but Paul was making his life elsewhere and wasn't around.

Gwendoline Lillian Trew had the softest skin I had ever felt. She believed it was from all the udders she had milked at the farm back in the day. Mum reminded me of a green-eyed Elizabeth Taylor. Unlike her name's sake, she had one husband and not seven, and like Liz, she had a massive crush on Richard Burton. With raven hair, a cute little nose, and a small, gracile jawline, she rarely wore makeup other than blusher and her beloved Coty L'aimant Perfumed Talc. Sharing a similar five-foot-two-inch height with the Hollywood bombshell, Mum had the biggest heart in the whole world. She also had a Celtic temper and strength that rivalled the incredible Hulk.

So, that summer, I listened to rock music and helped Mum look after my twin nephews. Mum also busied herself with her grandchildren, but I noticed she drank more alcohol than usual and had started smoking. From being the stricter parent, my mum sensed I was in an emotionally fragile state, and her rules and expectations appeared to go out of the window. I was also sensitive to the pain and loss she had been through, but I was in too much of a dark place to reach out to her. I felt lost, and without my dad, I began to feel life no longer had any meaning for me.

As September drew nearer and the thought of returning to school loomed, I wondered how to slip back into the crowd, becoming the unnoticed, inconspicuous person again. My deep passion for cricket saved me from contemplating the worst. It was the loophole I had been searching for. I still had an opportunity to release my anger, rage, and frustration by forcefully throwing a red leather ball at someone, perhaps even getting paid for it one day. Maybe Mum was right—returning to school might distract me from the dark thoughts with the prospect of boisterous and colourful classrooms and the scent of freshly sharpened pencils. However, the sights and smells were wishful thinking.

CHAPTER 14
ZEBEDEE AND THE GREAT BIG LIE
SEPTEMBER, 1975

THE COMBINATION OF ILLNESSES, FEAR, AND GRIEF LED TO ME missing a substantial amount of school, affecting my academic performance. I knew I had to catch up; I also had to stay under the radar, to blend in and not draw attention. Hopefully, dumbass Skinner and his gang of jerks wouldn't spot me. Miracles happen, don't they? When I returned to school, initially, no one asked me about my absence, and I was thankful for that. During my absences, I found it puzzling that the school failed to reach out to my mother to inquire about my well-being. Despite my struggle (twice) with double pneumonia and the passing of my father due to cancer, not a single letter or phone call came from the school.

The first class of the new academic year was geography, with Mr Boycott, the teacher with a broad, Yorkshire accent, affectionately known as "Zebedee." For once, I couldn't wait for a classmate to make the mandatory "BOING" sound, to break the ice and watch Mr Boycott go batshit again. On my first day back, I sat in the middle of the class, hoping to blend in and avoid eye contact with anyone, especially the teacher.

I've gotta lay low and not be noticed. Go under the radar, and Zebedee and my classmates won't know I'm there.

Mr Boycott welcomed us boys back from the summer break, which was odd. Mr McNeil, the English teacher, was the one who usually asked us what we did during the holiday. Anyway, Mr Boycott smiled and wrote the following on the chalkboard: "What ... does ... your ... father ... do ... for ... a ... living?" As I looked up and read his writing, a boy to my right shouted out an enormous "BOING."

Boycott's smile disappeared, and he smashed his fist onto the wooden desk. His large mug of tea leapt one inch off the surface, and hot tea spilt onto the table. "The next bloody bugger that makes that 'boing' sound is gonna get t'cane. D'ya get me?"

Front-row boys were wide-eyed. Some classmates were desperately trying to suppress laughter.

He pointed his chalky finger at a boy called Swanny. "Tha's numpties gone and ruined me brew. Tha lad, get us a rag and mop it up."

"Yes, sir."

What the flip did he just ask? His accent was almost too strong for me to decipher. Swanny left his chair, grabbed a cloth near the chalkboard, and mopped up the spilt tea. "Eh, tha's got to stop makin' them barmy 'boing' noises. Tha's in thy' third year, it's time tha grew up. D'ya get me?"

"Yes, sir" shouted back the class.

"Ah want to do an icebreaker. Like it sez on't blackboard, I want each of ya t'stand up when it's thy turn, and tell t'class what thy father does for a living."

Once again, I stared at Boycott's writing on the chalkboard; it was more comprehensible than what he was verbalising to the class. *Oh no. Please, God, no.* Each boy had to stand up, shout out their name, and tell Mr Boycott and the class what their *father* did for a living. *But mine just died. Oh, shit.*

So, in turn, each classmate stood up from behind their individual desk, introduced themselves, and stated their father's occupation.

"He's unemployed and on welfare."

"My dad is a butcher."

"He owns a fish and chip shop."

"My dad is a road sweeper for the council."

"My Pops is doing time (class laughter) in Her Majesty's Prison."

"Oh no," I whispered under my breath, feeling a knot form in my stomach as I panicked. *Oh no, no, no. This is literally the worst thing that could happen.* My heart sank. *Oh crap, I just can't.*

There was no way I could handle standing up and saying that my dad had recently died from cancer. I'd become even more vulnerable, and worse, I might start to cry. I'd be forever known as the kid whose dad died. Skinner would have a field day; he'd ask me how my wanker father died? Did he die of a venereal disease? Did he hang himself because his son was so ugly? My new name would be "cancer boy" or "the bastard." I wanted to blend in with the class, but I would now stick out like a sore thumb. Unless, of course, I lied.

Boycott continued his social experiment in humiliation, nodded, and accepted each boy's response. *Good, he's not questioning anybody about their answers.*

"My dad's a milkman."

"My dad is a brick-layer."

"My dad is in the army."

Shit, I was next. I took a deep breath, stood up and meekly said, "Trew. My dad's an air traffic controller." I sat down lickety-split.

"Speak up, lad," said Boycott, waving at me to stand up again.

I stayed seated, "My dad's an air traffic controller."

"What? Thy dad is an air traffic controller?" Boycott turned his neck from right to left as he addressed the rest of the class. "Didst thou hear that, t'rest o'thee?"

"Yes, sir!" a couple of kids in the front row answer, subtly wiping off the teacher's spit from their blazers.

"Stand up, young un'," Boycott said with a smirk as he looked directly at me.

I reluctantly stood up. I was paralysed with fear as I felt blood move from my extremities. I braced myself for what he was about to say. My stomach churned like butter. *Will he reveal my big lie? Teachers may have seen Dad's obituary. Is he about to humiliate me and say, "Laddie! How can your father be an air traffic controller when he's been dead for five months?" Why didn't I say that my dad worked in a shop or was a mechanic? Idiot.*

Mr "Boing" made things a whole lot worse. He commanded the class to look at me, and ordered me to become the focus (and ridicule) of the class's attention. "Stand thee up, lad."

I complied, staring down at my desk.

He told everyone my dad had an essential job—more important than anyone else's dad in the class. Trew's dad, in a nutshell, was unique. My dad, he said, had nerves of steel. I heard classroom murmurings.

Yes, I thought to myself. *Dad's uniqueness stemmed from the fact that he was now a corpse.* I hoped the ground would open up and swallow me whole.

Boycott gave an exhaustive lecture to the class, emphasising the necessity for air traffic controllers to have nerves of steel and a heart of ice.

How many times are you going to say nerves of steel?

He explained that working as an air traffic controller was a highly demanding profession requiring immense focus and attention to detail. Such responsibility. Such calmness under pressure. Mr flipping Zebedee wouldn't stop talking about my dead dad.

I often resort to gallows humour in stressful situations and stopped listening to Mr Boycott, whose lips kept moving. *Dad sure was calm right now. Yes, his heart was indeed colder than ice; in fact, it was so cold that it no longer beat in his chest.*

Boycott gained my attention. "Boy, sit thee down. Maybe we

can arrange for yer fatha to come int t' school and give a talk to the class?"

"Yes, sir." I sat down, having died the death of a thousand cuts. *Dad, come to the school? Good luck with that!*

The boys continued to share their dad's occupations. However, now the answers were tongue in cheek, and Boycott's body language showed he wanted to get on with his first geography lesson:

"My dad's an airline pilot."

"Pop is Nelson Mandela's bodyguard."

"Father landed on the Moon."

"My old man lives in Uranus."

"Pater is the President of the United States of America."

Blood rushed to my hot face. The class were taking the piss out of me. I stared at my maroon exercise book, desperate to leave Mr Boycott's lesson. *Great start to the day.*

Although there was the occasional "BOING" and one brave kid hummed the theme song to *The Magic Roundabout*, Mr Boycott managed to get through the lesson without throwing anything at a pupil.

Saved by the loud, clanky old school bell. "Zebedee" stopped me at the door as I was about to leave the classroom. "Mr Trew, can I have a quick natter with thee?"

Mr Trew? I have NEVER been called Mr Anything in my two years at the school. Please let me attend my next class—I can't be late.

"I'd like to scribble a letter to thee dad to invite him to pop in and have a natter wi t'class. Even better, mebby see if he could come and have a chinwag at t'school assembly?"

Let me get this right. You want to write to my dead dad to see if he can visit us all from the dead to talk to the class. Even better, could he visit from beyond the grave and spook everyone during an assembly? Perfect. Consider it done!

"Yes, sir, he'd be delighted." I walked away like I had a rocket shoved up my arse. On my way to Mr Biffen's French class, I imagined getting hold of a Tarot or Ouija board, setting it up, and seeing if Denis would say a few words to the class about his past-life career. I'd gone and screwed things up. I must come clean, and that would be humiliating.

I grabbed a set of headphones from the desk of one of the language lab's booths, lost in thought, ignoring Biffen's instructions as he talked from the front of the class. A sharp pain went from my bum up through my spine. I automatically pulled back the red vinyl chair I sat on.

"Arghh," I jumped up and looked down at what had caused the pain—then felt my behind.

A brass tack (drawing pin) was firmly lodged in my arse. I felt like I'd been stung by an angry wasp.

"Welcome back, Zebedee's pet!" scoffed a classmate.

Red in the face, I pulled the pin out of my buttock and threw it to the floor, rechecked my seat and pulled on the grey-coloured, plastic headphones. All I could think about was what I would do when "Zebedee's" letter arrived home. I must tell Mum. I take geography again next week. *Maybe he'll forget I'm there. It had worked for the first two years—it may work again.*

Desperate to find a solution, I prayed to a God I didn't believe in, hoping for a way out of the situation. The reason this memory is memorable is that a "miracle" actually took place.

No, Dad didn't come back from the dead, but my geography teacher disappeared—there was no more "Zebedee"—as if an alien had snatched him and he had returned to Planet Boing. A new teacher suddenly took his place. Boycott had been replaced, and the new guy appeared even more unhinged than "Zebedee." He also had a northern accent, but he was far more understandable. We took our seats and talked to each other, ignoring the curly-haired, shortish guy at the front of the class for a minute. He erupted!

He banged the desk with his closed fist more violently than I'd ever seen someone bang a desk. "SHUUUT UP! Shut up!

SHUUUT the frig UP!" Silence. "I will have order in this class, or by God, I will beat you half to death!"

The new geography teacher was Mr Dylan, known from that day by the rest of the school as "Psycho" Dylan. *What was it about Geography that brought out the best modern teaching styles?*

He told us he was the new geography teacher and was there to teach us about oxbow lakes, cumulous clouds, tectonic plates, and cartography—right up to our O-Levels. No reason was ever given for Boycott's departure. If God did exist, maybe he zapped him to spare me the grief of publicly summoning Denis Trew from the dead. No matter how angry and crazed he turned out to be, Mr Dylan would forever be my saviour and my hero. His screaming, yelling, punching the desk angrily, and throwing objects at my classmates was pure bliss.

Moreover, despite being batshit crazy, he was also a flipping good teacher and made the once-boring lesson come alive. He kept order in the class due to his rages and tantrums, but I really liked him, and he clearly adored his subject. I loved geography too, and did well in the final exams, thanks to Mr "Psycho" Dylan.

The class never learned that my dad was as dead as a doorpost; I told a huge lie, and I was fatherless. My dad may no longer work in air traffic control, but thinking about the Norman Greenbaum song, in my heart, my dad is currently controlling spirits in the sky rather than aircraft.

CHAPTER 15
DARKEST HOUR
SPRING, 1976

JUST BEFORE THE SUN RISES, THE SKY IS AT ITS BLACKEST. THE proverb suggests that when we feel at our worst, at our most depressed, and at our weakest, times will get better as the light of dawn breaks through and ushers in a new day. My hero, Winston Churchill, used the phrase in his "finest hour" speech in June 1940 after France capitulated following the German trouncing of her armies.

The teachers had arranged a trip to the Imperial War Museum in London, where I would have loved to visit with my dad. The school provided a bus, and I sat alone, looking out the windows. I was excited to see memorabilia from when my dad bravely served his country. I was fascinated by all things military and enjoyed re-enacting battle scenes at home, including Dunkirk, Monte Cassino, Stalingrad, and The Battle of the Bulge. I had hundreds of miniature soldiers, troop carriers, tanks, and planes, both Allied and Axis forces.

I loved the trip, and towards the end, I visited their fabulous store and purchased four large posters. Two were of Winston Churchill and the Battle of Britain; the others were German propaganda posters—fitting as they depicted Britain's darkest hour. One poster was of an image of Hitler looking very camp and pouty, posing with his hand on his hip. He looked like he was about to break into Gloria Gaynor's *I Will Survive* or Village People's *YMCA*, the disco anthems of the gay community in the '70s. The other poster was jet black, with a red swastika and the words "*Ein Volk, Ein Reich, Ein Fuhrer!*" sinisterly emblazoned on the print.

Arriving home a week or so later, I decided to revamp my bedroom to convey my darkest hour. I asked my mum if I could paint it, as this was a new season, and she gave me the green light. Mum was delighted I'd returned to school, thrilled I went on a school trip, and now elated that I had a spring in my step and wanted to decorate my room.

Mum wanted me to join the Air Training Corps (ATC) like my two pals, Billy and Angus, and some other classmates. They all seemed to enjoy themselves at the ATC. I didn't join because I refused the mandatory short back and sides haircut. I looked weird enough, and my very long hair hid my ugly face; I didn't want to draw any more attention to myself.

So, I painted my room, using very dark colours to match my "darkest hour" mood and put up my new war posters. I had black walls, a white window frame, and doors, with a light blue anaglypta ceiling to simulate the sky to help me imagine the dogfights between the heroic Spitfires and the Luftwaffe's M.E. 109s. The German posters were placed on my right-hand wall; the Allied ones were on the left, beside my bed.

Mum decided to check on me and see my creative efforts. I was on my bed reading a book about Douglas Bader, the famous RAF fighter pilot with tin legs that my dad had introduced me to back in the day. After a quick tap on the door, Mum's head appeared. She scowled as she stared at the walls; her eyes looked at the posters, then slowly went up to the blue ceiling. For a few seconds, she gawped, her little nose scrunched up. Mum broke her silence. "Gary, what on earth have you done?"

"What? It looks cool, don't you think."
She pointed at Adolf's camp poster. "What is HE doing on your bedroom wall?"
"I got it from the War Museum."
"He's disgusting."
I smiled. "His moustache is one of a kind."
Mum's lips came together like a puffer fish, and her meadow green eyes became paler—a sign she was about to lose her shit. "You need to see a shrink. I've had enough of your moods and sulky behaviour. You've clearly gone bonkers."
I dropped *Reach for the Sky* onto my lap, raised my eyebrows, opened my arms wide and then turned my hands inward toward myself. "Me? I need a shrink? I'm here, in my happy place. A shrink?" I pointed both hands towards my mother.
"What is that supposed to mean?"
"Um. Gwen. How about *you* going to see a shrink?"
Mum's eyes turned a light jade, but I didn't care. Bubbles of molten indignation formed deep within me, and the volcano was about to erupt. "You sit downstairs drinking whisky upon whisky, puffing away on your cancer sticks, feeling oh so sorry for yourself. I'm the one who lost Dad. I'm the one who loved him."
Her eyes blinked rapidly and were now wide open. I continued to vent. "You mocked him, remember? He was sick and dying and crawling up the stairs, and you and your daughter laughed at him."
"How dare you. I never laughed at your dad."
"I came home from school, and he was crawling up the stairs in agony. You and my sister stood there, cackling away, accusing him of an Oscar-winning performance because the pain was all in his head!"
Mum's face went white as a sheet. It didn't cross my mind that she could go batshit-psycho on me, and I had nowhere to run. I

THE HATE GAME

pointed at three of the walls. "This is how I remember Denis Trew, my dad."

"By worshipping Adolf Hitler?" she snapped back. "Your dad will be turning in his grave."

"Sure, if he had a grave to turn in. You had him cremated, remember? He was a Roman Catholic and would have wanted to be buried."

"You have a nerve! You didn't even bother to turn up at your own father's funeral."

I felt like my head was about to explode. I saw red mist before my eyes. I yelled at her to get out. Mum's head disappeared from my view, and she slammed the door. I heard her muttering that she was disgusted with me—ashamed I was her son. I sprung up, opened the door and yelled after her, "I have no one. Dad was my life. I'm better off dead!"

I lay back down on the bed, breathing heavily through my nose; my heart, once again, pounded in my chest. I decided there and then that I had nothing to live for. I was alone, heartbroken, and my life sucked. All I knew was I was going to die, and I'd die spectacularly. *I truly am better off dead.*

If Mum had walked into the bedroom rather than peeked in from the doorway, she would have seen I had two much larger posters on the wall depicting Churchill and the Battle of Britain. I'd created Britain's darkest as well as its finest hour. Churchill was the good; Hitler was the evil.

But now, I wanted payback. *If she accuses me of being a German sympathiser, then let's see what she thinks about my next move.* Different scenarios and options swirled around my head. Suffice it to say, I wasn't in a good place. Grief is such a strange phenomenon. I felt like I could fly into a rage at the flick of a switch. Pure, unadulterated anger seemed to percolate in my chest and tummy. I'd vowed not to love again or shed a tear in sorrow. *I wish I had painted satanic pentagrams on my walls and left voodoo dolls and library witchcraft books lying around the house.* Now, that would have been cause for her concern.

Honestly, I'd always hated black magic kind of stuff. I was angry with God and super-angry with Mum's version of faith, but deep down, I felt that something or someone outside of my being wanted to reach out to me. So, the dark stuff was off-limits, but I would indeed find something to drive her up the wall—something that would shock and horrify her.

Once a week, I'd ask Mum to buy the *Sunday Times* newspaper as I enjoyed catching up on the news happening around the globe. After our colossal row and fallout with each other, we stopped talking, and she refused to buy the *Times* for me to read. Mum continued reading the smutty *News of the World*, a gossipy rag. Ironically, while reading the *News of the World*, I saw a small advert on the classified page next to the sports stories. It read something like, "Brave warriors of the United Kingdom. Join the National Front Party." As the 1970s progressed, the National Front, a far-right political party, saw a surge in popularity among the public. I tore out the ad, made up a name and filled out my address to receive further information. Postage was free, so I popped the application form in an envelope, posted it, and forgot about it. A few weeks later, after Mum and I made peace with each other, she was visited by two sketchy-looking men wearing dark trench coats.

Thinking the men may be Jehovah's Witnesses, Mum was ready to shut the door in their faces. "Hello, Madam. Is Mr Schicklgruber at home?"

Mum gave them a puzzled look. "You have the wrong address."

One of the men was holding a clipboard. He looked at it. "This is number 3, Livingstone Road?"

"Yes."

"Well, we would like to speak to—" Again, he looked down to check the clipboard, then looked at Mum and said, "Doody."

THE HATE GAME

"Doody, you mean Gary?"

"Doody Schicklgruber. We have come on his request."

"Who the heck are you?" One of the men produced a business card. Mum looked at it and gasped.

"We are members of the National Front Party."

"You need to get the hell off my property."

"But, Madam—"

"Your 'Doody' happens to be *my* son. He's also underage. 'Schicklgruber,' you idiot, was Hitler's mother's name. Now, piss off before I phone the police."

Later, when I returned to the house, Mum told me that two perverts wearing long flasher macs called for me. I furrowed my brow, "Who were they?" Mum held up a business card and placed it in my hands. I looked at it, gazed at the ceiling, deep in thought and then burst into laughter.

Mum's solemn-looking face broke into a smile. "Gary, The National Front. Why?"

"Remember when we were angry with each other, and you accused me of worshipping the guy with the funny moustache—"

Seeing the prank's funny side, Mum started to laugh, too. "You . . . silly sod," she chuckled.

We hugged, and I tore the business card into pieces. Mum then spilt the tea on her interaction with the two Nazi nutters, verbatim, and swore they didn't just walk away from her—they goosestepped and made *Sieg Heil* salutes with their arms jutting out. I'm sure they didn't, but that was Mum's story, and she was sticking to it.

The funny thing about the incident was it broke the ice between Mum and me. I stopped hiding in my bedroom whenever I was at home and began hanging out with her and entertaining my twin nephews. We had several candid chin-wags that resulted in me apologising to her for my angry words. I felt bad for her and took the war memorabilia posters down. Mum suggested we both redecorate the bedroom, and she covered the black paint with wallpaper.

Over the next few years, I put up several less intense, teenager-type posters purchased from the Athena store in Brighton: John Lennon, George Harrison, and my favourite poster, the racy "Tennis Girl" print—a blonde female tennis player holding a racquet in one hand and holding her rather nice, bare bum with the other. Tennis Girl became my very first teenage crush.

I had survived that dark, horrible season of my life, and Mum had begun to get her son back, thanks vicariously to the National Front. However, I hadn't yet survived the horrors that waited for me back at the Knoll School for Boys.

CHAPTER 16
METAL GURU, IS IT YOU?
1972-76

I'VE ALWAYS ENJOYED BEING CREATIVE. HOWEVER, I WAS GENERALLY awful at crafty subjects like metalwork and woodwork. My dad and brother, the shits, were both gifted in these practical areas. I'm that person who is happy to take things apart but who can never put things back together again. There will always be components or vital parts that sit alongside the finished item. So, please don't ask me to look at your engine. I find solutions by kicking and banging the thing until it either works or breaks.

Mr Bird, a skilled teacher at the Knoll School, deserved credit for his expertise in teaching woodwork, metalwork, and technical drawing. I have no memory of him ever shouting or losing his composure. Some ex-pupils shared stories of the metalwork teacher resorting to using a metal ruler to smack the fingers or hands of miscreants, so I felt relieved that I had avoided such a fate. The constant awareness of Skinner and his team entering the workroom, where dangerous tools were present, made it difficult for me, at times, to fully engage in the lesson.

Many classmates made badass objects in Bird's metalwork class. It's not that I didn't try—I just sucked at it. This led to frustration and boredom on my behalf. I'd rather watch dressage at the Olympics, fly fishing, or, even worse, curling than try to create something out of certain craft materials. Metal and woodwork were mandatory subjects, like mathematics, but unlike maths, Mr Bird didn't hurl metal darts, hammers, or lathes at pupils.

At times, I looked enviously at other students' work—beautifully buffed and engineered garden trowels, a metal desk organiser, shiny pentagrams, or a toast rack—and I had to deal with my inadequacies and minor resentments. The kid working next to me appeared to be as thick as a plank in an academic class. Yet, he managed to turn a piece of metal and some nuts and bolts into a magnificent shiny giraffe ornament. I didn't want to wish Ebola on him; however, if he were to accidentally slice off his thumb, I'd take that as a win.

I was totally inept at metalwork. I didn't inherit my dad's genius for all things hand-crafted. Maybe his OCD and need for precision and perfection helped him focus on a particular project.

It wasn't for the lack of trying. At the start of a term, we were given a certain amount of free reign to make something out of the desired materials. I decided to "go big or go home," so I pushed myself to the max and tapped into my ancestor's warrior spirit.

I made one object during the two to three tedious years in these classes: a metal ashtray. My creation started as an authentic two-foot-long Viking shield. The technical drawing design looked incredible, but once I began to work on the damned metal, I soon lost interest.

As sabotage by him or other pupils was unlikely, in contrast to art classes, the metal canvas provided confidence that my work wouldn't be destroyed by any troublemakers in class. On the other hand, I had to keep one eye on my work and another on possible stabbings and circular saw-sawn-off finger "accidents."

However, as my craftwork was so bad, I would have welcomed the opportunity to start again, with or without missing digits. Anything to receive sympathy from Mr Bird.

Anyway, my two-foot buckler shield, a fancy small shield gripped in the fist with a central handle, was clamped, cut, ground, forged, bent, and battered. Then I'd cut some more of the metal, which would then be ground, drilled, ground, cut again, buffed, filed, ground, and polished. Finally, I presented my mum with the four-inch by four-inch (now miniature) shield. She told me it was a wonderfully crafted ashtray. Shocked by Mum's lack of imagination, I lied and told her it was an authentic Viking arrowhead. She loved it and asked if she could use it to flick ash from her cancer sticks. I shrugged, "Sure, why not," I said.

Woodwork class was a tad more interesting, possibly as stimulating as calling the speaking clock on the phone or listening to politicians debating in parliament. Mr Bird clearly recognised that I would have made a far better pilot than an artisan. He wouldn't let me make an authentic, mini seven-foot trebuchet or a medieval Norman crossbow. The silly man felt I should attempt something more suited to my practical skillset, so he talked me into making a serving tray for my mum. My rationale was that if I aimed to create a coffee tray, it might end up looking like a crossbow or practice sword.

According to what I'd heard, woodworking brings apparent benefits, such as enhancing fine motor skills, encouraging creativity, developing problem-solving abilities, and fostering a sense of pride in one's work. I couldn't think of any upsides other than admitting I suck at woodworking. I used to stress out when following food recipes or using woodworking plans from my Tech Drawing class. No matter how closely I followed the instructions, the end product was terrible.

So, I chose to liberate myself from conventional limitations, embrace my inner carpenter, and approach the meticulous measurements needed for a laborious woodwork project with a relaxed and laissez-faire attitude. Although disappointed by Mr Bird's lack of faith in my practical abilities, I accepted his non-negotiable position. I diligently measured and made the coffee tray's plywood rectangular base, which needed to be cut as a perfect rectangle and turned out more like a rhombus. *Why was this measuring lark so annoying?* I struggled with maintaining focus, not just because of daydreaming, distractions, and inattentiveness but also because of the sheer monotony. Despite the need for precision cutting, my mantra was, *oh, that should do,* or *Gary, just lob the pencil mark there—it's pretty darned close.*

However, I was satisfied. I managed to sculpt two very basic wooden handles. I sanded, cut, sanded again, cut again, spirit levelled, glued, re-sanded, made dove-tail joints, glued, super-sanded and varnished the beast. Three years later, I finally finished and proudly presented my tray to Mum for Mother's Day. She said she loved it despite its flaws—like removing splinters from hands after use and cups sliding off because of its warped and uneven surface.

CHAPTER 17
TREW RELIGION
1976

JOAN OSBORNE'S *ONE OF US* WAS ONE OF MY FAVOURITE SONGS from the 1990s. It explores the concept of believing in a God who is relatable to humans. Imagine if God was a random woman sitting next to you on a bus or a homeless person on the street. Pretty crazy, huh? However, I'm sure that God did not reveal himself through Knoll School's Religious Knowledge (RK) teacher, Mr Gully. While he taught RK, Gully was a fervent atheist who openly advocated against religion. Teaching atheism in RK was as odd as teaching Gaelic in a French class. However, this was the Knoll School, and nothing surprised me anymore.

Sitting next to my buddy, Billy, made the class enjoyable. On that rare occasion when Mr Gully was away, I was on the receiving end of the cane at the Knoll School. The attendance register was being taken by none other than Mr Oxford, the formidable head teacher, also known as "Batman." As the class began, Batman, with his half-glasses perched on his nose, scanned the room for Swanny, who was conspicuously absent.

"Swanny?" he asked.

"Swanny?" Another boy repeated helpfully.

"Swanny?" Batman said in a brassier voice.

In unison, the entire class called out, "Swanny!"

I found it funny that my class, often too scared of Batman to show even a modicum of defiance, had called out their missing classmate's name.

Without looking at Batman, I turned to Billy and squeaked, "Swanny?" Everyone else must have observed Batman's throbbing carotid vein and dared not say one more word.

"You, boy!" He was looking at me. His cheeks swelled and deflated like a couple of bellows, as he breathed from his nose. I made eye-contact with the most feared member of the teaching staff. "You, whatever your name is, come with me this instant," and he left the classroom with his black cape trailing.

The class giggled, and one lad said, "Now you're really in the shit!"

"Tell him you're Swanny," suggested Billy, unhelpfully.

I sighed, stood up, and followed in Batman's wake. Batman's office was a mere three classrooms away. His door was open. I politely knocked on the door; my whole body started to sweat. *Surely, he won't cane me for asking where Swanny is?*

"Come here, boy, and close the door behind you!"

I entered his study. He picked up a cane lying on his desk. SWISH. SWISH. SWISH.

As if that didn't terrify me enough, he walked from his desk and stood immediately in front of me. His face petrified me. He looked down at me like I was a cockroach he was just about to crush. I couldn't believe it—I wouldn't have said boo to a goose . . . or even a Swanny.

"Hold out your hand."

Oh, crap. I held out my right hand and grimaced.

WHACK! "Do not—" WHACK! "Be insolent—" WHACK! "With—" WHACK! "Me." WHACK! "Do you understand?"

I winced, tears forming in my eyes. *Don't you dare cry.* "Yes, sir." *Thank God that's over.*

"Flatten out your palm, boy, I'm not quite done!" I complied, looked away and grimaced. WHACK! My hand tingled and ached as if a bee had stung it. "Six of the best" for not reading Batman's demeanour and asking if dumbass Swanny was present. *Silly boy.* I left Batman's office and headed to the washrooms, where I ran cold tap water over my hand to try to mitigate the burning heat. *Why didn't I keep my big mouth shut?* Thank goodness his interpersonal skills were so bad that he didn't know my name, nor was he interested in knowing it.

I was never going to tell Mum what had happened. Despite it being my stupid fault, she would have raised hell and given Batman a taste of his own medicine. Being caned at the Knoll School was a rite of passage, and I could chalk that up on the "fun" experience board.

Despite the punishment I received, I found myself drawn to the Religious Knowledge class. Mr Gully's impassioned rants captured my attention far more than his lectures on world religions. I had already decided the Judeo-Christian God was probably a nasty piece of work, but I was curious that "something" had to have created the world in which we lived. Something created me, and this same something had stepped in and "disappeared" Mr Boycott, the deranged geography teacher who wanted me to ask my dead dad to tell the school about his career. So, with this in mind, I started to explore other faiths.

With his East-Indian-influenced music, George Harrison, my favourite Beatle, struck a chord with me. *My Sweet Lord* and *Give Me Love* were songs about his faith. Mum's version of faith certainly didn't attract me to Christianity. I had broken many of God's commandments, and, as a result, Dad was toast. Mum scared me as a child to be compliant or God would strike me down with a nasty affliction, or my penis would turn black with gangrene for thinking impure thoughts. On the other hand, George Harrison sang about love, peace, joy, and he played this funky sitar music—and was a believer in Krishna Consciousness.

Mr Gully loved to rant about religion rather than stick to the curriculum and teach it. He constantly made sarcastic comments about the different religions: "World religion has caused nothing but misery to mankind. Noah and his ark," he laughed, "what utter stupidity to believe such a fairy tale. Christian Protestants in Northern Ireland tie up children's swings in recreation parks on a Sunday to stop kids from playing on them, as the Sabbath is a holy day. What kind of miserable deity insists on doing that? Non-believers of Islam are beheaded for being infidels. Steal a loaf of bread for your starving family, and the thief gets his hand chopped off."

Gully went on and on about the different religions and how they all sucked. He smirked and asked if anyone wanted to disagree or debate with him?

I stuck my hand into the air. "Sir, Hinduism is interesting, especially the Hare Krishna movement."

"Oh, really?"

"Yes, sir. I borrowed a copy of the *Bhagavad Gita* from the library—it's the Hindu equivalent of the *Bible*."

"Hindus believe cow dung is sacred. Cows and cow dung. Yes, let's all follow the cow-dung God." Those who were awake in class laughed.

These days, Mr Gully would be fired lickety-split, but this was the Knoll School, and we were living in the 1970s. To his credit, I found my confidence and voice in Gully's classroom, having been on the receiving end of Batman's cane lashing.

"Hare Krishna, Hare Krishna, Hare Rama, Hare Rama," I recited. "Sir, that's what George Harrison sings on his album, *Extra Texture*."

Gully cleared his throat, "The extra texture truth is . . . Hinduism, like all mainstream religions, controls its followers through fear and oppression."

Yep, that's true of the Church and Christianity. "So, what do you believe in, Sir?"

Like, I don't know.

"Marxism. Because religion is the opium of the masses. The working classes accept their life of poverty and suffering, believing it's all part of God's plan. Be a good Christian; they tell you you'll go to heaven. Be a good Hindu, and you'll be reincarnated into something better in the next life. The classic psychological carrot and the stick. Unfortunately, I must teach about these religions, so let's not get too far off track."

Yes, I had borrowed a copy of the *Bhagavad Gita*, read some of it and couldn't understand a word of it. However, like the *Bible* and the *Koran*, it was considered a Holy Book, and, more importantly, George Harrison thought it was cool. The Knoll's Religious Knowledge teacher imparted to the class that God is one big myth to control the proletariat; religion was a load of crap, and it was all nonsense.

I liked Mr Gully's class; it was a safe space. Some kids would be slumped over their chairs with an arm dangling towards the floor. Mr Gully didn't seem to mind if pupils weren't engaged with the subject matter. His enthusiasm for *not* teaching about religion was commendable.

One afternoon, I sat beside Billy as we doodled on our exercise books. Doodling kept me awake, and it was less distracting than making paper aircraft and launching them when Gully had turned his back to the class. I drew the AUM symbol, the most important of Hindu symbols—the symbol that looks a little bit like a fancy curved number three—and next to the "heart sign," I wrote, "My Sweet Lord!"

I nudged Billy to show him my latest doodle. "Hinduism is the 'Trew' path to God." Billy nudged me back, showing off his doodle, "Jesus saves; Peter Ward scores from the rebound." Peter Ward was the prolific goal scorer who played for Brighton. Mr Gully was talking away, "Blah, blah, blah, religion is superstition, blah blah blah," and stopped at my row of desks.

I looked up at him. His arms were folded, his brow furrowed, and he craned his neck to make out what we had written on our notebook covers. Doodling on our notepad wasn't a Knoll School misdemeanour, so I wasn't too bothered—as many pupils decorated their notebooks.

I looked up at him and smiled, proud to show off my carefully drawn AUM symbol. Gully's upper lip curled. In a flash, he seized my exercise book and became unhinged. His eyes looked like fury, and with teeth clenched, he rolled up the book and beat me three or four times over the head with it. It was more of a shock to me than anything else.

That's a weird way to tell me you disapprove of my doodles!

He snatched Billy's exercise book that was too far away from him to read, brought it up to his face and read what he had written on the cover. "Jesus Saves" and "LUFC rule!" Leeds United Football Club held a special place in Billy's heart. Mr Gully rolled up his exercise book, leaned over me, and began hitting Billy on the head, too. We both laughed, nervously. However, Gully was not amused.

I briefly looked up; Gully's face was red and he looked genuinely pissed off. He moved to a position in front of each of our desks. With rolled-up books in each hand, he played the glockenspiel, using our heads as the wooden keys. He went from Billy's head to mine and repeated the action. WHACK! "Don't." WHACK! "Waste." WHACK! "Taxpayers." WHACK! "Hard-earned." WHACK! "Money."

I was still uncertain that he was being playful, in a Knoll School kind of way. This thought soon dissipated as the top of my head began to hurt.

WHACK! "Don't."

A harder WHACK! "Write on the—"

A very hard WHACK! "School's notebooks."

Finally, he imparted one more quick lesson, crucial for completing the Religious Knowledge curriculum of the Knoll School.

WHACK! "Trew."

WHACK! "You are a—"

The most brutal WHACK! "Disgrace."

He threw the workbooks onto our desks; the maroon covers separated from the pages. He walked to the front of the class and continued his "lesson" as if nothing had happened. The top of my head ached. I stared at the heavily graffitied wooden desk.

Thank God he didn't catch me doodling on the desk; I imagined him lifting the desk and crushing my skull with it. I dared not look at Billy as I didn't want him to pull a face and make me laugh. I didn't want to see him silently crying, either. After the initial shock of being assaulted by this man, I sat looking down at the desk and seethed.

I didn't attend a Mr Gully lesson again. He didn't report me for not attending and I didn't tell Mum about the beating. At the end of the term, Mum went to a rare teacher-pupil event and appeared in Mr Gully's classroom to get feedback on how her son was getting on following his dad's death. Gully mentioned I had defaced an exercise book, which had disappointed him. Otherwise, her son was a shy and withdrawn pupil. Mum shared with him I had lost my father due to cancer. Her son had been devastated, and seemed to find comfort in exploring different faiths.

When Mum returned home to give me feedback from the teachers, she said Mr Gully appeared genuinely shocked at the news of Dad's death. None of the teachers had known what had happened to my dad. Mum said she had informed the headmaster, who had not passed the news to the other teachers. Had he known my name, he may have thought twice about caning me a few weeks earlier. Then again, maybe not.

I dropped Religious Knowledge as a subject because it was utterly pointless, as nothing Mr Gully taught was in the curriculum; I also loathed the man for the exercise book incident. That said, Mr Gully became my new form master. He asked me to wait behind as he dismissed the class; Gully confided in me he had spoken to Mum about my dad's death. He expressed remorse for hitting me on the head and gave a sincere apology. Despite this, I couldn't shake off my confusion at his sudden anger towards Billy and me for simply doodling. Both of us were known for our good behaviour. Yet, it seemed like he and the other teachers turned a blind eye to the disruptive behaviour of other children and the Knoll louts that made pupils' lives unbearable. *C'est la vie.*

CHAPTER 18
MUSIC TO MY EARS AND PAIN TO MY HAND
1976

AFTER DODGING CHALK AND BOARD RUBBERS AND BEING humiliated in front of a classroom of laughing boys during maths class, it was time for music lessons with Mr Florence. As a music enthusiast, this should have been music to my ears.

Mr Florence was a man of enormous proportions—similar in size and weight to a minor planet. His beard was so thick and unruly that it swallowed his entire face. Taking his class after lunch meant we were often distracted by the remnants of his meal in his beard. While the boys sat in chairs arranged in a circle, he moved his lips, explaining chords and octaves. At the end of each class, we all chilled out and picked an instrument to play free-flow music.

Sounds fun? Remember, this was the Knoll School, and fun came with a cost. Mr Florence was known for his unique disciplinary method: using a gigantic slipper to correct his pupils' mistakes. If someone gave him a wrong answer or he thought they weren't paying attention, they risked receiving "the slipper" as punishment. I can count on one hand, no pun intended, the number of times it happened to me, and it was only twice.

Mr Florence was chewing on the remnants of his lunch. My

crime was to ask a chum to repeat what Mr Florence had just asked the class, as I had no idea. Reading lips helps sometimes, but Florence's bushy beard made it impossible. I could discern by the tone of his voice that he was pissed—his deep voice bellowed my name. Like most teachers at the school, he didn't know it, so he called me "boy."

The vein on his temple pulsated as he frowned at me. "You, the stupid-looking one," he yelled, pointing at me. "Come here, boy!"

Gingerly, I approached him, hoping in vain he'd ask me to have my first choice of instruments to play.

Florence grabbed the giant-sized slipper that was always beside him. I never witnessed him getting out of his chair, possibly as there was a high chance of him having a heart attack if he moved. "Show me your hand, boy!"

"Sir, what have I done?" I asked in a mouse-like voice.

"Done, what haven't you done?"

"I don't know, sir." His eyebrows raised, suggesting I knew and had one opportunity to apologise.

"Hold out your hand."

What if I didn't. What if I said, "piss off, you beached whale?"

I complied. I held my wee hand, palm upwards. *Here we go . . .* I grimaced.

WHACK! WHACK! WHACK! Three whacks in super-fast time. It didn't hurt much, and I was glad each blow to my hand didn't include a mini-lecture on why he had chosen to discipline me. However, I was embarrassed. Muffled giggles and coughs followed my slippering from my classmates. Returning to my chair and back to Florence, I crossed my eyes and put out my tongue to the other kids while shaking my hand to stop the stinging sensation. Three of four classmates sniggered.

Florence exploded—threatening to beat anyone who dared to laugh. "I will not tolerate insubordination in my class." He held up the colossal slipper in his hand and waggled it. "Anyone else want to test me?"

I assumed, like me, most pupils stared at the floor, trying not to make eye contact with the teacher.

The music lesson should have been a fun experience where we could relax, enjoy ourselves, and be creative. Music at the Knoll could have been therapeutic; on the contrary, it ended up being another reason to attend therapy later in life.

Most of the time, I struggled to listen to Mr Florence in class, as I was fascinated by two things: Firstly, what he had eaten for his lunch, as most of it remained in his fashionable salt and pepper Ayatollah Khomeini-type beard. Secondly, how far would the spit from his mouth travel as he spoke? Much akin to "Zebedee," Mr Florence was a spitter. I tried to sit as far from him as possible, which was challenging as we all sat in a semicircle in his music room.

When I received "the slipper" for the second time, my hand was met with a few whacks from what appeared to be an oversized Turkish baboosh. Apparently, my crime was that of gawping at Mr Florence. My mind, admittedly, had wandered. I became fixated on Florence's wild beard as I swore something was moving deep within it. I'm no ornithologist, but I pondered the possibility of a yellow-striped goldcrest finding refuge within the beard's chaotic tangle. It was almost as if a minuscule bird's beak was pecking away at the scattered food debris within his untamed bush. Once again, the slippering was more of an uncomfortable sensation than a painful one. The pain from being caned or beaten on the head with a rolled-up exercise book was much worse.

Although I would have loved to learn more about music, apart from practising a bit of ornithology, I learned very little in Mr Florence's class.

CHAPTER 19
AFRO TALES
1976

AT THE TOP RANK SATURDAY MORNING DISCO, I'D ONLY EVER danced with one girl, Connie, a pretty brunette with eyes that sparkled like sapphires. Unfortunately, she was super coarse and common as muck, which was not surprising to me as the Whitehawk estate was renowned for being a rough area of town —the Beirut or Stalingrad of Brighton. Connie was very touchy-feely, and I almost requested a translator when she talked to me. She was a pure-bred Brightonian with a very savage accent.

We sat drinking Pepsi, taking a well-deserved rest from the sweaty dancefloor.

"Oi! Gazza. You wanna come to my 'ouse lay-tuh? We can 'ave some 'anky panky." In other words, "Hello Gary, would you care to visit my humble abode later this evening? Would you care to get physically intimate if you are able and willing?"

Connie said she sometimes had *fun* with her *older brother* in *the same bed*, and he liked touching her below. My almost-first girlfriend told me her brother complained that she should improve her hygiene if they continued "doing it." I didn't know what "doing it" was, but Connie thought her brother was hilarious. The other concern was she had no idea how to read a room—or social cues. I gasped, narrowed my eyes, curled up my upper lip, wrinkled my nose, and recoiled from her as if she squirted pepper spray at me. Oblivious to my body language, Connie leaned into me, keeping eye contact, and pressed me on her invitation, "So, Gazza—come over at 5-ish and stay overnight. My mum won't mind at all. We can 'ave a nice snuggle too-geva."

Although naïve, I knew that going to bed with a sister and brother combo didn't seem quite right.

The other lesson I learned from Connie was that her medical advice was as sketchy as my mum's. Taking another break from dancing to the Glam Rock band, Sweet, and their *Wig Wam Bam* song, I sat on a chair and took another glug from my Pepsi. Connie noticed I had my legs crossed. I did this back in the day to a) stop my feet from jigging up and down and b) to make it more difficult for her to sit on my lap and make a grab for my nuts. "Oi! Gazza! Don't cross yer legs, mate!"

"Why's that?" I asked, sucking up the cold, sweet liquid in the straw.

"You are such a dickhead. Everyone knows that crossing yer legs gives you *the* cansa!"

"*The* cancer?"

"Yes, *the cansa*, init. If you cross yer legs, you'll get bone cansa."

"How do you know that?"

"My mum told me, she's cleva like that. I'd 'ate to see ya wiv yer legs chopped off coz yous got the cansa."

Attending an all-boys school really didn't help equip me in sex education or help me develop basic socialisation skills with the opposite sex. Back then, you were male or female in terms of gender identity. As far as sexual orientation went, a person was either gay or straight, with only Bowie and Elton John pushing out the bisexual boat from the harbour of sexuality. Most of us didn't have to run the gauntlet of deciding our gender or sexual orientation. Nowadays, there are gender reveals for six or 11-

year-olds. Life in the '70s was *much more straightforward*; pronouns were simply "he/him" and "she/her." I was kind of glad as it was stressful enough surviving school, never mind getting caned or slippered for not addressing a teacher by the correct personal pronoun.

I knew little about the opposite sex. The significant female figure in my life was my mother. My sister Carole had spent enough time looking after "the little brat." She was a good decade or so older than me. After Dad died, I saw very little of her.

So, when Sonya Kerchup came into my life, I was both excited and anxious, as there was a fair chance that I'd mess up the relationship due to my lack of worldly experience or sexual naïvety.

Having avoided Connie like the plague for a few months, I met Sonya at one of the Saturday morning trips to the Top Rank disco. Hundreds of kids gathered, sweated, flirted, strutted, and danced to Mud's *Tiger Feet* and Sweet's *Blockbuster*. Everyone had a great time.

My self-image was so low that I was shocked a nice-looking lass like Sonya would want to dance with me at the Top Rank Disco, never mind hang out with me. The only thing I felt I had going for me was my last name, as Sonya's sounded way too much like a red-coloured condiment.

A year or so older than me, Sonya was so much taller that if we ever were to kiss, I'd need to borrow a step ladder. The disparity didn't end there; she was self-assured and knowledgeable, and I was unassured and socially awkward. She was gorgeous, and I was an ugly duckling. However, we both attended a school with the same name; she went to Knoll Girls, and I went to Knoll Boys. Our respective schools were as different as we were to each other. Sonya's school was a modern building with adjacent green sports fields; mine was an old, ugly brick and concrete monstrosity with no green or playing fields nearby, and looked like a borstal or prison facility.

There was no romance, not that I knew what romance looked or felt like, but I hung out with her because she was a girl and an attractive girl to boot. We talked about Michael Jackson and Donny Osmond, Juicy Fruit chewing gum, and how we hated our respective schools. To stop any lull in the conversation, I desperately wanted to discuss cricket, football, World War II battles, or debate whether the best machine gun used during the war was the American Thompson submachine gun, the German MP40, or "Schmeisser." Alas, when I tentatively talked about such things, she bit her nails, yawned, and wore a blank expression. Anyway, despite our differences, we were building a solid friendship.

As we wandered through the nearby park, a sense of solitude enveloped us. Sonya suggested we sit down and continue our chat. Surrounded by oak and chestnut trees, we sat in a lush green field, listening to the delightful chirping of birds. The day was sunny and beautiful. I couldn't believe my luck in having the opportunity to hang out with such a beautiful girl. My life felt empty and devoid of purpose a year or so ago. Now, I wanted to live forever. I lay back, feeling the grass tickle my skin, and gazed at the fluffy clouds floating in the endless blue sky.

"Do you like me?" she asked.

"Of course I do, you silly goose!" I replied, "You're so pretty." *And tall*, I thought. She also had the right lumps in all the right places.

"Touch me," she said.

Lines formed between my eyebrows. *Touch you where?* As I sat upright, I brushed off the blades of grass that clung to my shoulders and the back of my head. I put my arm gently around her shoulder, feeling the warmth of her body against mine as I hoped to provide the comfort she longed for. Had I known about the five love languages, I would have told her that touch is undeniably one of my strongest love languages. I didn't, so I felt a tad awkward.

"Gary, I like how respectful you are."

"Thank you," I sensed myself blushing—it was nice to be complimented for a change.

She pulled away, smiled, looked at me, bit her lip, and whispered, "You can touch me down there if you want to?" She lowered her eyes towards her black slacks and lifted them up again to meet my eyes. *Does she mean inside or outside her trousers? Maybe she wants me to tickle her leg. Wait—eww, not her feet, surely?*

As Sonya stretched out on the grass, her head facing me, how she ran her tongue over her lips, leaving them slightly moist. As she turned her head, her smile widened, and her eyes locked onto the vast expanse of the sky. Her top and pants left just enough space for her pale, smooth skin to temptingly reveal itself.

I think she's waiting for me to make a move. I gently touched her tummy; my fingers felt her soft skin—she didn't swipe them away. Sonya had said, 'down there,' but, given a choice, I would rather go 'up there' and feel her boobs. I had heard kids at school asking each other about "bases" when discussing girlfriends: "Did you make it to first or second base?" I knew baseball had three bases, and then there was the home run. We hadn't reached first base yet—I'd not even kissed her. *Did second base refer to her boobs or her nether regions?* Shit, I had no idea. I prised open her top, slid my left hand up her blouse, and stopped when I felt what I assumed was a bra.

Crap! Wrong way! Put your hand down the top of her shirt, you donkey. I withdrew my hand and decided to get to whatever the base number was using my right hand. I awkwardly put my right hand down her blouse, and my fingers felt the top of her bra while she lay on her back. I couldn't believe it—I was going to feel a girl's boobs for the first time—*I'm not going to be a virgin anymore.*

I was a bit surprised as I had imagined her breasts would have been larger. My fingers slid under the bra; I felt something that resembled a hard and erect super-large button. I had no idea what to do next, so I rolled her nipple between thumb and forefinger. Sonya groaned. Her eyes were closed, her cheeks flushed red, and I wanted to gently kiss her lips. They looked so beautiful, but she unexpectedly took hold of my arm and lifted my hand from the inside of her blouse, then rested it on the front of her slacks.

"Gary, touch me," she whispered. *OMG, I'm going to second or third base or whatever the damned base number is!* With one hand holding mine, she unbuckled her belt using the other and then arched her back and used both hands to gently pull her slacks halfway down her thighs. Her head turned towards me; she smiled, took a deep breath, and said, "Go on!"

My heart pounded in my ears. I felt the strangest of sensations in my chest and down below. My fingers rested on her tummy. I was nobody's fool and knew what I had to do. I'd seen the advert for Yellow Pages: *Let your fingers do the walking*, went the jingle. So, I purposefully walked my fingers down her flesh and, as "manly" as possible, said, "Incy, Wincy, Spider, climbed up the waterspout. Down came the rain and washed the spider out."

Sonya giggled. The two-fingered spider carefully moved under her panties, "Out came the sun, and dried up all the rain—"

With one more assertive movement, the walking fingers went right under the panties. The spider was stopped dead in its tracks, and I immediately wanted to pull my hand away. *What the—*

I was shocked. The three other fingers met my two spider fingers and felt some very bristly fibres. Whatever it was had the texture of a Brillo pad—oodles of coarse, hairy stuff—and SO much of it! I had no idea what I was touching.

"Yes," she groaned. My brain told me she had some bush or hedge under her pants. *My God, she has some wild forest down there! What the flip*, I thought, trying to make out what I was touching. I moved my hand around, feeling, tugging, pulling, and then wrapping the bristly hair thingies around my fingers.

Sonya groaned once again. *Whatever you have down there needs a good trim.* I remembered a recent TV program I had watched with Mum, about "How to Maintain Hedges" or something. This dystopian-looking guy said, "Don't worry, pruning is easy once you get the hang of it," and "When you trim hedges, use shears— either hand-held pruners or a power trimmer—to snip off branch tips and keep them looking neat and tidy." At the time, it was the most boring programme I'd ever watched. However, the weird dude on the telly may have given me great advice.

Sonya grabbed my arm and pushed it further down to make my hands go further into the deep, hairy abyss. Initially, I resisted. However, curiosity killed the cat, and I asked her if I could see what was down there. "Yes," she panted,

Using my fingers like a surgeon's forceps or an arborist's pair of pliers, I pulled down the top of her panties. BOING! BOING! BOING! No, I wasn't in one of Mr Boycott's classes, but it was like an afro worn by the likes of Diana Ross, Lindsey Buckingham, and Mott the Hoople had jumped out headfirst from under Sonya's panty line, like a jack-in-the-box.

I had a crazy-arsed thought that the afro, also known as "Sonja's pubes," would grow lips and start singing *Blame it on the Boogie*. I sniggered with nerves as my fingers slowly retreated in disbelief. I had saved the day by moving my fingers away from the Amazonian jungle.

"And Incy . . . Wincy . . . Spider . . . climbed up the spout again!" Once free from her underwear, I yanked my hand out from the danger zone.

Sonya must have sensed something wasn't quite right as she sighed, reached down, and pulled up her panties and slacks in one go. I was as pale as a ghost. It was like one of those super-awkward moments in the classic movie *Trains, Planes and Automobiles*—when Steve Martin wakes up next to John Candy kissing his ear and snuggle-spooning him in the motel bed. We made small talk. *Don't mention orchards, rockeries, pruning or the Black Panther Movement.*

I desperately wanted to make her laugh, break the ice, and blurt out Lynne Anderson's song, "*I Beg Your Pardon . . . I Never Promised You a Rose Garden*," but lacked the confidence to practice dry humour on her. No, I had to face facts. The issue was mine to own: Sonya was a developing young woman, and I was just an underdeveloped and immature youth.

So, I said, "I hate that new flipping Telly Savalas song, *It*. OMG, *It* drives me bonkers. Whenever *It* plays on the radio, my mum shushes me, turns up the radio, and tries to serenade me with the stupid, bald guy crooning in the background. Funny. Not funny."

Sonya acknowledged my chagrin with a snigger. "I much prefer the Status Quo record," she said, patting grass and debris off her slacks and blouse as we walked towards the park's exit gate. I didn't know what to say or how to behave to break the awkward silence, so I hummed to myself. Sonya said nothing until we reached her home. She asked me if I had her phone number, which I had, but nevertheless, she scribbled her number on a piece of paper. "Will you call me?"

I was flabbergasted. With a broad smile, I told her I couldn't wait to see her again. Pulling me into a gentle embrace, she whispered in my ear, "Maybe we could go a bit further next time?"

"Sure," I lied and walked away, a relieved young man.

CHAPTER 20
COMING OF AGE: KNOLL SCHOOL SEX ED 101
1976

I NEVER MADE THAT CALL TO SONYA. WHAT I DID WAS RETURN TO my house, lock myself in the loo, pull down my pants and examine myself down below—I was bald as a coot. Although immature and verging on the stupid, I did know that "grown-ups" had masses of pubic hair.

In January, the same year as starting at Knoll School, I tragically discovered Father Christmas (Santa Claus) was not real. Mum would still get me excited about Christmas, so the following festive season, I thoroughly searched the house to discover presents I knew Mum and Dad would stash in the most unlikely places. We had a laundry cupboard in the kitchen, and while the house was empty, I searched it for yuletide contraband. My searches were super-thorough, and I discovered a few magazines hidden in a secret compartment. I opened one of the magazines, and the image made me gasp. A nude black man with a bushy goatee beard sat in various poses holding his willy, which was the size of a giant cucumber. The man was called "Jim Brown," and I noticed he had a thick clump of curly black hair surrounding his genitals. Shocked and confused, I replaced the magazine and gave up my search. When I listened in on Carole

THE HATE GAME

and Mum's chatter, they'd snigger and comment on what a "real man" this Jim Brown guy was. Stunned that they were talking about him, I assumed "real men" had massive peckers that were surrounded by an impenetrable jungle of curly, black hair.

Looking down at my silky-smooth Kojak of a pubic area, I realised I had yet to become a "real man." Sonja, obviously, was a "real woman," as I'd stumbled across her pubic bush. However, I had little understanding of bodily development, and it wouldn't be until my fourth and fifth school years that I would learn basic human biology—assuming I lived that long. Apart from Jim "real man" Brown, a girl by the name of Anna, who'd flashed her minnie at me under Ms Cameron's table at Middle Street Primary, and Knoll School playground were my only sources of sex education.

Attending the Knoll taught me to use vulgarity and profanity at a high level. Initially, it was all white noise to me, but on returning to school after Dad died, I began to understand a new vocabulary. The term "fanny" was commonly used to refer to a female's nether regions, albeit this uncouth term was at the lower end of the Knoll School vulgar word continuum.

My Knoll pals taught me an astounding array of rude words thanks to playground banter. I learnt that "fanny" was also referred to as; "C**t," "Twat," "Twot," "Pussy," "Vag," "Minge," "Box," "Penal Fly Trap," "Beaver," "Muff," "Gasp and Grunt," "Hole," "Snatch," and "Gash."

My use of Middle Street Primary and Mum's terms like "penny slot," "moo moo," and "minnie," elicited howls of laughter or ridicule from school chums. I had to adapt and improvise quickly. "Willy," "little worm," and "dicky-di-doh," were terms that not only elicited derision but also a punch in the face from bigger, rougher kids. Instead, I replaced my mum's vocabulary and used the following, instead; dick, prick, cock, knob, bell end, one-eyed snake, maggot, sausage, John Thomas, and pecker.

Clearly, James Brown syndrome had afflicted some of the

boys at Knoll School as some lucky lads even referred to their own privates as "anacondas" or "Mr Biggy that does the jiggy." However, not wanting to lie about the size of my member, all I could offer as a descriptor for what others referred to as their "boa constrictor" was my "little worm." It was one that Mum used and told me that birds (the feathered kind) wanted to peck off if it were ever exposed outside the safety of our home. These rough and ready terms were thrown around with abandon by my peers in both the classroom and the quadrangle during recess/break.

I have Neil O'Malley to thank for his practical masturbation tutorial—during a French lesson, of all places. Neil was from a large family that lived on the Knoll estate. He was a handsome, well-groomed, genial boy with a regular girlfriend. Neil was popular with his classmates.

I heard a "Pssst, Gary!" and "Pssst, Trew." Curiosity got the best of me, so I turned around in my seat to see what the lad wanted. His friendly smile and piercing blue eyes penetrated my drowsy state as he asked, "Do you wank yourself off?"

What kind of question is that? I nonchalantly shrugged my shoulders, trying to maintain an air of indifference.

"Gaz, do you ever toss yourself off?"

I shook my head and said, "Toss myself off?"

"Yes, you know—do ya mess around with your pork sausage?"

"Of course," I replied, my voice betraying the truth.

"How do you do it?" he asked.

I lifted both hands and rubbed them together, mimicking the motion of rolling a sausage between my palms, the mixture of pork and beef squishing between my fingers. O'Malley erupted in laughter, so much so that he had to wipe away tears with his jacket sleeve. My face turned bright red like a beet. *Shit—wrong answer!*

As his eyes met mine once more, he seemed to regain composure, and I asked, "Do you have any tips?"

Neil nodded, a small smile tugging at the corners of his lips. "I hoped you would ask," he said, mimicking holding something in his hand and shaking it aggressively. It was a familiar sign rival football fans made to each other: "Gaz, try it—it's the quickest and best way to come. I discovered the technique last weekend."

With a thumbs up and a grin, I let him know that everything was good. *What does he mean by "come?" I had heard other boys talking about "coming," but there was nobody I could ask to explain what it meant.* Maybe I should ask my mum?

"Mum, what do you think is the best way for me to wank myself off?" or perhaps, "Mum, I want to play with my sausage; what's the quickest way to come?"

Maybe not.

I was friends with Billy and Angus, but I felt uncomfortable asking them questions about "wanking" and "coming." What if I asked, and they responded, "Eww, you bender—why are you asking me?" No, the only way to deal with the situation was to roll up my sleeves and experiment. When the time comes, I will try the sausage rolling method and the O'Malley method to see which yields the best results.

My dad's warning about failing the 11-plus exam echoed in my mind, painting a vivid picture of a future spent cleaning toilets, and sweeping roads, or worse, serving time in prison. Little did my dad know that by sending me to the Knoll School for five years, instead of letting me bike to Varndean Grammar, I would be exposed to a wealth of colourful words and expressions. Furthermore, while the Knoll School fell short in teaching essential life skills, it excelled in immersing its students in a world of vulgarity and profanity. Equipped with an extensive collection of derogatory adjectives, I unquestionably possessed the ability to vent my frustration in any circumstance. Super handy when meeting up with fellow ex-Knoll School folks at the job centre or getting busted by the cops robbing a fancy house in a posh area of town.

Anyway, who needs to be taught about the birds and the bees

or human bodily development when you have mates like Neil O'Malley at school to help you understand sex and sexuality? My foundation of sexual education was based upon the following five tenets of playground banter, including Mum's profound worldly wisdom:

1. Shagging (and a plethora of other terms) is what a boy does with a girl, a boy, or a sheep.
2. It was okay and natural for some boys to shag sheep. I discovered this factoid after asking a friend why he thought Welsh people were sheep shaggers. "Gaz," he said, "No offence, as I know you are half Welsh, but Wales is a country where men are men and sheep are nervous."
3. If boys get frisky and sheep aren't available, never, *ever* try to shag a cow, as cows have super-suction sex organs that would suck out a boy's intestines.
4. It's *de rigueur* for posh girls to wank, or toss off a horse. This was a fact as Liz Jaeger, from the Girl's Grammar, did it to horses—regularly.
5. Too much masturbation makes boys go blind. Mum said that was why Stevie Wonder, Roy Orbison, and the old man a few houses down from us with the white stick went blind.

It was clear that the boys I hung out with had no understanding of the female anatomy, but they would never confess their ignorance. Naturally, we all pretended to be sexually experienced and hid our virginity, as admitting to being a virgin was considered the worst thing a teenage boy could do—a crime against masculinity.

Before diving back into the Sonja Kerchup situation, I want to share another conversation I had with a classmate named

Freddie Gates during my final year at the Knoll School. He approached me during "playtime," his voice hushed as he asked if I could keep a secret. I lied and told him I was known as "the vault" because I never revealed my secrets. Drawing closer, he cupped his hand near my ear and whispered, "Gaz, I've discovered an astonishing secret to reach a blockbuster orgasm that surpasses all others."

"Really?" My laughter bubbled up, and I couldn't suppress a giggle. I was all ears.

"I'd heard from a good source—"

Yes, Freddie, "good sources" are conduits for accurate information.

"If you stick your finger up your bum, you'll have an epic wank!"

I blinked rapidly. *What did he just say? Please, God, no!* Clearing my throat, I asked, "Did you test it out?"

"Yeah, and it totally blew my mind!"

The notion of Freddie possessing a stink finger and the position he adopted to carry out this astonishing act caused my eyes to widen in astonishment.

"Remember Gaz, Mum's the word! Don't let anyone know!"

I wanted to put his mind at ease, so I reassured him a) there was no need to worry about judgement and b) I would keep his secret confidential.

Without any delay, I shared the news with Billy and a few other close friends. In just a week or so, poor Freddie had earned the nickname "Freddie Brown Finger," and I felt a heavy weight of guilt as I recalled the sting of ridicule and teasing. It's a bit sad to admit, but the silver lining for me was that I became more invisible as Freddie basked in the limelight. In a reality where survival took precedence, a mindset rooted in self-centeredness prevailed.

Now, back to the Sonja debacle. I was extremely concerned about the next time I met up with Sonya. I, at least, wanted to play Incy Wincy Spider on an even playing field, and that meant me having an equally bushy "Jim Brown" on my nether regions. I regularly examined myself for weeks and weeks on end for my first ever pube. I couldn't believe it—not one solitary hair. If only there were such a thing as pubic toupees, I would have saved every penny from my paper route to buy one *tout de suite*.

Every self-assessment revealed no signs of growth. It was like checking lottery tickets, waiting for the winning numbers to appear. My heart sank every time, as the outcome never met my expectations. After school, I would hurry into the bathroom and quickly grab Mum's magnifying make-up mirror to closely inspect the pubic area. Disappointed and confused, I would emerge from the toilet, pondering Mum's occasional comments about the tragedy of going blind at a young age. Then, on one remarkable and magnificent day, I caught a glimpse and realised a solitary strand of hair had emerged from my pubic area. I couldn't believe my eyes. Happy? I confidently strutted around the kitchen, channelling the spirit of Muhammad Ali during his victorious match against George Foreman in the Rumble in the Jungle.

Puberty at the Knoll school was never going to be a fun experience. I had very sore nipples, as many boys going through changes had. It felt like I had hard disks behind my nips. Unaware of this natural phenomenon, I was scared it was breast cancer. My nipples were super sensitive to touch. Of course, Mitch Skinner and his merry men would seek out boys in the playground and "nipple-tweak" them. This was when my nipples were simultaneously grabbed, pinched, and turned 180 degrees, causing me to collapse on the floor in excruciating pain.

One advantage to being a late bloomer was that while my peers had to deal with different skin problems, such as pimples or "zits," I avoided being called names like "pizza face" and the accompanying ridicule. Other than my freckly nose, I was super lucky with my skin.

By the time I had a reasonable collection of pubes, I was too late to call Sonya as she was already dating other boys who weren't half as weird as I had been. As the legendary Doris Day once sang, "Que Sera, Sera (Whatever Will Be Will Be.)"

CHAPTER 21
THE LUMP
1976

AS SURE AS EGGS ARE EGGS, I DID NOT WANT TO HAVE DAD'S OR anyone else's cancer. I had a basic understanding of what it felt like to be sick, but my dad's pain from this illness was on a whole different level. Deep down, I felt like a ticking time bomb, my nerves on edge, dreading the Big C would make its presence known. My mum never missed an opportunity to point out how much I resembled Denis. She recounted the bizarre incident of her uncle Patrick's head spontaneously exploding in his mother's kitchen, attributing it to his refusal, like me, to eat Brussels sprouts. As she described the violent scene, comparing it to a watermelon exploding under the impact of a dum-dum bullet, I reflected on the shared genetic makeup between Dad, his brother, and me.

To remain sane and cancer-free, I was determined to do the following:

1. Avoid atomic bombs.

2. Disregard old wives' tales and treatments.

3. Become an oncologist and self-medicate with top-of-the-range chemo, if necessary.

I began to dive deep through various medical texts to discover ways to reduce the impact of the disease as I realised it was the start of my long journey to become an oncologist. It meant going to medical school. Alas, I had to put on hold my desire to become an aviator and bomb the shit out of the Soviet Union.

I knew getting into medical school would be no mean feat, especially as I attended the school from hell. I had to pick up the slack and opt for the "self-taught" route to stand any chance of making this happen.

I started reading through my mum's mammoth circa 1952 illustrated medical textbook. The common diagnoses were pox, plague, lunacy, or cancer, regardless of the symptoms. The sheer thickness of the book was intimidating, and the images of people with squamous and basal cell face cancer, lockjaw, syphilis, and penile gangrene were so graphic it was hard to look at. I checked myself several times to ensure my pecker wasn't rotting.

Mum had frequently warned me about the Trew madness genome, describing it as "a ticking time bomb" in the genetic makeup of specific individuals who err on the side of Roman Catholicism. She insisted Dad's ancestry could be traced back to King Henry VIII, who she claimed had contracted syphilis. The fact that Dad and King Henry suffered from gout proved, in her mind, their solid genetic connection.

As I looked at an image in her medical book of a man with a foot the size of an adult orca, I asked my mum what measures I could take to prevent gout. "Just eat your veggies, no red meat, and stay away from red wine and stuff."

Frowning, I pointed out, "Dad never touched red wine or red meat. He loved eating fish. What do you mean by *and stuff?*" I asked, my eyebrows furrowed in confusion.

"Fish, fish fingers, tobacco, can cause gout. So can swing music, liver, bacon, and Roman Catholicism."

Coincidentally, I started experiencing severe migraines with distressing light patterns, visual impairment, and ringing in my ears around the same time, which was then followed by waves of nausea and an agonising headache. Mum, once again, nudged me after my first attack, whispering, "Just like your Uncle Patrick," while mimicking an exploding watermelon with her hands (complete with sound effects). "Gary, you're a mini version of your dad. Eat your veggies—they could totally save your life!"

When I looked up my migraine symptoms in Mum's ancient medical book, I had a clear case of cancer (meningioma) with a dash of lunacy, pox, or syphilis. Maybe she was right after all these years. I decided when I stopped throwing up, I'd start on her regimen of sprouts, broccoli, cabbage, and green beans. "Remember your onions too. They'll relieve the pressure on your swollen brain," my mum said, in a kind of told-you-so way. Then, without touching her green diet, the migraine symptoms went away. I sighed with great relief and carried on my boycott of all things green.

I realised that reading Mum's medical book wasn't helping me get into med school. So, I decided to visit the nearby library, which housed the latest medical books. It felt like I was in Heaven. While my Knoll buddies were learning prison shank skills, I was deep into Robbins' *Pathologic Basis of Disease* and mastering Prior and Silberstein's *Physical Diagnosis*. I gobbled up Grant's *Atlas of Anatomy* and had a total nerdgasm over Goth's *Medical Pharmacology*. I memorised bizarre medical conditions, their symptoms, diagnoses, prognoses, and the wide range of pharmacological interventions used to treat them.

Mum thought I was reaching an age where boys spend all their time masturbating everywhere, even at the library. She decided an intervention was necessary and approached me that evening after returning from the library. "You'll go blind," she warned, her voice filled with concern.

"Why?"

"It's a well-established medical fact. Pastor Gwyn, the pastor at my Baptist Church in Pwllheli, used to caution the boys during choir practice that excessive indulgence could cause blindness."

I wrinkled my nose and let out a deep, heartfelt groan. *Pastor Gwyn this, Pastor Gwyn that.* "There's nothing wrong with my eyesight!"

With a knowing nod, Mum recounted Pastor Gwyn's extraordinary encounter with a boy at the library. The boy had been pretending to read books, but to everyone's astonishment, he was struck blind.

I rolled my eyes so much that I'm sure I caught a glimpse of my amygdala; Mum must have thought I had turned into Regan of *Exorcist* fame. "Mum, for Heaven's sake. I'm at the library *reading* medical books."

Her head bobbed with a sagacious understanding, whispering with conviction. "That's what they all say."

The intense book study helped me to check for signs of cancer. I examined my carotid glands, then moved down to feel the lymph nodes beneath my clavicle. Next, I checked for any lumps under my arms. I carefully felt around my sternum for any signs of an enlarged spleen, which could indicate leukaemia. After that, I inspected my groin area, and finally, I checked my pecker to ensure there were no signs of gangrene.

It was during one of my twice-daily exams that I first felt it. A small, mysterious lump caught my attention—in the area around my buttocks, quite near my bum. As my dad had died of colon cancer, the blood drained from my head, and I fainted beside my bed. When my senses returned, I summoned the bravery to poke and prod in that area. I felt it. It had a solid and rigid feel. Indeed, it was huge. Every time my hand reached the spot on my buttock, I felt like it was growing bigger. I could feel the tumours, like ticking time bombs, threatening to burst through my skin and spread throughout my body, resembling the grotesque fungating tumours I had learned about days ago.

I thought about asking Mum to check out the lump herself. But it was way too close to my bum, and there was no way I'd let Mum go anywhere near it. The lump consumed my thoughts for an entire week. The more I prodded and probed, the more aware I became of its immense size and how it was causing me to walk with a distinct difference. I had no choice but to book a doctor's appointment.

I phoned the doctor's office; the receptionist took the call. Mum couldn't stand her because she asked too many questions.

"Why do you want to see Dr Harris?" the receptionist inquired, her tone tinged with impatience.

"I have a . . . a . . . lump."

"Mr Trew. That's T-R-E-W. Gary, G-A-R-Y?"

"Yes." I tried to pace around the front room, but the short phone cable was stretched to the maximum.

"A lump, you say?" I imagined her filing her nails, chewing gum, and rolling her eyes in the overcrowded doctor's office with everyone listening. "You're in luck. Two o'clock this afternoon," she said abruptly and ended the call.

Later that day, as I waited in the doctor's office, I found making eye contact challenging. I felt ashamed I was a cancer patient, like my dad.

I'm too young to die.

The old bag of a receptionist eventually pointed me in the direction of Dr Harris's surgery and told me to go inside. I sat across from Dr Harris and was immediately drawn to the impressive collection of diplomas adorning the wall behind him.

If only I could have lived long enough to collect a few of those. Dr Trew, M.D. Oncologist. Damn you, cancer!

Dr Harris scribbled on his notepad. He put the pen down, smiled, and looked at me with his large brown eyes. He wore round, John Lennon-type glasses and had a full head of thick brown, slightly curly hair. I inhaled deeply. The air filled my lungs as I met his intense gaze.

Both hands suddenly smacked his knees. "So, you found a lump?" he asked, his tone warm and calm.

I took a deep breath and sighed. "I have a sizeable lump, most likely a premetastatic tumour, located in the gluteus maximus region.

"I see," he said, raising his eyebrows. He pointed to the examination table. "Drop your trousers and lay face down over there."

I gingerly slipped off my trousers, climbed onto the squishy surface, lay face down, and wiggled my pants halfway down my buttocks.

"Can you point to where the lump is?"

Um. Has he taken off his glasses? It's huge. The Kilimanjaro-like mass on my bum.

I gestured towards the lump's summit; my finger landed on the spot where the enormous tumour loomed. "There!"

After a series of prods and probes, he released a worrying grunt that made me super-anxious. It was the kind of sound a doctor makes when the patient is in a critical condition. *Grunt. I'm sorry, you only have four days left to live.*

"Can you feel it yourself?" asked the doctor. "When you find it, keep your finger there, and I will follow it with my hand so I can feel it too."

I did what he said. I became a bit frantic, not because the tumour had doubled in size in under an hour, but because I couldn't find it. *Shit. Shit. Shit. Lump, where are you?* "It might be easier if I stand and try to find it for you," I said.

I got to my feet. I felt. I poked. I prodded and pushed. There was nothing to be found. I couldn't freaking believe it! "Honestly, doc, it's been there for two weeks."

No, no. He's thinking I'm Gary Munchausen.

I needed to convince him, so I carefully chose my words. "I can't stand visiting the doctor. My intention in coming here is not to waste your time. I promise the lump used to be there, but now it's gone." I tried to reassure him to prevent him from thinking I was a total loser. "I have read medical school books and regularly conduct self-examinations."

With a quizzical expression, Dr Harris arched his eyebrows. *I think I've impressed him.*

"What's upsetting you? How's school? You must have missed a lot with pneumonia and your dad's passing." I watched him in silence, absorbing the intensity in his eyes. "Let's examine you."

The doctor looked away, his fingers probing my neck gland. He shone a light in both eyes.

He's looking to see if I have a brain.

He asked me to get on an old-fashioned weight scale and tweak the weights on the top of the device. Finally, he locked eyes with me and delivered the news, "Gary, there's nothing wrong with you. You're underweight for your age. Maybe a tad undernourished."

I frowned. *How the heck would you know that?*

"You've been quite ill. Your mother's chief concern is that you're not eating enough. Enjoy your studies; they will open doors to a world of knowledge and opportunities. Also, remember to eat your vegetables."

Thanks, Mum!

"Anything else bothering you?"

"Are my eyes okay?" I blurted out.

"Your eyes?"

"I get teased a lot by this one kid at school."

"Your eyes are fine. You have nice, big, blue-green eyes."

"I do?"

"Yes."

"No iodine deficiency? Too much thyroxin? A brain tumour?"

"No, absolutely not."

I sighed in relief, and then my heart started to beat faster. *Why did I ask him that? He's going to think that I came here for reasons other than a lump in my bum. I'll be forever known as the Munchausen Syndrome kid.*

Despite everything, I couldn't help but love Dr Harris. There was no lump. It had disappeared, just like "Zebedee," the geography teacher. Maybe there is a God, after all? Dr Harris was a perfect professional who didn't scold me for wasting his time. I wanted to be like him when I had my own practice. He presented as a kind and respectful adult. I hugged him. I felt I wasn't quite ready to die—yet.

CHAPTER 22
BENT AS A FIVE-BOB NOTE
1976

HERB BARKER, THE CRICKET COACH WHO NOTICED ME AT THE academy, confidently said I had great potential. He appeared for the school's first cricket net practice the following year. He headed straight for me and mentioned that had tried to locate me the previous year, but I had disappeared from his radar. I didn't explain why. I told him I continued playing for the men's team at the British Legion. With a hopeful tone, he asked if I was interested in joining his team. He advised me to aim for the stars and join his club, which offered top-notch facilities and connections.

Barker was an odd-looking bloke in his late forties; he was very noticeable and stood out from the crowd. Although he bore a considerable girth, he seemed fit and healthy and was tanned from many hours spent in the sun. A coarsely textured Dickensian beard adorned his jowls, extending to the corners of his mouth and adding a touch of old-fashioned creepiness to his appearance. The coach's prominent sideburns were two large, salt and pepper-coloured tufts of hair that resembled mutton chops. Multicoloured bristles erupted from his eyebrows, nose, and ears, creating a striking visual display.

Barker would have made a fabulous double for Mr Brownlow of *Oliver Twist* fame.

I politely declined the invitation. I enjoyed playing for the Legion. The guys knew each other well; their salty language and conversation were hilarious. I was just in my teens, and the average age of the rest of the team was about thirty. Afterwards, we would head to the Legion's clubhouse, where I'd enjoy a refreshing shandy and a game of darts or snooker, just a short walk from my house. With each step away from my home and sad memories, I felt a weight lift from my shoulders.

Barker suggested I take some time to consider it, and he promised to ask me again in a few weeks. He surprised me by bear-hugging me from behind at the practice nets. It felt uncomfortable. The coach put on his batting pads and asked me to bowl at him; my school cricket buddies noticed that this influential coach was focusing on me when he should also be helping them develop. I agreed and found the attention embarrassing since the school Phys. Ed. master, Mr McDougall, was present; I assumed Barker was there with his knowledge and blessing.

Afterwards, one or two players said they were thrilled he wasn't focusing on them, as Herb had a particular reputation in the community. "Like what kind of a reputation?" I asked.

"He's an influential coach," said one.

"He's too intense," said another.

"He's bent as a five-bob note," laughed an older boy as he winked and punched me in the arm.

Bent as a five-bob note? What's that supposed to mean? That he's dishonest? The school staff wouldn't let him near us if he was a sketchy character.

Herb Barker attended the following few practices and coached the other kids. Then, out of nowhere, he came up behind me and told me he had some tips for me. He told me to face away from him, and he would show me how to improve my accuracy as I bowled fast deliveries for my age but was occasionally wild. I'd received coaching in the past and was keen to improve. Barker placed his hips against my backside, taking my left arm, raising it into the air and instructing me to look through the gap between my arm and head; this was sound advice.

The sensation of something hard pressing into my buttock area caused me discomfort. The coach stood so close I could feel the warmth of his breath on my neck as his coarse beard brushed against my skin. I shuddered. He started grinding himself into me, pushing my hips forward.

What's he doing? What's pressing into my bum? I felt super-self-conscious and uncomfortable. I broke free and thanked him with a cherry-red face, hoping I wasn't the recipient of any sarcastic comments. Barker moved to the next practice net and coached another lad a few batting techniques.

I avoided Herb Barker like the plague as much as I could for the rest of the summer. He and some scouts attended some of my games and approached me again. "Well played. You are impressing quite a few scouts." Compliments were always welcome when it came to playing cricket. "We want to help take your game to the next level."

We? That sounds promising.

I noticed the scouts he was with were talking amongst themselves, nodding, and referring to their notepads. "We all think you can go far. How far would you like to go?"

Barker had got my attention. I looked away from him towards the centre of the cricket field and sighed. I stared into his eyes, "I want to play for England." A few seconds of silence followed.

The coach chuckled. "First things first, we must get you up to County standard." Kev, a cricket buddy, called me and waved for me to come and join him.

"Gotta go. See you later, Mr Barker," I said, jogging over to see what my pal wanted to talk to me about.

"You owe me one," Kev laughed.

I frowned. "What for?"

He playfully pushed me away from him, smiled and said, "Rescuing you from Pervy Herby."

"He was talking to me about cricket."

"Yer, right. Just be careful, Gaz, in case he's got the hots for you."

I punched Kev in the arm. "Shut up, you donkey. Now, who's the jealous one?"

It was pretty common for kids at school to tease each other about being gay. Mostly it was playful banter; sometimes it became downright nasty—especially when the same old bullies labelled their peers as "benders," "queers," "fags," and the like.

Becoming a professional cricket player in England was challenging, especially having attended a secondary school. The typical practice was to exclusively scout cricketers from high-ranking grammar or private schools and colleges. Despite Barker's outstanding reputation as a cricket coach and the assistance he could give in realising a dream, I avoided Barker to prevent being mocked. He also gave me the creeps.

When I returned home from school one day, my mum informed me she'd had a visit from a gentleman who was a cricket coach. She said he and a few other coaches had taken notice of her son's talent. My mum believed the man genuinely wanted to help me and was dedicated to making me an elite player. He stated he had helped many other players fulfil this dream. Knowing my deep love for cricket, my mum was overjoyed. Unfortunately, Mum, a social butterfly, couldn't help but overshare. She spoke about the unfortunate death of my father. Her recommendation was that I should have strong and dependable male role models to support me during my grieving process and assist me in overcoming it. The man promised my mum he would mentor me and help me reach my full potential in the game. He advised her that coaching could be the key to success, and he offered to coach her son free of cost. As a cherry on the cake, he volunteered to take Mum to practices until she became more comfortable with the new role model in her son's life.

"He gave me his business card and asked me to discuss it with you when you return from school."

I took the card from her hand, looked at it, and rolled my eyes. "Herb Barker came to our house?"

"He sure did."

How the heck did he know my address?

"Gary, he's a top coach."

I sighed. "I know."

Deep in thought—I was annoyed, yet I was also stoked.

Mum said, "He mentioned that you were distracted when he suggested coaching you a couple of weeks ago. He came here to show you and your mother that he was serious about his offer to help."

Distracted? No, my pals were laughing at me.

Barker proposed that I switch teams from the British Legion to his more professional team and sign a contract. That wouldn't happen because I was happy where I was. I wasn't prepared to sign anything, but the coaching sounded fine, and if this Herb guy was as "bent as a five-bob note," my mum possessed supreme predator senses—she would be the first to chase him from the house. This dude's presence made me uneasy, but most people in authority did. The male teachers at the Knoll School were abysmal examples for young boys—just sayin'. Mum suggested I give the coaching a few weeks trial to see if it was helpful.

A few weeks later, Barker turned up in his car. He asked if my mum wanted to join us, but she was at the park with the twins. Barker took me to his club's practice nets—they were excellent. He batted; I bowled at him. Barker coached and gave some tips. I listened and did what he'd asked me to do. When the coaching was over, he talked to me in his car before going home and then dropped me off. I was acutely wary of him and said little in response. Now that school had ended, he agreed to coach two or three times a week. All seemed fine and dandy.

A few days later, Herb Barker brought me to the practice nets. Bowling to him made me feel more at ease—like I had more control over the situation. I goofed around and mimicked the bowling actions of famous cricketers, which I found hilarious. Irritated, the coach told me to focus on my bowling style, likely in response to a few deliveries that whistled past his ears. When I played cricket, I became lost in what I was doing; I felt free. In the movie *Billy Elliot*, when Billy started to dance, something inside of him came alive, and he just wanted to dance. When dancing, he forgot about poverty, his dad's unemployment, and the misery of the coal mining strikes; he just danced, and everything else became moot.

As I bowled a cricket ball, the wind whispered past my ears, and the solid ground beneath my feet filled me with a liberating sense of exhilaration. I entered a world where there were no school bullies to torment me, no fear of death looming over me, no complicated relationships to navigate, and no stressful math classes to worry about. A force surged within me as if a whirlwind of pain and fears found solace in hurling a cricket ball with all the strength I could muster.

On the third and fourth occasion, it was evident I had started to relax and smile. The next time he picked me up, Barker told me he had to grab something from his house before we went to the nets. We drove to his home. He stopped and invited me in. "I'm good. I'll wait here," I said.

"Don't be daft, I can't leave you in the car. I need to grab a couple of things."

Why can't you leave me in the car?

He was insistent. I sighed loudly and joined him. The coach asked me to close the front door behind me. I gazed at the front room. I felt uneasy. Clothes and a newspaper were scattered over the floor. *Yuck. This needs a good clean.*

Barker suggested I follow him upstairs as he'd like to show me some fascinating memorabilia. "Nope, I'm good."

"Come on, lad. I'm not going to bite."

My mum taught me about stranger danger. My eyes opened wide as I gazed at the clutter. I shook my head, not wanting to make direct eye contact with him.

"Why are you looking like that?" he asked. "We're hardly strangers, for goodness' sake. I've met your mum, been to your house, and I'm your friend, your coach, Herb." He threw back his head and let out a loud, humourless laugh. "Okay, your loss."

He went upstairs. I stood by the door, rooted to the spot. I could hear a few things clattering above me. He sounded angry. I gently undid the latch and pulled the front door slightly ajar. Barker stomped down the stairs, and by the time he was in the living room, I was halfway along the short walkway to his parked car. He didn't make conversation on the way to the practice nets . . . it was an awkward hour or so. *Something's off. He's mad. I don't want to be here.*

I had to admit I could see a marked improvement in my bowling. Barker made helpful remarks, and like a sponge, I listened and applied what he suggested I did.

"Great delivery," "good ball," "wowzah . . . that was fast," he said. I felt like a million dollars as he poured compliments upon me. He's a nice bloke when he's not acting weird—when he's not pressuring me.

When we packed up, like every other time before, I sat on the left-hand side in the car's passenger seat, fastened the seatbelt and waited for him. Barker got into his car from the driver's side. He put the keys in the ignition but didn't start the car—he just sat there. There was a short, awkward silence.

"You've improved in a very short time."

"Thanks," I nodded.

"You're short and skinny but bowl with a ridiculous pace."

THE HATE GAME

Please don't tell me my mum told you I'm a fussy eater. "Yup. I need to grow and fill out." I felt he was staring at me.

"You know, despite your size, you're strong. Your shoulders are broad. I bet your thighs are athletic."

Quick as a flash, he leaned in toward me and grabbed my right leg, which was covered with my white cricket flannels. He gripped my thigh and repeatedly squeezed. His large, hairy hand reminded me of a tarantula.

I turned my head and looked at his mutton-chop sideburns. His eyes were cold and dark, fixated on mine. "You have nice legs."

My eyes widened, and my mouth felt dry; it was hard to swallow. Barker felt my scrawny thigh muscle and didn't release his tight grasp. I turned away from him and looked out of the windscreen, stunned. "You know," he began squeezing again, "you have plenty of raw talent, and I have the connections and the ability to make you an outstanding player."

Like a deer caught in headlights, I completely froze. His sizeable tarantula-like hand slowly moved up my leg. "You are a lovely boy. I scratch your back—"

I steadied my breath, trying not to panic. My mind echoed with silent screams, a paralysing terror gripping my entire being. Barker's hand had now moved up onto my thigh and rested on my crotch; he squeezed again. The suffocating grip of fear immobilised me, just as it would in the presence of any predator.

The tarantula groped for my zipper, not realising my cricket trousers did not have one. I was now petrified. I couldn't move away from the man; I couldn't get out of the car—I was held in my prison by the seatbelt.

"Look at me," Barker said. I tried to swallow and failed; I complied. He winked at me with one hollow, dark eye, "I think you know what I mean?"

I did, but I shook my head in response. I reached down and tried to remove his hand from my groin. "I scratch your back—

and connect you with scouts and selectors. I coach you to become the player you dream of becoming. Then—you scratch my back." He rubbed my groin with one hand and moved my hair away from my ear with the other.

I couldn't bring myself to say anything. I sat there, my body rigid with fear, unable to even blink. My own small and bony hand was trying to pull his hand away from my crotch. "Please, no. Stop. I don't . . . I don't like that."

I felt his fetid breath close to my ear. "Then, what do you like, Gary Trew?"

I dare not turn to look at him. The pressure on my crotch lessened. He sighed, laughed, and finally shifted back into a driving position and started the car. "Now we understand each other. Do you want to come back to my house?"

Are you kidding me? Eff off.

I wondered what I had done, what signals I had given him? How did we 'understand' each other?

"You can use my phone to call your mum and tell her you might be a bit late if you like. Do you want to relax? I have some booze in the house."

Not a word escaped my lips. I was thinking of an answer. I needed to escape.

"Is that a . . . yes?"

I had to stall and get the feck out of this situation. "I need to think about it. Please take me home."

"I have connections that you wouldn't believe. I can make it happen," he clicked his fingers, "just like that."

"Yes, I believe you. Are you able to drive me home now?"

"So, this is your last chance for this evening. Come home with me or maybe we can clean up in the changing rooms. Maybe a nice shower?" He was relentless.

"No, I'm not feeling great," I said, which was true. The butterflies in my tummy were now making me feel like puking. I asked Barker, once again, to take me home. I said Mum would get worried. I told him I'd consider what he said. I even made him a promise. However, I knew there would be no next time; I just needed to get home. The fear was morphing into anger. If I had a blade at hand, I would have put it through his eye,

He wouldn't take no for an answer, "I can smooth it over with your mother?" He leaned over to me again and ran his hand through my hair. A shiver went down my back. This was never going to end.

"Stop. I want to go home."

I saw a middle-aged guy walking a dog about 100 yards away. Barker must have caught a glimpse of him from the corner of his eye because he pulled away from me, reached for the keys and started the car. Barker thrust his hand down his own cricket trousers like he was tucking in his shirt or adjusting his privates. I hate to wonder what would have happened if that man with the dog hadn't appeared that early evening. While driving me home, he acted like nothing had happened. "Gary, I like you. I can be a father figure to you; you are like a son to me."

I said nothing while he continued to make conversation. When he finally dropped me off, I grabbed my kit from the back seat of his car, slammed the door behind me and ran to my house.

I was extremely relieved. I ran through the hallway and kitchen and headed straight to the toilet, locking the door behind me. I had a terrible dose of diarrhoea. I sat on the toilet for a while. I was consumed by feelings of shame and filth, and I felt the overwhelming urge to wash my hands and face repeatedly as if trying to rid myself of an invisible stain. I could still feel Barker's wretched whiskers on my face. Mum called out jokingly, wondering if I was taking root in the loo. She was laughing; she had no idea.

What do I do? If I tell Mum, she might not believe me. If she does, she'll kill him. I don't want the twins or me to be taken into care. I couldn't see any way of being coached without being abused. I wanted to play cricket so badly—but at what cost?

Maybe it was your fault. You ignored your mates—they knew he was "bent." There's something wrong with you. I felt like I was in purgatory. *I had no girlfriend—my lover was cricket. Cricket was my life. Now what?*

I couldn't share this with anyone, especially school friends. I couldn't tell a teacher. In the claustrophobic toilet space, my mum's voice echoed, encouraging me to come out and talk to her. But once again, my screams remained trapped in the silence of my mind. I left the bathroom and told Mum the coaching didn't work out.

"I didn't like Barker—he was too pushy." Like the moody teenager I was, I stormed up the stairs, went to my bedroom, slammed the door, fell facedown onto the bed, and bawled into my pillow.

Barker continued to appear at the house—Mum made excuse after excuse before she told him I wasn't interested in cricket anymore. Sometimes, I'd see his Rover car parked on Livingstone Road. He was waiting for me. After a few weeks, he must have lost interest and targeted other boys.

Several years later, I reported Barker to Sussex police for a historical sexual assault. I also discovered he had spent time in prison for sexually abusing several children. This man ruined countless lives. I was fortunate, but it was a close call. As for cricket, my dream had been shattered; I would play for fun but had no appetite to be an elite player anymore.

CHAPTER 23
IT'S LIKE TAKING CANDY FROM A BABY
1976

IN GERMAN-OCCUPIED FRANCE, JACOBUS VAN NIERON, A 51-year-old Dutch dentist, committed heinous acts by joyously massacring over one hundred of his victims' mouths—allegedly causing considerable pain and suffering. After being arrested in Canada, they deported him back to France in 2014. Despite his protests, the court ruled he was unfit to practice dentistry again. No shit, Sherlock!

In the 1976 film *Marathon Man*, Laurence Olivier played the part of a Nazi dentist, Dr Christian Szell, who violently and sadistically tortured "Babe" Levy's (Dustin Hoffman's) teeth. I'd heard about the movie from my mum and watched it by sneaking into a movie theatre (illegally), as it was "X-rated" at the time. In one vicious scene, Sir Laurence cruelly interrogated Hoffman by drilling into his healthy gnashers, causing screams that would make even the most hardened individuals shudder.

While *Marathon Man* was being watched and enjoyed by thousands upon its release, many of my past dental issues came to the surface. I confess to having a sweet tooth. Thanks to my tender-hearted mum, I developed a deep love for all things chocolate. As she went without in her childhood, stealing sugar cubes from the mouths of the farmyard horses, she made sure little Gary would never complain about not being provided with enough sweet things as a kid. Mum was very generous and enjoyed treating me with bars of Cadbury's Dairy Milk slabs, Tiffin, Crunchies, Fry's Chocolate Cream, Milky Way, and Mars Bars. There were also non-chocolaty, and "healthier" gifts that she provided me with, like Flying Saucers, Spangles, Love Hearts, Everton Mints, Polos, Fruit Pastilles, Refreshers and Sherbet Fountains. My Mum was the real-life Tooth Fairy, without having to give her teeth in exchange, or so I thought.

However, being the generous mum that she was, she continued to supply me with my daily sugar fix. It never crossed her mind to remind me about brushing my baby teeth; I often found myself without toothpaste or a toothbrush. As a result, I was pinned down on the dentist's chair, unable to escape the overpowering, sweet aroma of nitrous oxide and the smell of rubber emanating from the dentist's gas mask. In a blind panic, I kicked the dental nurse and grasped the dentist's arms during the procedure. Afterwards, the fuming dentist forcefully rolled up his sleeves to reveal the numerous red, angry fingernail marks crisscrossing his forearms, leaving my mother visibly startled and taken aback. Mum had been too worried to warn her young son about the forthcoming mass teeth extraction. I was utterly traumatised by the experience. However, having rebuked the dentist for being a dumbass, she also chastised her sweet-toothed, five-year-old child for eating too many sweets. Mum rewarded me after my ordeal with a large bar of Cadbury's Tiffin. That was Mum, and that's how she rolled.

As a teenager, I did my best to make up for the early years of poor dental hygiene and brushed my teeth twice daily. However, it had been 10 or 11 years since I had been for a check-up and thought it was time to make an appearance. Dentists gripped me with fear, having been "gassed" back in the day by the angry "Gas Mask Guy." My mum told me she knew of a friendly, elderly

Polish dentist called Dr Podanski, and I should get my teeth checked out by this kind old soul.

Terrified by the thought of another gas mask being placed over my nose and mouth, my sister assured me any required work would be done under anaesthesia. No gassing would occur. At the time, in the United Kingdom, all essential dental services were free under the National Health Service. Carole made an appointment for me to see the charming old dentist, whose hair was as white as snow and who referred to himself as "a doctor." I must admit I was nervous, and when I saw him, he looked a bit like the crypt keeper from a B-movie horror story. I tried to overcome my through-the-roof anxiety by thinking positive thoughts. Dr Podanski would have made a great Father Christmas. He was a rotund, amiable-looking man with unattractive, chubby, sausage-like fingers; his fingernails had been noticeably gnawed down to their cuticles. Although he sported a buzz cut, his bristles were snow white—nothing a red floppy Ho! Ho! Ho! North Pole hat wouldn't fix. He wore white facial stubble and a thick, droopy moustache, a bit like Kaiser Wilhelm's. Unfortunately, up close, when he was a few inches from my face, his ice-blue irises were neither warm nor kind.

The "doctor" had a marked East European accent and sported half-rimmed glasses. When he spoke, his "Ws" became "Vs," and his "Vs" became "Ws." There was no dental nurse or assistant, just him.

With my mouth open wide, he prodded and poked with the metal instrument he held. Dr Podanski scheduled another appointment for a few fillings the following week.

On my return home, Mum had been shopping and treated me to chocolate, a bag of crisps and cola. I hesitated for a nanosecond and finished the treats, thanking Mum for her kindness.

I returned the following week to have the dental work completed. I was highly anxious. As I sat in the dental chair, a metal suction device was inserted under my tongue, and my mouth was wide open. The old dentist grunted, huffed, and puffed.

Don't look at him. Take deep breaths. Close your eyes and calm down.

The drill's high-pitched noise made me shudder as vivid images of Sir Lawrence and Dustin Hoffman flooded my mind.

Gary, stop it! Don't be an eejit; don't be a baby—it's just a couple of fillings. I wondered if he intended to use anaesthesia—my ultimate fear was the thought of pain. Damn movie.

Despite the suction thingy gurgling and sticking to the base of my tongue, I opened my eyes. I asked, "Aw, u oozing nowacaine?"

With instruments in his hand, he stopped what he was doing and said, "Vhot?"

"Aw, u oozing nowacaine? Nowacaine, to rumm me?"

"I don't know vhot you ask? Stop talking."

I furrowed my brow. I tried to swallow but couldn't—my mouth was too dry.

The drill's high-pitched whine began. I closed my eyes and gripped both armrests in anticipation. The dentist drilled into the lower left molar, and the air was thick with the acrid smell of burning enamel.

"Argh," I cried out. My face twisted in discomfort, and I held onto the armrests for dear life, like a woman in labour holding onto her partner's hand. Podanski continued with stoic determination. My mind whirred round and round as the shrill whine of the drill excavated the decayed section of the molar. He stopped and interchanged one drill bit with a new one. Relief.

The speed of this drill was slower and made a whirring sound.

"Relax," he snapped. He began to drill.

The pain was shocking. "Arggggh!" Loud, guttural sounds filled the room. There was a moment when the sounds emanated from the drill, and my mouth perfectly synced.

Dr Podanski stopped the drill, raised his white eyebrows, and stared at me.

"It 'eally 'urts," I said.

"Young man, you are baby child."

Baby child? "Naw, I not . . . it huurts."

"Nonsense!"

The drilling continued; I had never felt so much pain. Each time he drilled, a fire shot up my left eyeball. He switched the drill again, opting for the faster, more high-pitched one. The stench of burning teeth and decay in my nostrils was overwhelming. My face involuntarily contorted. Sweat poured down my face from my temple.

"Zer you go, baby child." He stepped away, his back to me. He turned on a machine that made a deep, humming sound. He made amalgam fillings, and before he placed the amalgam into my super-sensitive molar, he blasted the cavity with air. I almost passed out. It felt like my mouth had been open wide for decades—my jaw ached. He took the spit-sucker out of my mouth and commanded that I take a plastic cup of blue liquid, swirl it around my mouth and spit it into a small bowl attached to the chair. His mouth moved beneath his white beard. I'd had enough; I was out of there within a minute.

Of course, the molar "Dr" Podanski treated began to pound. I developed an abscess. Mum found me a different dentist, an Irish one whom Carole had recommended. Euon MacSweeney, a softly spoken, dashing, and handsome dentist. He treated the infected tooth by prescribing me antibiotics. Ultimately, the abscess cleared up, and I was back in the dental chair for root canal treatment.

I begged him to use novocaine. My plea fell on deaf ears as he drilled the tooth. The pain was intense, akin to a mantis shrimp striking an exposed nerve. Suddenly, without warning, my knee launched upward. The force was so fierce, and the reflex was so quick that MacSweeney couldn't avoid my knee—he was sent crashing to the ground. My knee had smacked him on the side of his face. It was an event that belonged on YouTube or TikTok. However, the internet wasn't around then. No wonder Jacobus Van Nieron and the fictitious Nazi dentist Dr Christian Szell used sadistic dentistry to torture and extract not teeth but information from their victims. If it were me who was in the dental chair and I was being interrogated, I would have confessed in a heartbeat. I'd admit my guilt, even though I was as innocent as a newborn. In fact, I'd admit to being Jack the Ripper, Charles Manson and even to assassinating JFK.

When I returned home, I was flustered, white as a sheet, and incapable of smiling. Mum was kind and made me a bed on the sofa.

"Son, you really must take greater care with your teeth."

"I know, Mum, I brush them twice a day."

"Good lad. I have something for you," she said as she left the room.

I took a couple of paracetamols she'd left on the table beside the sofa. Mum returned to the room with a bag of goodies that sent me into Candy Nirvana. Maltesers, a Crunchie, Cadbury's Fruit & Nut bar, a Topic and the *pièce de résistance* was a massive slab of Bluebird toffee.

"Mum, remember all those years ago when I had half a dozen teeth yanked by the dentist."

"How could I forget?"

"You told me if I kept eating sweets, I'd look like Mr Ed, the T.V. horse with big, artificial gnashers."

Mum laughed, stuck out her front teeth, moved her jaw from side to side, and made her eyeballs look at her nose. "I can always take my gift away and buy you some dental floss?"

I laughed. "No, I'm good," Mum joined me on the sofa, and we shared the bag of sugary goodies.

Mum's way of comforting me hadn't changed in a decade; neither had my common sense.

CHAPTER 24
THE BIKER DUDE
1976

THE FRIENDS I MADE OUTSIDE OF SCHOOL WERE FEW AND FAR between. However, after Dad died, I made one or two, and they proved to be a godsend. Each of them lifted my spirits immensely. Bob came from a nuclear family with his mum and dad, two older brothers, and a younger sister, creating a bustling household. Bob's dad was always busy with construction projects, while his mum dedicated her time to homemaking. Bob completed his education at The Neville, the rival school of Knoll's. A handsome fellow with an athletic build, he had an eye for the ladies and had no end of admirers. Super-confident and equipped with 'the gift of the gab,' Bob was older than me and was earning a decent income working as a roofer.

I can't remember how we became inseparable despite being complete opposites. We shared a few things in common: a love of heavy metal rock music and a passion for cricket. Bob, the mischievous yet lovable rascal, captured my mum's heart with his cheeky personality and unwavering respect for her. Bob's always warm and unobtrusive parents welcomed me into their home with open arms. I liked anyone who didn't pry into my personal life, avoiding questions like, "How's your dad doing?" or "Where is your father?"

Bob had other pals the same age as him but often encouraged me to go into town with him and have a shandy or the occasional underage beer, which I was thrilled to do as it got me out of my house. However, he had the propensity to get himself and me into unnecessary conflict. I didn't like that aspect of our relationship. However, having a buddy who could handle himself was also a big plus. Bob was one of the funniest (and friendliest) guys I'd ever met, and I watched in awe as he pulled lady after lady on a night out. I didn't care that it never happened to me. Hanging out with him was just fun.

A middle-aged biker dude moved over the road from us into a basement flat. His colossal BMW motorcycle was parked outside. Every day, he suited up in his full leather ensemble, donned his helmet, and rode off. An hour or so later, he would return.

My mum was the first to notice something odd about this chap. Several boys riding pillion appeared at his home daily and she grew concerned. He would glance around furtively, checking no one was watching, before slipping into his flat with the young boy. My mum's words were clear: stay away from the biker dude. After the Herb Barker situation, I found it ironic she hadn't picked up the same protective Mumma Bear vibe around him. There was no way on earth I would have anything to do with the guy.

Whenever the biker dude saw me, he smiled and said, "Alright?" I continued with my business, keeping my eyes downcast to avoid meeting his gaze. I felt his eyes follow me everywhere, making me feel super uncomfortable. The last thing I wanted was this guy's attention; I was still hiding from creepy Barker. I had trouble looking into the eyes of adults. Whatever little trust I had with people had long since departed. I tried hard not to feel disgusted with myself, like it was my fault somehow. I often wondered if something was inherently wrong with me. The biker dude's intense stares gave me a sense of unease. At least Mum was aware of the guy. I knew she'd be looking out for me.

The sun was already beating when I grabbed my cricket gear from the shed one summer morning and headed to meet Bob to play cricket. We were all set to play at Hove Recreation Ground, but first, we had to walk for 10 to 15 minutes to get there. The Biker Dude was outside cleaning the chrome on his motorbike. From the corner of my eye, I saw him stop what he was doing. I kept my distance from him while crossing the road. Summer had arrived; I had a tan and was dressed in a T-shirt, shorts, and trainers.

"Hey, how's it going?" he called out. "That tan looks great on you!"

My jaw clenched. I pretended he wasn't there.

"Wow! You look fantastic," he said.

I immediately had flashbacks of Barker's complimentary words to me. I felt as uncomfortable as a person would feel if their adult diaper leaked in public. I was a very live-and-let-live young man, but this guy's comments crossed a boundary. However, I knew Bob, my pal, was way less tolerant and had already mentioned he wanted to punch the guy in the face. Bob would say things like this, but wouldn't always follow through with action. I often acted as Bob's calming influence in tense situations, knowing that my dry humour would diffuse rather than inflame.

Bob collected his cricket gear and joined me at his door. I told Bob that the Biker Dude was shining up his motorcycle, and he'd tried to start a conversation with me. I suggested we take the longer way to the park, avoiding him altogether.

Bob disagreed, "No way. I'm not going to take any shit from him, and neither should you."

Gary, you donkey, why did you tell him? I tried to backtrack, lied, and told Bob he was being friendly. It was easier to avoid him, and I wanted to get on with our game.

So, with cricket gear in hand, we headed to the sports field, the same route we took every day. Bob told me, in no uncertain terms, that if Biker Dude said anything to *him*, he was going to "fuck him up." This made me even more stressed. We walked towards the flirtatious biker as he shined up his BMW. I felt a code-red situation on the cards. Biker Dude stopped buffing the chrome on his bike, stood up and faced the two young guys walking along the street, sports gear in hand. I looked right past him and carried on walking. *Phew!* I breathed a quiet sigh of relief.

As we ambled past him and his shiny BMW bike, we both heard a wolf whistle, followed by, "Nice pair of bums!"

Bob stopped in his tracks and turned around to face him.

"What did you say, mate?"

I sighed deeply. I just wanted to get away and play some cricket with my friend.

"I was only admiring two handsome young lads walking past me on a fine summer's day. There's no law against it, is there?"

Bob put down his cricket gear and clenched his fists. I nudged him on the arm.

"Come on, Bob," I said. "Don't let him wind you up."

With an ashen face, Bob stared at him and decided to use his best diplomatic skills, "Fuck off, paedo! Do you want to eat my fist?"

Biker Dude looked stunned; his wide-open eyes blinked rapidly. "What did you say to me?"

"You heard! We all know—" Bob said, pointing his unclenched hand towards several of the neighbourhood houses, "what you get up to with all the young kids you take to your flat!"

Biker Dude, now puce of face, said, "You better watch your mouth, son!"

"What are you going to do if I don't? I'm not a little 12-year-old."

I felt brave standing by Bob, who had gained some local

notoriety for being tough. I saw my friend reaching for the top of his cricket bat in his bag.

I wanted us to go on our way. I felt okay with Bob alongside me. However, what would happen when I was alone when Bob was at work? I didn't want to be a prisoner in my own house, too afraid to go out. I tugged at Bob's sweater, laughed nervously, and asked him to walk away— like I'd done many times.

"Leave it, Bob. He'll go in for the kiss, and you might not resist giving him one back on his lips." It worked; he laughed.

Biker Dude smirked, adding fuel to the fire, "Come on then, pretty boy."

What's wrong with him?

Bob yanked the cricket bat from his bag, held it upwards and said, "Maybe, you'd like some of this rammed up your arse!"

I stood before Bob and pushed him back with both arms. Bob's face was flushed with rage, his nostrils flared, and his eyes avoided mine, looking daggers at Biker Dude. I reminded him of our cricket game, and this guy wasn't worth getting into trouble for. Still staring at the guy, Bob felt for his bag, put the bat back into it, and then let rip with an impressive array of expletives.

The biker dude's response was to blow Bob a kiss. The stocky biker dude looked like he could hold his own in a physical altercation. Be that as it may, Bob was born into a sizeable family. Biker Dude would face an incensed Bob and his entire clan, some of whom had an even more notorious reputation than himself.

So, we turned our backs on the source of our chagrin, walked towards Hove station, went over the railway bridge, and arrived at our destination—Hove Recreation Park. We found a level-ish spot, set up our wickets, measured twenty-two yards between stumps, and played. Bob's mind wasn't on the cricket game at all. He was pissed and bowled at me like a man possessed, at times hurling the ball without it bouncing (a beamer), narrowly missing my head. After a while, Bob calmed down, and started to make jokes again. As we took a break from our game, ate the sausage rolls and crisps Mum had given us, and swigged iced juice, Bob said, "That guy is so dead!"

I changed the subject quickly. I didn't want him to get into trouble with the police; he was my link to a world that didn't involve the Knoll. Our strange friendship was one thing that kept me sane.

The following day, as I watched TV with Mum in our living room, there was a loud BANG! Followed by an explosion of noise and light against our front window. We looked at each other and asked simultaneously, "What was that?"

Mum headed to our large windows, opened the curtains, and exclaimed, "That bastard!" Biker Dude was scampering down the stairs to his flat. As Mum opened our door, I followed. We glanced at our windows, and I saw a black, sooty mark. The smoky remains of a firework rocket had been ignited in our small front yard. Mum slipped on her shoes, kicked the remains of the smouldering firework, and marched towards Biker Dude's basement flat.

I shook my head, knowing what was about to transpire. This would not be pretty, but it may be quite comical. My mum was a very laid-back lady. Everyone loved her. She was hospitable and social and almost always wore a lovely smile on her pretty face. That is unless one of her cubs had been threatened. When the latter happened, like the change from Bruce Banner to the Incredible Hulk, Gwendoline Lillian Trew transformed into a superhero character, the Savage Mumma Bear.

Mum reached his house and walked down the stairs that led to his flat. She pounded at his door with a clenched fist. I followed closely behind her and waited on the pavement, looking down for Mum to go atomic. Her back was facing me, but as she rained blows onto Biker Dude's door, she turned her head slightly, and I saw her cheeks were vermillion. The transformation was almost complete. Let the countdown begin.
THUMP! THUMP! THUMP!

THE HATE GAME

Finally, the door opened, and Biker Dude appeared. I winced. *Three . . . two . . . one . . .*

My five-foot, two-inch-tall mother was *face to chest* with the guy in his black bike leathers. Quick as a cheetah, Mum grabbed the lapels of his leather jacket with both hands. The biker dude looked down in shock as her hands locked onto the robust-looking black leather like a guided missile. She lifted the guy into the air and, swear to God, his boots left the ground. She held him suspended in the air for a few seconds, snarling in her now, very Welsh accent, "Don't you ever, ever, come near my house, or my family, ever again, or—" her spittle splattered his face, "I will effing kill you!"

I'd never heard my mum swear before, or at least never heard her say the F-bomb in English.

The biker's eyes looked like they would pop out of their sockets; his face was devoid of colour. Mum released her grip, and he was back on solid ground. Her face was still a few inches from his. *Oh no—don't headbutt him, Mum.*

He tried to re-organise his jacket and composure. Just as serendipity would have its last say, a confused-looking 12 to 13-year-old, topless boy appeared behind the ruffled Biker Dude, having come out to see what the commotion was about.

My mum's eyes widened, "I swear to God, I will report you, you filthy bastard!" She was snarling like a wild animal. Biker Dude gulped, spun around, and closed the door in her face. I heard the sound of a chain being put on the door latch. As Mum walked up his flight of stairs, joining me on the pavement, her pale green eyes were almost translucent. She was heading home, then, the chained door of the Biker Dude's flat opened a few inches.

"You crazy bitch! Keep that brat of yours and his half-witted mate away from me!"

Brat? Half-witted mate?

Witnessing the scene from above, I broke out laughing. With a squint and a shake of my head, I yelled, "What are you talking about, you plonker?"

He shouted out to Mum, "Your son and his punk-arsed buddy pushed over my motorbike last night. The mirrors have been damaged, and the chrome was scraped up. He's lucky the cops didn't come and arrest him. The firework, you mad woman, was tit for tat!"

Mum stopped where she was, turned her head towards his door, scowled and replied, "Better your bike lay on the road than me having to shove it right up your hairy arse!" Mum motioned for me to follow her back to our house—there was no way I wouldn't comply!

Hairy arse! Priceless.

Now full of confidence, I winked, smiled at Biker Dude, and then blew him a kiss. He slammed his door.

I didn't know anything about his BMW motorbike being pushed over. Shockingly, Mum didn't ask me either. I thought it was *always best to come clean*. "I promise I didn't do anything. I never touched his stupid BMW!"

"I know, son," Mum said. She was still visually wound up. "When you see Bob, tell him this from me—good job!"

And she, like all Brits do when they are stressed or have to deal with a traumatic situation, put the kettle on and made us both a cup of tea! Even though we had our regular parent-child conflict, Mum was the kindest, gentlest, most positive person I knew. Although I do not share many of her positive traits, it's safe to say that I did inherit the same genetic on/off "go nuclear" switch as my dear mum.

We never heard a peep from the biker dude again. Over the next few months, we knew the police had arrived at his home several times. Mum saw several officers lead him into a police van, much to the merriment of her and some of the other occupants on Livingstone Road. I was relieved when his BMW bike was no longer there, never to be seen again.

I touched base again with Bob a year or so ago and have remained in contact. One of the first things he asked me when we chatted after all these years was, "Do you remember that biker guy, the one your mum scared the shit out of?"

I chuckled, "Of course—how could I ever forget him."

"I loved your mum," he said, "she was a wonderful lady."

"Bob, after all these years, I've never asked. So, was it you that pushed over his motorbike?"

"Now, Gary, my son—that would be telling."

Mum certainly was a character adored by almost everybody who met her. However, the guy with the BMW who lived across the road from her may beg to differ.

CHAPTER 25
LIE DETECTORS, MARS BARS, AND A COMING OUT SURPRISE!
1976-1977

IT WOULD BEHOVE ME NOT TO MENTION A PARTICULAR CAVEMAN who taught biology at the Knoll School during my penultimate and final years at the dreadful academy of non-learning. Only a couple of teachers come to mind when I reminisce about teachers at the Knoll School. Mr McNeil, my English teacher and a gentle Scot, was a pleasant and peaceful man who taught rather than intimidated. Bob "Caveman" Tanner was the other.

Mr Tanner was a heaven-sent addition to my school life. He was yet another bearded man with a crazy, wild barbarian appearance. He looked highly intimidating, a bit like Fred Flintstone meets Neanderthal Man. However, Bob Tanner became my educational hero. It took just a few words in class to captivate me, and I adored his biology classes. It was the only subject I looked forward to attending during my last season at the Knoll School.

It was shocking. When he taught, I understood everything he said. No coercion, no throwing rats soaked in formaldehyde, scalpels, or skulls at the boys in his class, no humiliation, and no detentions, slippers, or canes. He controlled his class without having to shout or scream. Bob Tanner appeared to love his subject and wanted the boys in his care to do the same. Tanner helped me find my first love in the sciences, and he alone gave me the foundation I needed to study biochemistry later at university.

I didn't have the opportunity to study physics, as pupils had to choose between that and biology, which was a bummer—another roadblock to entry into medical school as physics, chemistry, and biology go hand in hand. However, one member of the physics class left a positive impression that was quite shocking and hard to forget. Phil was a tall, skinny boy with dirty blond hair and a very noticeable military side parting. He spoke crisply and quickly, with a robotic tone, and often spoke aloud to himself. Phil was pressured to compete in Knoll's Fight Club sooner than expected. He didn't want to resort to violence; however, an older boy threw a few wild punches at him, and Phil ended up leaving the flabbergasted assailant bruised and well-beaten. When he fought, Phil's arms were a blur, like he had pistons up his sleeves. Nobody messed with him after that. He was a peculiar fellow and became one of the toughest kids in school.

Phil's love for electronics and engineering was evident, and he was never happier than in physics class with our mutual friend, Billy. During our final year at school, a commotion broke out in one of the corridors. Phil bought a lie detector device for school, and a rumour was going around he was looking for volunteers. Phil had told a half-truth, as his device, "Boris," was an electric shock device. A slew of idiots tested Phil's lie detector's veracity. Boys lined up for Phil's simple truth or lie questions. He cautioned them that the device would detect a lie if they dared to hesitate in their answers. If a boy tried to lie to Boris, he would always be caught out, no matter how convincing the story was. The ear lobes of the first guinea pig were held in place by two crocodile clips, which made it difficult for the recipient to move.

However, Phil's "helpers" held the boy's arms down if they resisted the interrogation.

"What is your full name?" he asked the boy.

"Michael David Smith."

The growing audience hushed as Phil announced the news. "Michael Smith's full name is Michael David Smith, which is true. Boris has an exceptional level of precision in its readings."

Phil asked the second question. "Boris would like to know the first eight digits of Pi."

"Um..."

Phil pressed a button sneakily, causing Michael Smith's head to jolt back like a heavyweight boxer had punched him in the face. Phil admonished the boy. "Boris will mess you up if you hesitate!"

The lads surrounding Phil were laughing their heads off. The next person volunteered. Classes were about to start, and the bell was about to ring. Phil attached the clips to the sucker's ears. "Name?"

"Gordon..."

His head snapped back, and he screamed, more from being surprised than hurt.

"What the..."

"Your name is not Gordon," Phil interrupted, his words staccato and emotionless. "If I am correct, your first name is... Mary. You were born a biological female. You lied. *Boris* detected the lie." Gordon joined in with the raucous laughter.

Predictably, Skinner and his cohorts had witnessed Phil's crazy antics and elected to grab a few kids for obligatory "volunteer" work. Billy and I skulked away before someone could observe us.

∼

THE HATE GAME

I HAD no idea whose brilliant idea it was to allow Deon to attend Knoll School. I first saw him in the quadrangle for senior boys. Positioned in the far corner, the large boy muttered under his breath, his smile widening as people approached and greeted him. Minding his own business, he exuded an aura of meekness and harmlessness. Not only did the boy refrain from playing games, but he also appeared solitary, without any apparent friendships. In the corner, Deon stood motionless, his face devoid of discernible feelings. His school jacket no longer fitted him, and his mouth was filled with overcrowded teeth.

Deon, a pupil with a brain injury, was placed at the infamous Knoll School for Boys, thanks to the brilliant idea of someone on the school board or during a governor's meeting. During that time, he was left without the support of special education teachers or assistants, and no classes provided the nurturing and safe environment he needed. I did not know where he spent most of his time. Nonetheless, during breaks, he would invariably be found in the corner of the quadrangle.

Playtime was never enjoyable for me, especially during my early years in school. I felt on edge, ready to flee or defend myself to avoid encountering Skinner, Arnold Fickle, and the older children. Thoughts of the Holocaust games, chaotic fights, and crowded "bundles" filled my mind. No matter how old I got as a pupil, I could never shake the feeling of being unsafe or unsettled on any given day. The bigger kids shouted "bundle," leading to a chaotic pile-up of students on an unsuspecting, more petite student. The experience of being at the bottom of the pile, face pressed against the cold quad concrete, was not enjoyable. Occasionally, a bigger boy would grab a classmate's hair and guide them around the schoolyard. Anyone could become ensnared in a headlock by a mischievous bully, who would then confidently strut around with them, treating them as if they were a valuable possession.

Meanwhile, Deon positioned himself in the corner of the

concrete recreational area, minding his business and conversing with himself. He was often subjected to the cruel taunts of the kids, who took pleasure in calling him pejorative names. However, Deon was also required to put on a performance. He was frequently instructed to lick the brick wall. On various occasions, pupils were brought to him against their will and told to kiss him. Deon was reluctant to do so. Seeing a boy screaming and begging his captors to stop the terrible act probably terrified him. The bullies tried to bribe Deon with chocolate to manipulate him into doing what they wanted.

The memory of a Mars bar being offered to him lingered as I watched the boy struggle, surrounded by a gang of tough kids. There was no way for Deon or the other boy to escape from their predicament. There were no teachers to intervene and protect him or the other children from inappropriate behaviour in either of the two courtyards. More often than not, break time was traumatic for many of the pupils.

By the fourth year, although still scrawny, the other children didn't pick on me as much. I was angry and had the demeanour of a trapped, feral animal. I would also fight anyone, as I'd demonstrated several times.

The worst part about recalling school days at the Knoll was the overwhelming feeling of helplessness, constantly at the mercy of the bigger thugs. I experienced a sense of relief knowing I wasn't the one being singled out. Still, I couldn't ignore the possibility that I might be the next one to suffer. Nobody wanted to be noticed. You hoped to reach home without being physically, mentally and emotionally harmed, handling each day as it came.

BRIGHTON AND HOVE is renowned for the public's tolerance toward minorities and is known as one of the most diverse and exciting cities in the United Kingdom. Known globally for its gay village, Brighton has an impressive cultural scene that caters to all. For years, Brighton has been hailed as the gay capital of the UK. In Brighton, specifically on St James's Street in Kemptown, there are numerous LGBTQ pubs, clubs, bars, restaurants, cafés, and shops.

Sadly, the Knoll School for Boys failed to embody the same inclusive spirit as Brighton and Hove's rainbow flag. The atmosphere at the Knoll School was marked by negative behaviours, intimidation, abuse, victimisation, bullying, and a disregard for diversity. I can't even fathom the experiences of those who didn't fit the mould of straight, white, "Christian" males at the school. Steve Knight, a young man, caught everyone's attention with his confident personality among the pupils. Steve was a kid who stood out from the rest, the subject of whispered conversations among the other boys.

I didn't understand what this meant, as my worldly knowledge was as limited as a baboon's arse—that's how naïve I was. For me, you love who you love . . . so, what's the big deal? Steven's public declaration of being "different" instantly made him the school's sensation and my personal hero. For once, and only once, a modicum of credit to the headmaster, as the incident had to have been bizarrely pre-arranged with his consent. During one school assembly, Steven walked into the jeering lion's den of the assembly hall dressed in a dapper checked suit. He climbed up onto the stage, with the headmaster by his side, and announced to all and sundry: "I am a gay man!"

Many pupils laughed and treated the incident as a big joke; others were stunned into silence. I understand that Steven was literally run out of the school after the brave proclamation by some of his more Neanderthal peers. If the headmaster hadn't had the visual acuity of Stevie Wonder, he would have realised the consequences of such a proclamation for one of his pupils. "Batman" neither saw (nor wanted to see) the bullying, toilet duckings, sexual assaults in the toilets, the beastings, classroom chaos, assaults, after-school, and playground fights.

To me, Steven was the epitome of bravery—it certainly made me feel like a wimp, complaining about this and that. I've no idea what happened in Steven's life. Still, he made a lasting impression on many of us, witnessing his unbelievable act of bravery that day.

CHAPTER 26
PANIC AT THE DISCO
SPRING, 1977

APART FROM A BRIEF ENCOUNTER WITH AN IRISH GIRL NAMED Siobhan in the cloakroom at Middle Street School, I had never experienced the thrill of a kiss or the joy of having a girlfriend. There had been that brief encounter with Sonja Kerchup and her incredibly bushy bush, but there were no passionate kisses or hint of romance. Just like any other insane teenage boy, I'd lock myself in my room and practice kissing with my pillow, hoping to perfect my technique. Unfortunately, this would be disappointing, as the feathers in my pillow became wet and soggy, and I had to sleep on it afterwards. I soon came to the realisation I needed to find myself a girlfriend.

When I heard there would be a disco at Brighton, Hove & Sussex Sixth Form College, the school I planned to attend after the Knoll, some friends and I decided to go. The idea of going out and having a blast was really appealing. But honestly, it was hard to imagine any girls being nice (or desperate) enough to dance with us Knoll School boys.

At the disco that evening, we were immediately drawn to a group of girls dancing energetically, their purses and handbags swinging in rhythm. They were all attractive, but one really caught my attention. Her petite stature was a bonus for me, along with her alluring figure and lovely face. I found myself constantly battling with my self-doubt and lack of confidence. I wanted to approach her and start a conversation, but my fear paralysed me. My friend discovered the girls dancing without partners were all Hove Grammar School for Girls students. The grammar school girls were bright and carried themselves with poise and respect. I worried that if I mustered the courage to ask this girl to dance, she might quickly leave once she discovered I attended the notorious Knoll Boys school, and wasn't the sharpest tool in the shed.

I waited until the last slow dance songs were being played. It was some godawful tune: *When I Need You* by Leo Sayer, the singer with a hairstyle like a toilet brush. I swallowed my pride and nervously approached this grammar school girl with her ponytail and bright blue eyes. I had options with several smooth pick-up lines.

I could go all mathematical and say, "Hi, sex bomb! If you were a triangle baby... you'd be an acute one!"

However, I was so crap at maths because of Hippo Grippo's lessons that she may have told me she didn't like my angle.

It needed to be really cool, like saying, "Hello, gorgeous. Do you enjoy drinking Coca-Cola? Why? Because you are so soda-licious!"

Maybe not.

I had one more up my sleeve that my pal Bob had often used, with surprising success: "Hi there, I just shit my pants. Can I get into yours?" *I'll try this one. It works for him. It's funny, and it might make her laugh.*

I tapped her on the shoulder, and she turned around. I was instantly overwhelmed by a wave of panic, thankfully forgetting my chat-up line.

She smiled. "Is there anything I can do for you?" she asked kindly.

Crap. She's super posh and formal. "Yes, um... err, you wouldn't want a dance with me, um, er... would you?"

"Sure."

"What?"

"Yes, I'd like to."

"Really? Why? I mean... awesome."

Leo Sayer was crooning away, and I was praying my eardrums wouldn't burst and cover her hair with my brain or, worse, my ear blood.

This song is so awful.

We stepped on each other's toes a few times, and I felt like I was as nimble on the dance floor as Frankenstein's monster. Her hair smelt divine. I realised I didn't want Leo Sayer's song to finish. I felt like a million dollars. *I am dancing... with a girl!*

My saving grace was making her laugh. It wasn't intentional; I was just so nervous and super awkward. Walking together from the dance floor, I noticed my pals had all found someone to dance with. We chatted briefly, and she told me her name was Kathryn, but she liked to be called Kathy. I asked her if she'd like to meet up the following day, and she said yes; we exchanged phone numbers. I thought I might strike when the iron was hot and asked for a cheeky kiss, and to my astonishment, she said yes. Kathy became my first-ever girlfriend, my first-ever love. I felt like I was walking on a fluffy cloud. Why would anyone so lovely want to hang out with me?

When we started to meet and go for walks, Kathy appeared reserved and shy, often keeping to herself. Neither of us had been in a relationship before. Some of my friends started dating and hanging out with her friends, which led to forming a new social group.

I had made a few new Knoll buddies, including Merv and John. These lads were intelligent and funny, and we had something in common—several beautiful, bright grammar school ladies.

Kathy's friends from school had charming personalities, and it was surprising how the girls were willing to include us Knoll boys. They were a breath of fresh air. It felt like a collision of two worlds, each with distinct energy, but we gelled well. There was no doubt that times were changing in a positive direction. When Kathy visited my house, she had the chance to meet my mother and twin nephews. She was adored by everyone. I tended to do most of the talking, while Kathy was a great listener. Kathy's close relationship with her parents extended to her younger brother, and she always looked out for him like a protective older sister.

Kathy told me her dad was looking forward to meeting me. I felt uneasy. I won't lie—adult mistrust kicked in. The meeting with her dad took place in the early evening, and we chose to go for a walk. After chatting briefly, we went to a pub near Hove station, and he offered to buy me a beer; I declined and accepted a Pepsi instead. The conversation was occasionally uncomfortable. He inquired about my family, school life, and career aspirations, the usual topics. I told him it was my first relationship and wanted to ensure I didn't ruin it or offend Kathryn's parents.

He was a nice, sincere man; he discussed his expectations of his daughter and me and asked if I thought they were fair and reasonable. They were. He wanted Kathy not to go out during the week, during school time. I agreed to have her back home at a reasonable hour on the weekend. Kathy's family appeared to be lovely. I felt like I was a fortunate guy.

CHAPTER 27
LONE THE AUSSIE, DICK THE PRICK, AND UNCLE GAZ
1976-1977

LONE BUNTYNE WAS AN OLD AUSSIE EX-MERCHANT NAVY OFFICER who came into our lives after Dad died. Mum and Carol had met him at the British Legion club, where they went for a cut-price beer or whisky and ginger ale. Lone was about 25 years older than my mum and had a massive crush on her. The crush wasn't reciprocated, but he became a good family friend nonetheless. I remember him as this Methuselah-type character who looked about 562 years old. He was balding but still had white whisps of hair and pale blue eyes. He claimed that he came from Wagga Wagga (pronounced Wogga Wogga) and argued that the Indigenous people, the Wiradjuri, were *his* people. Lone was as indigenous to Australia as I was. However, he did have an Aussie accent, peppered with sayings like "Struth," "Fair dinkum," "Bonzer," "G'day," and "Crickey."

Due to our Australian adventure in the 1960s, Mum disliked *all things* Australian, as well as *all things* French (because they were French), Irish (because of the Pope), American (because a GI had run off with her mum), Moroccans (as they ate horse meat and were "shifty"), Italians (because the Pope, the antichrist, lived in Italy), and probably most of the other countries in the world, apart from Canada, Spain, Wales, and New Zealand. The Australian abhorrence was negated a wee bit by Crocodile Dundee, Paul Hogan, and Barry Humphries (Dame Edna), whom she adored. When I challenged Mum about this anomaly, she insisted they all came from The Cook Islands rather than Australia.

So, whenever Lone opened his mouth, Mum was triggered, and Lone opened his mouth *a lot*. He was a very outspoken cobber. Lone loved horse racing, cricket, my mum, and Carole's twins. He tolerated me as he tried to get into our family's tight inner circle. Like most lads who had lost their dad, I didn't want any guy sniffing around my mum, as I certainly didn't want a new daddy. However, Lone amused me, and he helped Mum get over her grief and encouraged her to manifest her angsts, frustration, and anger at him rather than the rest of the world.

Lone shared that he raced horses and was a champion jockey in Australia. Mum found this hard to believe as he was about six feet seven inches tall, and most British jockeys were under five feet. He loved horse racing and enjoyed having a "flutter" on the "gee-gees." On the other hand, Mum hated horse racing; she loved animals and thought the sport was cruel and boring. Mum would rather have her arm dunked into caustic soda than hear Lone discuss geldings, fillies, or handicaps. However, her strong views certainly didn't stop Lone from telling Mum about the "Three-thirty race at Kempton Park," or the "One O'clock at Haydock Park," and how "this beautiful little filly" was going to win the race—every single day.

AFTER THE BIRTH of her twin boys, I believe my sister, Carole, went full-on into post-natal depression. Dad died, and her relationship with Mike, the boy's dad, deteriorated. My sister's personality changed so much that we could no longer tolerate each other. Mum looked after the boys full-time. Carole lived away and popped over to see them. Unfortunately, she started dating a particularly odious guy. His name was Dick. Mum would refer to him as "Dick the Prick," and I soon understood why. I sincerely disliked this guy. Each time I met him, he bragged about how much money he had made or why education was a waste of time. I don't think we spoke to each other until the day of the chess incident.

Dad taught me to play chess at an early age. I began beating him when I was about nine or ten. I'd play my brother Paul, and much to his chagrin, I beat him, too. As a teenager, I read books on chess and knew most of the classic chess opening moves. One day, Dick the Prick accompanied Carole to our house. I had the chess board on the kitchen table, with a chess book in front of me. I was playing against an imaginary Bobby Fischer.

Dick appeared. He grunted and said, "Oi!"

Without giving me a chance to respond, he said, "It's Carole's bruvva— the lickle brat who wants to be some kind of docta?"

I looked up at him from the chessboard. *Lickle brat?* Oh, the *Li-TT-le brat?*

I sighed. "Yes, well, maybe one day."

"You's a wastin' yer time."

"I am?" *Excellent career advice from Dick . . . the "Brain of Britain."*

He reached into his jacket pocket and produced a large wad of bank notes. He slammed them down on the table, which annoyed me because he did it with such voracity that my chess pieces moved from their positions. "Look at this lovely moolah!" he bragged. "That's what makes you successful. Money talks, my boy. You don't need to waste yer time with educa-shun. Get into construc-shun, like me—you'll earn a stack of it!"

He glanced at the chess set, "What you playin'?"

Rugby? Tennis? OMG! Just go away. "Chess."

"Chess? You ain't no good at that!"

I rolled my eyes. He picked up the wad of cash and waved it in my face. I could smell the aroma of the construction site. I pulled away from the shaking wad of money.

"You wanna play me?"

I continued to ignore him, wishing he'd go away. He slapped a five-pound note onto the table—his large hand covered the note.

An Elton John album. Maybe the new Carole King or Carly Simon one?

"Sure, Rick."

"It's Dick!

Yep, Dick the Prick.

"Mmmn," I pondered. "Say if I win—"

"You won't."

"And I win in, say, eight moves or under—you pay double."

Dick guffawed, pulled out a chair and announced, "I'll go first."

Perfect. It's more fun playing second.

I studied my opposition in a Garry Kasparov versus Bobby Fischer kind of way. *Gary, no one thinks you'd be good at chess. Everyone underestimates you—don't underestimate him.*

Dick was a well-built, tall, balding, sun-tanned fellow whose skin was embedded with grime and dirt. He smelled of Hai Karate aftershave, the budget men's aftershave that (I imagined) smelt like a rugby player's jock strap.

I positioned the board so he played first with the black chess pieces. "Stop!" he yelled. I looked up, startled. "I wanna be white. I don't like black." He turned the chess board around so that his pieces became white. "ME first," he snapped.

"No," I groaned, "Black gets to move first. If you want to take the first move, then be black."

He tried to make a joke. "Not in a month of Sundays. I'm white and proud of it—there ain't no black in the Union Jack!"

What?? That's so not funny. Dick the Prick was now known as Racist Rick. I couldn't wait to tell Mum.

I pushed my black pawn to the square E-6 on the chessboard.

I wanted to see if Dick was as gormless as he looked. *Gary be careful. He wouldn't bet money if he was crap at chess.*

Dick defied my inner thoughts; he responded by stupidly moving a pawn to square F-3. *Surely, he's not going to do it?*

I pushed another black pawn to square F-5. Immediately, Dick moved his pawn to G-4. I tried very hard to control myself. *Don't smirk or laugh—he may take the move back and play a different pawn.*

He looked up at me. It was my move. I reached over, took my beautiful, black queen with the tops of my fingers and slowly and calmly pushed her diagonally to square H-4. My queen faced Dick's white supremacist king. He cannot move or protect his most important chess piece on the board.

"Checkmate." A classic "fool's mate," fitting for my sister's new boyfriend. I'd never played that move before.

I grabbed the fiver; he slammed his large, grimy hand on mine, covering both my hand and the five-pound note. I looked up at him, my heart skipping a beat.

Gary, shut up. Don't open your mouth.

I couldn't resist. "Double or quits, Mr You-Don't-Need-No-Ed-You-Kay-Shun?" I asked with a smirk.

Dick was red-faced, and his carotid artery looked like it was going to pop. His brown eyes were full of hate.

"Piss off, you little brat," and he took his hand off mine. "Keep it—that's like a year's wages for a pauper like you."

Whoopsie Doodle. You sure got under his skin. Be a good sport. Thank him. Or...

I looked at the chess pieces, moved the four pieces back to their starting positions, and then, with a nod, blurted out contemptuously, "Rick is thrashed by the 15-year-old brat."

He pushed his chair away and stood, towering over me. "It's Dick, dummy. You can't even remember my name. You ain't nuffin'," he hissed, leaving the kitchen and heading towards the basement door.

Yep, Carole. You've totally chosen a winner, dating this clown.
As the basement door slammed, I held up the fiver and flicked it with my index finger. The smell of cement filled the air. I grinned and smugly hummed Carly Simon's "You're So Vain."

I caught just one last whiff of Dick the Prick's overpowering aftershave as he loitered by the front door, eagerly awaiting Carole. Happy to stir the pot, I couldn't resist sharing Dick's controversial views on "education" with my mum, and the news left her absolutely fuming. She made it clear that she didn't want him waiting for Carole in our house. I couldn't help but feel a hint of satisfaction at the turn of events. Too bad—so sad.

LONE WAS, at times, a fantastic helper, assisting Carole, Mum, and I look after the two rambunctious twins, Michael and Gary. Mum became their beloved "Nanna" and guarded them with her life. Carole was in and out of their lives for a season, so Lone often took them to Hove Park on his own to give Mum a break. Lone would drive an ancient, light blue Bedford Brigand camper van, which, I swear, seemed older than its owner. He'd open the doors of the Brigand and ask them to wait until he was ready to put them into their children's harnesses and take them for a walk. Then he'd hold their reins like a pair of can't-wait-to-run-away huskies.

The twins were very observant and quickly learned Lone's routine. They knew his habits well and anticipated what would happen when the ageing Lone harnessed one of the boys and left the other waiting on the pavement. Once harnessed, Gary would make a run for it in a specific direction. Lone's first instinct was to grab the runaway husky, ignoring Michael, the unharnessed twin. As Lone struggled to capture Gary, he realised Michael was free and running in the opposite direction. With Gary in his grasp, Lone charged through the park, trying to capture Michael.

The boys' raucous laughter filled the air as spectators cheered them on. Lone, despite being close to a cardiac arrest many times, still volunteered to take them out repeatedly.

They did this to Bob, Kathy, and me when we walked them to the park in their twin buggy. The difference was that we were much younger and fitter than Lone and caught them swiftly. It was hilarious to us—likely encouraging the boys to do the same in Lone's company.

Lone, flustered and sweaty, returned the boys to their nanna's care and breathlessly recounted what had transpired. Mum ended up scolding Lone, accusing him of attempted infanticide.

I loved the boys dearly and, at times, played the role of a teenage dad to them. Poor lads, I wasn't the greatest role model. My twin nephews became a reason for me to live during dark times. They were happy and full of beans, and Bob, Kathy, and I played with them regularly. These two blond-haired, blue-eyed identicals were my heart. They were the only humans I ever felt truly and unconditionally loved by. The fishing rod that dangled love over my life always seemed to have a barbed hook on it. There was a catch. I will love you—*if* you love me. I will love you *if* you obey me. I will love you and leave you. Too many barbs that stuck in my soul and made me shy away from taking any kind of bait. The twins were the only humans I ever felt love from that did not come with any attached conditions.

I kept them laughing by acting silly during the daytime and making up ridiculous bedtime stories. They were both intelligent and shared their dad's playfulness and zany humour even at a young age. Michael and Gary were truly double trouble; they both adored my mum and me. Mum made our home like Fort Knox to prevent the little buggers from making a break for freedom. She purchased and fixed a door latch outside their reach, but Michael climbed onto little Gary's shoulders and undid it. The next thing I knew, Mum chased them down the street, desperate to grab them before they ran into traffic.

At one point, I acquired a pair of leather roller skates and travelled everywhere. I quickly learned to perform tricks, skate backwards and show off with the twins watching in awe. The boys desperately wanted to be like their uncle Gaz, so Mum purchased them a pair of children's toe-in skates with no ankle support. One day, after much nagging from my nephews, I took them out for a trip around Livingstone and Clarendon Road. I skated ahead and waited for Michael. He fell over, landing on his wrist and started to cry. I skated back to the little lad; he was sobbing and clearly in pain. My reaction was typical—I channelled my inner mum. "Don't be a wuss," I told him sternly. "You're crying over nothing. You fell. Big deal. Get over it!"

We returned to the house; he was snivelling and holding his injured arm. Mum ended up taking him to casualty with Lone. He had fractured his wrist. When I found out, I felt terrible. *Great job, Uncle Gaz. The little guy idolises you, breaks his wrist, and you tell him not to be a wuss.*

I still feel bad about the incident. I was a dysfunctional teenager, desperately trying to find my way through the challenging circumstances, surrounded by the deafening silence of my own struggles. Deep down, I knew I couldn't fill the void of the father figure they craved, no matter how much I wanted to.

CHAPTER 28
ART FOR ART'S SAKE, CHEMISTRY FOR GOD'S SAKE
LAST TERM, 1977

HOWEVER BAD I WAS AT METAL AND WOODWORK, I MADE UP FOR IT with art class. Now, this was a different animal for me. As Dad was once offered a job as a commercial artist, although passing his practical metal and woodworking genes to Paul, I received his creativity and talent in art; I loved to paint and draw. So, typically, one would expect to excel in the school's art class and enjoy art lessons in Mr Ramsey's classes. However, this was the Knoll School. What should have been a joy for me tended to be a frustrating and wretched experience. I was in a class with many pupils who detested art, including the brain-dead Reichsführer Mitch Skinner, the Nazi versus Jews thug who felt it was his divine mission to not allow other pupils to enjoy the lesson.

"Oh, that's so pretty," he said condescendingly, looking at a classmate's art. He picked up a full red or black paint pot and tipped it over his classmate's artwork. "Whoops, you Jewboy," he would grin. Then, he'd approach another victim. Spilling paint onto the art, he'd squawk, "Aww, now, that looks so much better, you faggot!"

On more than one occasion, Skinner took a paintbrush saturated with black paint and daubed my artwork with a large penis or a swastika. If it weren't Skinner, it would be some other knucklehead who also hated art and had the IQ of a pebble.

Mr Ramsey appeared oblivious, often dozing off to sleep and smelling of alcohol during the afternoon classes—much like his colleagues' absence during the antisemitic playground games, the fights and intimidation during breaks, or the name-calling, homophobic bullying, or the berserker activities of some of the kids inside the classroom. At least he wasn't physically or verbally abusive to me.

The one blessing about the art class was that it was close to the senior toilets. It never ceased to amaze me that the senior boys' loos rarely had partitions separating the cubicles—as they had been repeatedly damaged and destroyed. I did not wish to go to the toilet area during the mandatory breaks. It was far wiser and safer to ask permission to go to the bathroom in one of the more affable teacher's classes. As Mr Ramsey was present, yet not present, I'd sneak out to use the toilets if I had a strong sense that no yobs were hanging about the area.

The "O" Level public exams were approaching as the final year at the Knoll School was coming to an end. Ramsey instructed us to present a portfolio of artwork to the examiners. I was thrown into panic mode because of this. The still and real-life work would be fine, as third-party observers would regulate the exam. The portfolio was problematic, as all my work had been ruined. I would have to submit art that had a swastika daubed upon it or the words "wanker," "c**k sucker," or "c**t." My interpretation of Van Gogh's *Starry Night* was unrecognisable. There were no stars but a background of thick, black paint.

Guffawing with laughter, Skinner bragged to his pals, "Look, Trew's Starry Night has become Nighty, Night."

Although I tried painting over most of the graffiti, the colour was so thickly slapped on by my cover-up job that the artwork became virtually three-dimensional. The final straw was that I

THE HATE GAME

completed work at home and hoped to slip it into my exam portfolio file in Ramsey's care in art class.

I tried to paint a copy of Vermeer's *The Girl with a Pearl Earring*. It wasn't great—but handing it to the examiners was acceptable. Back at school, I discovered an enormous phallus had been drawn onto the painting, entering the subject with ejaculate coming out of the phallus. Unless the examiners viewed it through a modern art/porno comedy lens, the painting was ruined. Many years later, I watched a *Mr Bean* movie where he attempted to restore the same Vermeer with hilarious results. I wondered if he had stolen my idea after seeing my post-vandalised work of art.

I didn't give up and attempted to paint simple images or splatter colour onto a canvas, insinuating it was contemporary artwork. Each time I returned to check on my work for the following class, it had been defaced again. Out of frustration and anger, I found Skinner's "portfolio" of work, ripped some pieces into two, or added my own personalised graffiti. I knew it was so wrong, but it felt so right.

Since the year was ending, I was confident I wouldn't face any consequences because Skinner was unpopular. Anyone could have tampered with his artwork. In light of the numerous vandalised art pieces, Mr Ramsey suggested I search for old, discarded ones at the back of the classroom and add some fresh paint as a temporary solution.

THOUGH THE ART teacher's lack of classroom management was disheartening, it was nowhere near as dreadful as the frustration accompanying every chemistry class with Mr Sparks. Skinner and his gang first called him the derogatory name "Reptile." It was a cruel and heartless nickname, mainly due to his rough, scaly skin and small, snake-shaped eyes. Mr Sparks was also a yeller and had the reputation of being a bit of a bully and losing his cool with pupils on many occasions.

Ridiculously, the headteacher or someone in authority merged the "O" Level class with the remnants of the year that had either checked out already or were the thickest of the thick. Some of the biggest louts at the school took up residency at the back of the large classroom. The few trying to learn tended to be near the front. As we had some big and aggressive teenagers in the class, Mr Sparks became way more passive, and the bully became the bullied.

As I couldn't take physics at this school, chemistry was do or die for me; I needed a good grade to stand any chance of progressing into further education. For the first time in my life, I sat in the front row of the lab beside my best chum, Billy. We both enjoyed chemistry class, and we were keen to do well. Unfortunately, this was a challenge as the bullies and the miscreants sitting at the back of the class rarely allowed a lesson to proceed without interruption.

Mr Sparks was a good and patient teacher, but he had zero control over the dynamic in the classroom. Had he been allowed to teach . . . he could have been outstanding. However, this was not to be.

When Mr Sparks pulled down a dry-erase whiteboard and turned his back to the class to write or draw something, on Mitch Skinner's command, the class bombarded the board with a sea of projectiles. These flew past our heads like they emanated from a Katyusha rocket launcher and landed on the board with a SPLAT! SPLAT! SPLAT! These Stalin's organ missiles were paper put into the pupil's mouth until soaking wet with saliva. Dozens of spit-paper gob-mâché shots covered the surface, making the whiteboard unusable.

This kept happening repeatedly. Sparks would freak out, yell, and scream, so we never received the chemistry tuition we desperately needed. The vein on his temple visibly pulsated.

THE HATE GAME

Rather than command silence, send the miscreants to Batman's office or demand an apology, the boys in the back of the class hurled further abuse at him. When it became too much for him, Sparks disappeared into his backroom to regain his composure.

The idiots in the rear of the class taunted him, saying: "What's the matter, Reptile?"

"Are you going to cry?"

"Will you send Mrs Reptile to our school to tell us all off?"

"How do Mr and Mrs Reptile have sex with each other?"

It was brutal. He threatened to report each lesson's behaviours and send students to Batman, the Master of the Cane, for punishment. Still, he never followed through with the threats.

Instead, to alleviate the big kids at the back of the class, he allowed them to smoke cigarettes, or rather, he'd pay no heed to them lighting up with Bunsen Burners and smoking their "roddies," as they were called. Billy and I often laughed; we never learned anything, so we felt we might as well sit back and observe the circus.

On one occasion, when Mr Sparks was teaching us about isomers, some of the larger kids asked him to unlock a cupboard to "see" what was in it. Mr Sparks broke away from the lesson, walked to the cabinet, opened it, and continued talking about butane and 2-methyl propane. Suddenly, several large boys grabbed him, pushed him into the cupboard, and locked it from the outside. One of the bigger kids went to the front of the class, pretending to be Mr Sparks. The pupil proceeded to teach how Mr and Mrs Sparks, as reptiles, procreate. Mr. Sparks, trapped, frantically banged on the cupboard door and screamed for them to let him out. Finally, they obliged and released him. He then went to the reagents room at the front of the class, composed himself, and returned, red-faced, to a maelstrom of noise and jeering.

We were in exam revision territory. Sparks had utterly lost control and asked the class what revision topics needed to be addressed. Someone asked for a vote and a show of hands and asked Mr Sparks if he would abide by a democratic decision of the class. Sparks agreed. Someone from the back of the classroom suggested the class vote to play a game of football in the rear playground. Everyone raised their hands. I did, too, as I thought it was a joke request. One of the bigger lads reminded him he had to abide by the "will of the people." Sparks barked, "If the class elects to play football rather than review elemental stoichiometry, so be it." Our chemistry teacher had given up by this point and shrugged, saying, "If that's what you want, then damn your learning." The class left their bench chairs and marched towards the north playground, where there were two five-a-side goals. Someone produced a ball, Sparks watched, and the rest played football.

It was all fun and games until the headmaster opened the door to the playground. He yelled at us: "You lot back in your classroom." To Mr Sparks, he cried out for him to visit his study immediately. We returned to class. Mr Sparks returned twenty minutes later, ashen-faced. Yet another lesson down the toilet.

To reiterate, it wasn't that the students who wanted to learn also encouraged and enjoyed the madness. To remain a non-participant, there was a danger that I may be locked in a cupboard, have a Bunsen burner light up my school jacket, or be picked on the following day during break time. It was like being in a zoo. I'd rather the teacher bear the brunt of the chaos than me.

One kid, who I despised, was one of Skinner's pals. He was a bully with a brain. He sat in the middle section of the class and wore a distinctive pudding-basin hairstyle. I was in the front row, trying to listen to Mr Sparks' lesson. This kid was berating the front row, hurling names at us, and verbally abusing Mr Sparks. There was so much noise it became difficult to hear what was being taught. Frustrated with the heckling and stupid behaviour,

THE HATE GAME

I turned around on my stool and asked him to be quiet. I returned to Mr Spark's teaching.

The next thing I knew, I was seeing stars. I'd seen comic characters like Tom and Jerry and cartoons with some character receiving a head injury, and stars, butterflies, and birds appeared on the screen as an expression of concussion. This kid had walked up and sucker-punched me in the back of my head several times. All hell broke loose as I sat there, stunned. One of my classmates, a lovely lad called Mike, was shocked and intervened, telling the pudding-basin boy to leave me alone, almost resulting in another physical fight between the two bigger kids.

Mr Sparks witnessed the whole incident. He said nothing. He did nothing. He just told the attacker to sit down. I sat there, dizzy, my head aching, and wondered how to retaliate. Sparks continued the lesson. I needed to get pudding-basin boy back, or I would lose face. I felt the only way to succeed and avoid an after-school fight with basin-boy was to go behind him, lift a lab stool, and lamp him with it. Billy didn't say much; he was shocked at what had happened. I just stared at the front of the class, with my head spinning. My blood boiled.

It also dawned on me that retaliation might make me unable to attend the final few weeks of school and prohibit me from attending Brighton, Hove & Sussex Sixth Form College (BHASVIC), which I was desperate to attend the following September. I also was cognisant I may have to cause him serious harm and possibly break his skull with the stool. Otherwise, there would be trouble after school, for sure. I had gone from an innocent who wouldn't say "boo" to a goose pupil to a fifth-former that was prepared to commit a serious crime against another boy. Thankfully, I chose to leave it. However, it's not something I would forget in a hurry.

The sad thing is that there were never consequences for the kids who bullied the class or even this teacher. Sparks could have

193

reported the incident, and the assailant would have been suspended. Moreover, it was an assault. I would not have reported it as such, but the school could have. The incident concussed me. Yet, there were no ramifications for the miscreant.

My five-year sentence at "Stalag Knollditz" was nearly over, apart from one last incident. However, the five years enduring the Knoll School was down to me and me alone. Dad may have chosen this school for me, but it had come down to the 11-plus exam. Stupid balls, Gary, who didn't know the colour of the black mat the stupid black cat was sitting on. My bad.

CHAPTER 29
VLAD THE IMPALER
LAST FEW DAYS OF SCHOOL, 1977

THE KNOLL SCHOOL WAS A HELLHOLE. BULLYING WAS EVERYWHERE, and you had to fight back to survive. Fights would happen in the corridors, classrooms, during breaks or after school. They would even happen on the bus if kids were dumb enough to travel home that way. It was a real jungle out there. Sometimes, you didn't have a choice, and other students would just say, "I'm going to fight you," or "I've been told to fight you." I wasn't ready to fight anyone, mainly because I was scrawny. Nevertheless, I understood I could go cuckoo psycho if I had to, which was often a deterrent.

Most students hailed from a notorious, rough neighbourhood that encircled the school. The student body at The Knoll comprised individuals from local primary schools who, like me, didn't pass their 11-plus exams. It was rare for a student at Knoll Boys to not have connections in the area due to the close-knit community. I lived in a different location and only knew a few pupils from the school. Apart from the first few days at the Knoll, when Pete interdicted further toilet baptisms from happening, I never had the comfort blanket of protection from other folk. When challenged to a fight, the choices were to fight, walk away, or stay under the radar to survive like other outsider kids. Not accepting a challenge from a classmate would have repercussions and might lead to never-ending bullying.

I had my debut fight at the Knoll. Someone instructed a kid I didn't know to challenge me. Older kids surrounded us in a circle, and I knew the teachers would not intervene. There was no point reasoning with my opponent—walking away wasn't an option, as I'd become an easy target for anyone wanting to flex their muscles. I stared at the kid's angry face as he postured.

"Come on, Trew, I'm going to beat your ugly arse into the ground."

It was inevitable that this would happen. The kid was a year older than me and a little bigger in stature. "Fight, fight, fight!" the circle of boys bayed.

Clenching my fists, I stared into his eyes and waited for the lad to make the first move. He obliged, shoved me, "Come on, you wanker!" he said with a contorted face. So, I did. I unleashed a flurry of punches and kicks on the kid like a deranged banshee, relenting only when one of his companions intervened. I was shocked at my rage; it was like a year of pent-up anger. That fight gave me a modicum of respect and clarified I wouldn't back down from a fight. Sure, bigger kids would likely win, but peers knew I would fight back when physically picked upon.

Moving ahead to the last weeks at Knoll School. I was waiting outside a classroom for my first lesson of the day. The corridor was very crowded, with the usual commotion and noisy bustle. Angus, a pal living near Billy, and I were chatting. He was likely recounting his latest sexual escapades with his girlfriend, Diana. Out of the blue, a kid pushed through the crowd and sucker-punched him in the face twice. I noticed the kid was getting ready to strike Angus again, so I took action and delivered four or five punches, which caused him to collapse to the floor. He rose to his feet, holding his head in shock. Because of the commotion, the deputy headmaster, Mr Woolley, flew out of his office. With a furious look, he signalled towards me and yelled, "You, boy!" and ordered me to go to his office immediately. Angus and the kid went about their day, albeit with black eyes. Woolley asked no questions, and I expected six of the best from his cane.

I entered his office. His cold eyes glared at me; his upper lip curled in a snarl. "You are a disappointment. Get out of here!"

Five years at the school, and he can't recall my name.

I shrugged my shoulders. That was it. He didn't ask who, why, what, how, or anything about the incident. I returned to the classroom and pondered what had happened.

Nevertheless, the idiot who punched Angus in the face was affiliated with one of the most brutal boys at school, who I called "Vlad the Impaler." Despite his intimidating size, reputation, and Russian name, I had never had any issues with Vlad. He was vulgar, oppressive, loud, and at the top of the fighting food chain. The ones who acted tough and were mouthy were usually the hangers-on, working vicariously through him.

Later, at break time, I received "the word" that Vlad would knock my head off after school because I interfered in his friend's "business" with Angus. Suddenly, it was the talk of the school. I was going to get beaten to shit near the school gates. Word was I was a dead man walking. I felt sick.

My crime was to defend my friend, who was sucker punched by a moron with the IQ of a tangerine. Now, because of some "relationship" between the toughest kid in school and Tangerine Boy, I would get a beating from Vlad the Impaler. The war between the two mindsets began in earnest. *Wear it like a badge of honour. Shut up, mind, I have a few days to go before I leave this purgatory. You have every right to worry. Just go berserk. Take a few punches. Tap into your inner-psycho. Jerk! He'll skin you alive. Beg for mercy.*

Don't get me wrong, I would've done the same for my friend, knowing what would have transpired because a friend is a friend, and I was tired of kids picking on Angus, who didn't harm anyone. Angus's only crime was not wanting to fight back, making him vulnerable. What would have been reasonable was to get the idiot who sucker punched him to fight *me* after school. Fair enough. Yet, cowards tended to hide behind their protectors, so I would have to deal with the consequences of my actions after school.

As thoughts of exams and summer filled my mind, I yearned for the freedom of attending a proper school where I wouldn't have to deal with this nonsense daily.

Angus thanked me for doing what I did, but he also said I shouldn't have because I would get a hiding after school for sticking up for him. He'd already been told to fight the kid who punched him on another occasion.

Bill and I joked during lunchtime. "I'm dead," I said.

"No, you're SO dead," Billy responded helpfully.

I nervously laughed with bravado, not wanting to look weak in the eyes of my best pal. Billy continued, "Vlad will leave you brain-dead. You idiot . . . he's Vlad the Impaler!"

"Will you be at my side? My buddy, my pal?"

"Eff off, no way," he laughed. Then, frowning like he was asked to solve Schrodinger's equation, he asked, "Why did you stick up for Angus?"

"He's a friend. I would do the same for you."

"Well, count me out being your friend until after you get beaten half to death by Neanderthal Man."

My last lesson was in Mr Tanner's biology class. Vlad the Impaler had already discovered this. I had a clear view of the exit route from the classroom, which was good news since I could see the outside passageway leading to the school gates and into freedom. Possibly.

As the 30-minute mark approached, everything seemed fine. I could swiftly exit the school and escape through the gates, avoiding encounters. Their threats might have been empty, causing unnecessary worry and wasted energy.

Then I saw him. *Feck. Feckedy, feck feck.* Vlad the Impaler appeared and hovered menacingly near the lower school gates, flanked by a handful of his companions. I could see him guffawing and throwing phantom punches in the air as if sparing with George Foreman.

I had an idea—I left the class to use the bathrooms. I grabbed my parka from the cloakroom and stuffed the four large pockets with biology textbooks; I'd use them as body armour. The image of Tennyson's poem about the Light Brigade charging to certain death during the Crimean War crossed my mind. I'd walk towards Vlad the Impaler and his gang of hangers-on and take a few of his punches. I had decided that if his buddies joined, I'd target one of them and go berserk.

When I returned to the class wearing my super-heavy armour-plated coat, Mr Tanner asked why I was wearing a coat in the classroom. "I'm cold, sir," I said.

"Become un-cold, he responded. Take it off—you look ridiculous!"

Delicately, I removed the cumbersome coat, mindful not to disturb my book-body protection. I continued to look odd. Tanner approached me and asked if everything was okay. I had been quiet in his class, which was unlike me. I loved his teaching and often contributed during lessons. I took a big gulp of air and blurted out in one breath, "Everything is fine, sir." I stared at the classroom clock. *I ain't no snitch.*

Tick, tock. Tick tock. Tick tock. My guts were doing summersaults—my heart was thumping. I realised I was rocking back and forth. *This is just like D-Day five years ago. Now it's a different D-Day. Ducking-Day had become Death-Day.*

More and more kids were joining Vlad well before school ended. I wondered why the school's teachers allowed this. They were so strict and harsh, yet they couldn't stop one fight or scuffle. What had been brewing all day was more than apparent.

The school bell tolled, signalling the end of the day. I wrapped myself in a heavily armoured parka, bracing myself for what would come. As I approached Vlad the Impaler, a group of 30 or 40 kids gathered around him, eagerly waiting. His face bore a twisted, menacing grin that sent shivers down my spine. Amidst the tension, I envisioned various scenarios, including the possibility of shedding my coat and confronting him, akin to a mismatched battle between a featherweight and a heavyweight. A classmate asked me what I was going to do. Vlad the Impaler stood forty yards in front of me. I swear he looked forty feet tall. I said I didn't know. A glom of boys called out, "Fight, fight, fight."

Our eyes met in a fleeting moment of connection as I approached Vlad, attempting to maintain a chilled-out demeanour. I was about ten yards away from him. He pointed his finger towards my face and snarled, "Keep your nose out of my mate's business. They'll have a rematch, but I don't want you to interfere!" *Rematch? He sucker-punched Angus. A rematch would give Angus a better chance of defending himself.*

I carried on walking towards him. I recited Tennyson's poem I'd learned at Middle Street Primary: *Half a league, half a league, half a league onward. All in the valley of Death rode the six hundred.* Vlad snarled and stepped aside. *Cannon to the right of them. Cannon to the left of them. Cannon in front of them...*

"Fair enough," I said back at him and continued to walk toward the gate. I winced, expecting a blow to the back of my head.

Into the jaws of Death. Into the mouth of Hell rode the six hundred.

The kid who sucker-punched Angus was standing with Vlad, scowling at me. I was prepared to confront him or anyone in their group. I was angry and pumped up with adrenaline. *Let Vlad punch you, but make sure you deal with Tangerine Boy and give him the hiding of a lifetime.*

Nothing happened. Nothing. I left the exit gate and walked briskly, not turning around. Billy joined me at my side.

"Well, that wasn't too bad," he said, "I thought I'd find you lying on the pavement with Vlad the Impaler standing over you, eating your liver and smearing his face with your blood, Viking style."

"Well, my best pal . . . thanks for your support."

We burst into laughter and confidently strode back to Livingstone Road, chuckling with amusement.

I could forget about the horrors of the Knoll School in just three more weeks. No more beatings, no more Vlad the Impaler, no more swastikas drawn on our foreheads, no more electric shock devices attached to our ears, no more ducking in the toilet, no more art being destroyed, torn up, or having a Star of David daubed on it. No more having your clothes soaked in the showers; no more pneumonia. No more nipple tweaks, or dead arms or legs from punches or kicks. No more being put into a bully's headlock. No more sucker punches in the back of the head during class. No more being in an all-boys environment, or no dodging chalk or board rubbers thrown by the teachers. No more humiliations and no more of that tosspot, Skinner. Billy and my time at Knollditz was ending, and we roared with laughter in pure relief of emotion.

I'm cognisant that many kids at the school had it way worse than me. I wish I would've been bigger and bulkier. I dearly wish I would've been more kind to others' suffering than I had been. I just wanted to blend in and do my best to survive. I had the whole summer ahead of me. Things were looking up. I had a lovely girlfriend; I could start afresh at the Sixth Form College. I was looking forward to being educated—I couldn't wait to start.

CHAPTER 30
BEWARE OF LIFE'S SUCKER PUNCH
1977-1978

OH, THE JOY OF ESCAPE. I LOVED THE BOOK *PAPILLON* BY HENRI Charrière, the petty criminal convicted of a murder he didn't commit. Spared the guillotine, he was sent to a penal colony called Devil's Island in French Guiana and became obsessed with escape. All he could dream about was escaping, returning to France, and clearing his name. Against all odds, he did so. It took him a lifetime to achieve this, and he became a Venezuelan citizen en route. He wrote his memoir and released it in 1969. It became a best seller and a blockbuster movie in 1973 starring Steve McQueen (as Charrière) and Dustin Hoffman. In 1970, nearly forty years after the wrongful conviction, he was granted a pardon by the French Government.

Henri was a hero of mine. His indefatigable spirit and determination to escape the brutalities of the penal system were incredible. Having received curve ball after curve ball, even after escaping the inescapable, he became a free man, only to be struck by one more savage delivery three years after being pardoned—Charrière died of throat cancer in 1973.

Sometimes, life throws curve balls at you that you can do little about, like Henri's throat cancer (incessant smoking would have had an effect—like my dad's pipe smoking and exposure to atomic radiation).

Escaping a situation, albeit a terrible one, is not the be-all and end-all. Yes, things can get better. However, they can take on a new trajectory and dynamic. Papillon escaped and tasted the freedom he had craved for many repressive years. It wasn't to last very long. I was about to savour the freedom I craved from an unfair and archaic school system. A new chapter, a new reality, and hopefully, a new norm. Surely, unlike Charrière, life would be smooth sailing from now on?

The new chapter of my life at BHASVIC would be an adventure. I had developed a sharp, noir sense of humour. There would be no more bullying or crazy-arsed teachers. I had developed muscle mass and a ton of confidence. I would be surrounded by friendly peers and have fabulous sporting opportunities, excellent teachers, and a real opportunity to get back on track and fulfil my dreams of becoming a doctor or an aviator. What could possibly go wrong?

BRIGHTON, Hove & Sussex Sixth Form College is a sixth-form college in Brighton and Hove, England, for 16 to 19-year-old students. The college was formerly Brighton & Hove Grammar School, which I wanted to attend before my 11-plus disaster. Britain's sixth-form colleges provide some of the best non-paying, post-16 academic provisions in the UK, and the better ones have a reputation for inspiring and nurturing a love of learning and academic excellence. BHASVIC allowed students to find their paths while providing the educational support they needed to thrive. The old grammar school motto was *"Absque Labore Nihil"* (Nothing without effort). I was determined to live up to this motto by studying hard.

Arriving at BHASVIC, I was greeted by a crisp autumn

morning. The sky was a vibrant blue. I inhaled the fragrance of freshly mowed grass on the expansive 15-acre playing fields, starkly contrasting the concrete jungle playground of the Knoll and the dog poop-infested Greenleas fields. That first morning, I rode a recently purchased motorcycle to school; the parking lot was full, but there was space for motorbikes.

Out of nowhere, I pictured myself leaning over a white school toilet, arms pinned behind me, hovering mid-air, with my head moving towards the bowl. I shuddered, remembering my first few minutes at the Knoll School. Walking towards registration, I reminded myself not to stand out—every school had bullies like Skinner. I wondered where I'd find BHASVIC's antagonist?

When I eventually saw the interior of BHASVIC, I experienced a mix of pride and relief. I'd never seen anything so grand. My jaw dropped as I walked into the magnificent main hall. The vibrant colours of the stained-glass windows and the intricate beauty of the murals decorating the walls immediately caught my attention. Solemn lists of ex-pupils who had made the ultimate sacrifice for their country in the two world wars adorned the walls. It was a relief not to see a school uniform; the absence of conformity allowed for a more relaxed and diverse atmosphere. BHASVIC stood out for being a school that welcomed both male and female students. The students were friendly, respectful, and intelligent, and I didn't have to worry about some moron sucker-punching me on the back of the head. My Knoll buddies also started at the college, including Billy and Angus. That made it easier to relax and not be 'Mr Norman No-Mates.'

Education was a priority at this college, and everything was geared towards transitioning to university or entering one of the professions. I loved being there. Football was fun. Cricket was fun. Classes were co-ed. The teachers were fantastic, and it was weird not to watch out for flying board rubbers or chalk missiles being hurled at anyone from the front of the class. I no longer experienced deep-rooted anxiety. One maths teacher took me under his wing, realising I had maths trauma. He made it his personal goal that I would find mathematics fun and easy. This was everything I ever wanted in a school.

In my mind, I felt different from the other students. I initially found solace and familiarity with the few other ex-Knoll pupils who had started a similar journey. We all felt a massive relief and were determined to not look back.

But I still felt like a fish out of water. Many of the students' accents differed, especially the grammar school students who had merged with the new college. Several had a lilting cadence that signalled lar-de-da and a chirpy accent; they sounded refined and educated. I tended to babble and mumble, more out of nerves than anything else. I felt like an imposter. I chewed my lip in class. It was one thing being singled out as a thicko at the Knoll School, but here would be much worse.

The students, for the most part, wore a variety of different clothes—many were super-fashionable. One guy, Jeremy, who I came to like over time, noticed me walking into the refectory. He was an ex-grammar schoolboy. He looked me up and down and stared at my best pair of Wrangler jeans. They were pleated, high-waisted, and very 'Oxford bag' style. "Hey, Gary, you don't want to be caught downwind wearing those things."

"Why?"

"Because you'd end up blowing away to Calais, over the English Channel." I frowned as my brain processed the comment. He interrupted my thoughts. "They are so wide and baggy that they'll act as a windsail."

I feigned laughter. *There you go, Gary, you are an imposter here.*

"Mate, they went out about four years ago," he said, chuckling.

I went red and wanted to die on the spot. I had little idea about fashion. I couldn't wait to get home and take the jeans off. Poor Mum. She had spent money on new jeans, and I was thrilled to wear them to my new school. I never wore them again.

Every school must have a Skinner character—where's the BHASVIC one? What if the college bully is a girl? A female bully would be hard to swallow. There'd be no fighting back; it would also be devastating as I was enjoying interactions with the female students in class and in the two leisure areas of the college. I cared more about my appearance and watched my words as I didn't want to offend or push girls away. I was also ridiculously self-conscious about my appearance. I waited for the dagger in the heart. *It will happen. It had to happen.* This experience was too good to be true.

Skinner's words flooded into my mind. "You, ugly frog," he'd goad and mock. "You are so ugly that your mum and dad couldn't believe that their son looked so handicapped. I bet your mum threw up when she saw you. Trew, you are a walking abortion." I expected this to happen sooner rather than later, but this time, I wouldn't let them finish what they were saying—my fists would be clenched and ready.

A super trendy young lady stopped me as I worked my way past students exiting the doors of the changing rooms. I had an instant flashback and imagined my clothes in the shower area, lying sodden on the wet floor. I shook my head to embrace the new norm.

It will be okay; this place is okeydokey and safe—damn flashbacks.

The girl was named April; she was stunningly attractive, and it was well-known she was dating a lad who didn't attend BHASVIC. She had sandy, dead-straight hair, a freckled face, and sparkly blue eyes. April brimmed with confidence and was dressed immaculately.

"Hey, it's Gary, isn't it?" she asked.

"Yes," I replied, my voice breaking.

"You're an ex-Knoll Schoolboy, aren't you?"

I grunted a nonchalant, "Uh-huh."

April stared at me. I looked into her eyes and looked away as if I wasn't paying her attention. She was known to be part of BHASVIC's 'in-group' of students.

"We've been talking about you," she said, gesturing her hands towards invisible friends back in the refectory.

They've been talking about me? April's friends—Why?

"I wanted to tell you something. Your eyes—"

Here we go. My face has gotten fuller. I was enjoying my time here.

"Have you watched Jesus of Nazareth on the TV?"

"Yes, I have." *I loved that show, even though it was religious. I daren't tell her that I cried when they crucified him.*

"Robert Powell, the guy who plays Jesus—"

"Yes, he's fantastic."

"Your eyes are as captivating as his. They're big, beautiful, and filled with blue-green hues. Whenever I gaze into them, it's as if I'm beholding the eyes of Robert Powell himself."

I was speechless, but my face lit up with a big smile. *That is the nicest thing anyone has ever said to me.* Tears welled in my eyes, and my heart skipped a beat. It was clear that April wasn't flirting—she was showing kindness.

She returned my smile, started walking away, then turned her head, winked, and jokingly said, "See you later, Robert Powell, or should we start calling you Jesus of Nazareth?"

At any minute, I thought she would say, "Just kidding. You're so ugly. My friend, Mitch Skinner, told me about you." She didn't. She walked out of the changing room entrance doors and into the distance. Mum was so wrong about her sticks and stones garbage. Words really can hurt you; they can also be used to heal. Words can tear down; words can be used to build and edify. This was the life lesson that April taught me that day, and I still remember it.

ANGUS'S PASSION for motorcycles led him to convince Mum that I should have my first motorcycle, a neat little Suzuki 100cc trail bike. This would allow me to be more self-sufficient and not rely on public transportation. However, I couldn't take anyone else on my bike because I hadn't passed my full motorcycle test. The only time I risked a ticket from the police was when I took Kathy to the Hungry Years Club to make it to her parent's house before curfew. Everything was fine until I reached a street close to my destination.

A policeman appeared out of nowhere and gestured for me to pull over. Although calm on the outside, I was freaking out inwardly. Before the cop could speak, I said, "Sir, I am so sorry. We is not from around dese parts, in it?"

To this day, I have no idea what possessed me, a whiter than a white guy, to talk to the copper with a reggae lilt.

"Do you know why I have pulled you over?"

"No, Mr Officer. Whatever I is done, I is truly sorry. Me first time in de area."

The police officer was surprisingly friendly and told me I was going the wrong way down the street. I couldn't believe the police officer had let me off without a ticket for riding the wrong way down a one-way street or riding with a passenger without a full license.

On our way home, Kathy chuckled and asked, "What's with the weirdo accent?"

"I don't know. It must have been my ancestors speaking through me."

I had to present my documents at the police station within a week. The angels were on my side the day I produced my license. The duty officer failed to notice that I didn't have all the correct documents. After that incident, Kathy and I agreed that I would be riding solo from now on.

CHAPTER 31
KILLER DARTS
MAY, 1978

THE GAME OF "KILLER" DARTS STARTS WITH THE PLAYERS THROWING a dart using their non-dominant hand. The digit struck on the dartboard becomes the player's designated number. Then, every player attempts to hit double their number using their regular throwing hand. Upon scoring a double on their number, the player ascends to the status of "Killer." Killers have the letter K placed after their names. The dart 'killer' then aims for the doubles of their opponents' numbers. Every player has a total of three lives. The opponent loses one life when a killer hits their double. If a killer mistakenly hits their double, they will lose a life. One can die from self-inflicted dart wounds. The last person with any lives left is the winner or ultimate Killer!

My first year at BHASVIC was relatively uneventful. I worked hard and was quickly accepted as a football and cricket prodigy. I had almost forgotten how wretched the Knoll School experience had been. Sure, apart from biology, geography, English, and, surprisingly, art, I had to take several exams to catch up and start my journey into university. I would never have thought it a possibility a few years ago.

However, the next few months would change my life for the

next decade. The term was winding down, and most students were preparing for their exams. BHASVIC had two recreational rooms where folk hung out. One of them, the old grammar school refractory, was where the British game of darts was played. One game and one older student will always stick in my mind.

"Killer" would often be the go-to game if a student played during the breaks. I only played darts once with him, and I didn't even know my opponent's name; however, he beat me, which was pretty easy as I wasn't very good. John Tett had been a grammar school boy who was not only sharing the Sixth Form with his all-boys grammar school peers, but also an influx of girls and kids like me who had escaped from the Knoll School. It was on or about the early part of May. Tett and I didn't speak during or after the game, apart from me thanking him for the game and saying, "Well done!"

The following day, the rumour was this innocuous, intellectually gifted 18-year-old, ex-grammar school boy brutally murdered his mother and five and six-year-old relatives with a knife. The two children, a little boy and a girl, with their whole lives to live, were killed in a fit of rage. The gossip mill flourished at BHASVIC that day and the following week. News from the media was in scant supply. However, some of Tett's acquaintances and other sources claimed he had gone berserk over a trivial matter.

Nobody believed the shocking triple murders at first, and many found it hard to believe that John Tett, who seemed quiet and distant, could have killed his mother, never mind two young 'uns. It was just too preposterous. But Tett was no longer at the school playing darts in the refectory—he was no longer a BHASVIC student.

As the news spread of Tett's arrest and subsequent conviction for the triple homicide, the community was filled with shock and disbelief. Found guilty, the authorities dispatched the ex-grammar school student to Broadmoor . . . "indefinitely."

Broadmoor has hosted the likes of Charles Bronson and other prisoners considered so dangerous and so criminally insane that they were better off being separated from the general prison community. Peter Sutcliffe, the Yorkshire Ripper who murdered 13 women in the '70s, was sent there. Other dishonourable mentions go to Kenneth Erskine, known as the Stockwell Strangler, who was guilty of seven murders in 1986. It was hard to imagine an ex-BHASVIC student had been sent to Broadmoor.

Tett's file was then closed for eight decades. A local newspaper reporter, James Wallin*, from *The Argus*, brought the murders back to the public's attention in 2011 when the mother of the two young murdered children had finally been reunited with a long-lost picture of them. According to the article, the children's mother returned home with an Indian takeout meal only to find police everywhere. The police officers wouldn't let her into the home, finally telling her that her two children had been murdered. I can't even begin to imagine what she went through. John Tett admitted in court that he killed the children because they were screaming, and wanted them to shut up. The judge described Tett as "not normal" in the court case, as a "normal person" would have turned away from the situation in the house, left the room, and slammed the door behind them.

I'm sure the incident occurred in the blink of an eye, and his state of mind at the time likely triggered his reaction. I'm reminded that I nearly snapped, having been punched in the back of the head during a chemistry lesson a year before the Tett tragedy. I had been that close to a red mist forming before my own eyes.

---

* Wallin, J. (2011, May 19). Brighton mother of murdered children reunited with lost photograph. The Argus. https://www.theargus.co.uk/news/9034842.brighton-mother-of-murdered-children-reunited-with-lost-photograph/

I often think of the two children who were killed and his mum and the tragedy that unfolded in Tett's house that day. I have been reminded that I was lucky to not have been the one to make him snap that day when we played darts. I haven't played the game "killer" since that time, and I don't believe I have any desire to do so in the future.

CHAPTER 32
BILLY BIG BALLS
MAY, 1978

Approaching the end of my first year at BHASVIC, I couldn't help but feel a deep sense of satisfaction and enjoyment. I now had to swot for my exams, and I had a long summer to look forward to my first-ever summer job working for a store called *Brentford Nylons* to earn some much-needed cash. And to top off a great year, I was still dating Kathy, an absolute gem of a girl I wanted to be with forever!

However, as George Harrison of Beatles fame once said, "All good things must come to pass," and my throat started to hurt. As I glanced in the mirror, I noticed my face had become rounder, giving me a somewhat fuller appearance. My neck felt swollen like one side of my face had been inflated. Soon, the other side swelled.

"You have mumps," Mum declared confidently. "You never received a mumps vaccination as a kid."

"Thanks for that, Dr Mum," I said, rolling my eyes.

Mum shook her head in an "oh dear" kind of way. "Ga, the swelling in your neck will go down to your goolies," Mum continued, not thinking about the consequences of what she said: "If it spreads to both your balls, you'll end up being sterile."

There was little I could do, and now, with sterility staring me in the face, I looked on the bright side of life. I imagined the money I'd save on contraception, babies, nappies, formula milk, my children's school costs, sports gear savings, and parent-teen conflict. The more I thought about it, the more attractive sterility sounded. Moreover, I could grow up to be an utterly self-indulgent guy, buy sports cars, pay for season tickets to football games, witness the world's seven wonders, and be debt-free. If I didn't have daughters, I could envisage a world without *Coronation Street, Neighbours,* and *Crossroads.* No more passive-aggressive comments about my football and cricket addiction, no more awkward discussions about tampons versus sanitary pads, and I'd not have to stress about any of them dating drug dealers or, much worse, Arsenal or Crystal Palace fans. On the other hand, if I didn't have sons, I wouldn't have to nag about the toilet seat being left up, clean pee off the bathroom floor, or worry that they may prefer golf over football and become a Catholic priest or worse, vote Liberal.

Enforced sterility had its perks. I could buy a dog for companionship—not a yappy Jack Russell like Marcus, my childhood dog, but a Bernese or a long-haired German Shepherd.* Of course, my sterility would have to remain a secret to any future partner. I'd not say a word, and my wife would hopefully want to try, and try, and try to have kids. But, alas, after years and years of endless humping and shagging, I'd suggest to her the mumps had made me sterile. I could blame Mum or her looney pastor, Gwyn, and claim they had put a Pwllheli (Welsh) curse on me, like the (English) one I put on Dad that ended up killing him.

So, I shared my plight with Billy at the kitchen table while Mum was beavering around, pretending to look busy. Billy

---

* The 'Pet Sounds' chapter covers the Marcus incident in *I Think I Killed My Dad.*

always made me laugh and guaranteed to lighten up my mood.

"Gaz, you'll be a Jaffa!"

"A Jaffa?" I furrowed my brow. "What do you mean?"

"Yeah, a Jaffa's a seedless brand of orange, and colloquially, you'll be a man without any seed!"

"You'll fire blanks," added Mum helpfully, "At least you won't be passing on any of your father's madness genes."

My other concern was the looming presence of my pending exams. I couldn't afford to miss these and have my stay at BHASVIC delayed for another year because of the damned mumps. I'd already missed way too much school due to illness. Eventually, even though I desperately tried to avoid Mum due to her annoying flippancy and sarcasm about my "seedless Jaffa" condition, our paths crossed again.

"How are your balls?"

My face went red. "Mind your own business!"

"On the bright side, when you start to bulge down there, the girls will think you've got an enormous packet." Mum's dimples on her cheeks became prominent when she was in a convivial mood.

"Not funny, Mum. Enough already." I went to the bathroom, pulled down my trousers and underwear and self-examined—they looked like my regular balls. I breathed a long sigh of relief.

Erring on the side of caution and to be helpful with my exams looming, Mum called the doctor to help me obtain a sick note.

Ugh! Dr. Harris will dismissively shake his head and inform the inquisitive receptionist that he has a house call scheduled at the house of Gary "Munchausen Syndrome by Proxy" Trew.

"Oh, is that the guy who said he had a lump in his arse and believed he had three days to live?" chortled his dumbass receptionist, snapping her gum loudly.

"The same guy, yes."

Dr Harris appeared at the house. I sheepishly welcomed him.

Dr Harris looked at me, felt my glands, took my temperature, sighed, and nodded. "You have mumps."

Three seconds passed, maybe four, when Mum butted in. "Told you so," she said, lingering in the background. "Dr Harris, we're all worried about his testicles."

My eyes opened wide. My thoughts wandered uncontrollably through a haze of incredulity. "No one is worried about them apart from you!" I said, like a snapping turtle.

Dr Harris frowned, his large brown eyes accentuated by John Lennon-style glasses, stared directly into mine. "Are you experiencing pain below? Have you noticed that your testicles have swollen?"

This is so awkward; I wish Mum would go away!

"A little discomfort, but—"

"We call him Billy Big Balls," Mum said as if my condition were hilarious. "Gary mentioned that one of them is the size of a coconut!"

I prayed that her God would chastise her about the Bible verse that mentions parents shouldn't annoy their children. I found it once in Mum's ancient copy, with its gnarled pages and dog's ears that made it look well-read. Mum *constantly* quoted (and misquoted) from it.

Finally, I said, "No, Dr Harris, I didn't say such a thing." I glared at my mother, "Can you please ask my mum to leave the room? Doctor-patient confidentiality and all that!"

Dr Harris, an excellent doctor, smiled. He said orchitis was a common symptom of mumps. He clearly wasn't going to ask a parent to leave the room. This was the United Kingdom in the 1970s. I wanted to give my mum a dose of her medicine.

"Dr Harris, my mum has this medical encyclopaedia dating from the 1920s, and she bases her diagnoses, remedies, and cures upon it." Mum adored her medical book and appeared offended as I dared to comment on it. "And, she said that to stop me going sterile with the mumps, I needed to put Vick's vapour rub on the soles of my feet, spread Robinson's strawberry jam on my scrotum with a desert spoon, and wear a woollen sock on my privates for a week."

Dr Harris stepped back and pulled a "what the heck" face at Mum. It worked. Mum went bright cherry red. "No, I didn't, you fibbing little bugger!"

The physician composed himself, smiled, patted my mum on her shoulders, and packed his black medical bag. His final words were for me to ice my gonads to help with any future pain and inflammation. He kindly wrote me a medical note to present to the school.

"I can put the ice on them for you," Mum said with a grin.

A day later, ignoring the fact that I had a communicable and highly contagious disease, I sponged some money from my mum and decided to catch a bus into town and visit a record store. I chose not to ride the motorcycle because straddling the seat would have been a Herculean feat, as things down below looked a bit swollen. Blondie's latest album, *Plastic Letters*, had been released, and listening to it would help with my exam prep and take my mind off the uncomfortable heartbeat sensation in my groin.

While waiting for the bus, I started to feel my testicles pulsate and ache, so I gingerly walked back to my house. As I approached Livingstone Road, my gait resembled that of a weary traveller who had spent an entire year on horseback. On self-examination, a couple of basketballs were showing through my undies. My parotid glands were swollen, making me look like Alvin the Chipmunk. Mum helped me to not be self-conscious by calling me "Moon Face" and "Silly Balls."

BHASVIC allowed me to take the exams in isolation, which was nice. No one wanted to go anywhere near me, especially males, for fear of catching this atomic-ball disease. So, apart from the throbbing bollocks, I could concentrate on the test papers in silence, without teachers walking around looking for cheaters and listening to annoying students clicking their pens and muttering to themselves.

Finally, exams and college were over for the year. I looked forward to hanging out with Kathy, taking my twin nephews to the park, and playing my beloved cricket with the British Legion team, or so I thought.

CHAPTER 33
A BIT OF SLAP AND TICKLE
JUNE, 1978

SLAP AND TICKLE. THE NOUN IS OFTEN COMBINED WITH "A BIT OF." *Used to describe romantic gestures of lovers such as kissing, hugging, cuddling, and petting, or sexual activities that involve playing and joking.*

I WAS IN FULL RECOVERY, and Mum felt safe leaving her now sterile son alone with his girlfriend. Mum accepted an offer to go away for a few days with her grandchildren and her friend, Lone. I was hoping to reach more than first base with Kathy, and like most frisky teenagers, I wanted some alone time with my girlfriend. In contrast, Kathy was relaxed. She knew it would be a night of rebuttal, further explaining why she didn't want to lose her virginity. Whatever was going to happen, it was lovely for me to have some alone time with her and enjoy a snuggle. I fully intended to raid Mum's stash of hidden alcohol, as while the green-eyed cat was away, her teenage son would play.

Friday night was date night for Kathy and me. As soon as Mum left, I made a beeline for her secret cache of Canadian Club whisky and a few cans of Harp lager. I was happy that my body was virtually back to its normal state; my gonads were no longer floating aids and were now at their usual size. I was grateful for this, as the idea of playing cricket in the summer—wearing a protective box—was not something I was keen on. Being a virgin, I rationalised that a "successful" romantic evening with Kathy may be the only way for my testicles to return to their normal state. The equipment down below had to be tested out. What better time to experiment? No need for condoms because my mum and Billy had all but confirmed my sterility. Zero swimmers or sperm meant no need to waste pocket money or weekend wages earned at Tesco's on contraception: winner, winner, chicken dinner.

I rehearsed the night in my head, and although I was certain Kathy did not share my desire to lose my virginity—you never knew. However, some *Eagles* music, a few '70s power ballads, a night of "White Lightning and Wine," and who knows, maybe this night would be the night 'lil Doody popped his cherry? Kathy got a late curfew from her dad because she said she'd spend time with me and my family at my house. I was trying to play it low-key this evening. However, I felt somewhat weird, and my legs were a bit achy. *I guess this was what it felt like just before guys lost their virginity.*

I had a hunch my legs' dull aches were fuelled by adrenaline and sexual chemistry. I mentioned the leg ache to Kathy. She believed my leg discomfort was due to playing too much cricket too soon after my mumps episode.

My heart was pounding out of my chest as we walked along Sackville Road, hand in hand, heading towards my empty house and (hopefully) a little bit of "slap and tickle." When we got to the railway bridge, I stopped and hugged her. I closed my eyes and tried to focus on slowing my racing heart. *Was this to do with the prospect of nookie with my girlfriend? Don't be such a loser.* This was uncharted territory. I hadn't faced the prospect of bonking my girlfriend before, so I decided to go with the flow.

Unfortunately, other feelings soon manifested. My head thumped, and I needed to lean against a wall to steady myself. Kathy commented on how pale I looked. I was in shock as I contemplated abandoning the date night. Nausea, headache, and restless legs overwhelmed me.

The sickness came rapidly—in fact, so quickly that I felt way too ill to walk Kathy the eight hundred yards back to her home. I felt terrible about this. Kathy wanted to walk me home; I refused and wanted her to get home quickly. We parted ways. Unknown to me at the time, our lives would never be the same from that day forward, and sadly, our relationship would never be the same again either.

I kissed her goodnight and staggered home minutes later. My head was now pounding like a jackhammer. I thought about John Lennon's song *Cold Turkey* as he wrote about his high fever, heavy feet, aching body, goose pimples on the skin, and his experience of acute pain. Lennon was referring to withdrawal from heroin; my biggest faux pas is my addiction to cricket.

Once inside my home, I felt relieved, but I dearly wished Mum hadn't gone away. She wasn't due home until Sunday afternoon, and it was only Friday evening.

An hour later, I grabbed some paracetamol (acetaminophen) from the medicine cupboard to help with the headache. It was so bad I was dry-heaving over the toilet basin.

THUMP. THUMP. THUMP. Heart and head pound in sync. We had a phone, but Mum locked the dial to stop me from calling Billy every hour or so—as he lived five minutes away. I didn't consider reaching out for help. Although I felt very poorly, I reminded myself I was 17 and fit as a fiddle. Dialling 999 for an ambulance was the last thing on my mind. No, I'd be okay in the morning; I just needed to ride this out. I boiled some water, put menthol crystals in a Pyrex bowl (a cure for cancer in Mum's fifth-century medical book), leaned my head over the steam and breathed in.

THUMP! THUMP! THUMPETY THUMP! The headache was now unmanageable. I passed out, thankfully missing the glass container that was in front of me on the kitchen table.

I felt my shoulders being shaken. It was Mum. Her mouth was moving, and unintelligible words came from it. The room was spinning. I felt like I was in a psychedelic sequence of the *Magical Mystery Tour* movie.

Mum had come home early; she'd had a premonition to get home to her son. She arrived at two o'clock in the morning, twins fast asleep in Lone's campervan, and found me unconscious with my head on the kitchen table next to a bowl of tepid water. Paracetamol tablets were scattered over the table. There was a strong smell of eucalyptus and camphor. A plastic bowl containing clear, sticky liquid was on the floor next to me. Mum panicked; I was white as a ghost and super-delirious. I semi-woke, winced in pain, and mumbled, "My head is killing me." I felt queasy. Mum assumed I had too much to drink the previous evening. I was unable to tell her when or how much paracetamol I'd taken. She made me take aspirin with water and helped walk me upstairs to my bedroom.

I remember waking up feverish and babbling, with a bone-dry mouth and chaffed lips.

You're going to die.

I had a cognisant moment. "Mum," I called out.

Mum appeared; she looked stressed. She had been berating Lone for taking her away for a break. He had been pissed that she wanted to abandon the mini-break and return home.

You have such a warm and pretty face. I'm lucky to have you as my mum.

"What is it, Ga?"

"I think I have meningitis!"

"What, why, son?"

I lay on my back; I tried to touch my chest with my neck. I

can't move it more than an inch. "I can't move my neck to my chest, and my legs are aching. Mum, call the doctor."

Mum mumbled something stupid. "No, you have your father's genes. Uncle Patrick's head swelled up to the size of a watermelon and exploded right there." She moved her hand to the side of her head and made a loud BOOM sound, her arms simulating the graphic.

I was too sick to reply to her pep talk. I now had hallucinations—my head was swelling and exploding, with brain, eyeball and jaw fragments covering the bedroom walls like one of Regan MacNeil's victims from *The Exorcist*. Mum was wearing a vicar's dog collar and held up a string of Brussels sprouts in the shape of a cross.

Thankfully, Mum called the doctor via the phone in the front room. I heard her arguing with someone. It was Saturday, and Dr Harris only accepted house calls if there was an emergency.

Dr Harris arrived. It was early morning, and he was pissed off with Mum for calling him at home. He was due to visit the synagogue with his family. Mumma-bear Gwen had torn into him and told him her son, *who was almost a doctor*, knew he had meningitis, and if he didn't come, my death was on his head! Bearing in mind Dr Harris had the experience of my cancerous lump self-diagnosis, and Gwen Trew may be struggling with Munchausen's Syndrome by Proxy, I think I'd be hacked off to get a call on my day off.

Dr Harris asked what was going on with me. I was coherent and very much awake. "I have meningitis. It's bad, Doc," and shared my list of symptoms.

Harris cocked an eyebrow and made a "Humph" sound. *He doesn't believe me.* I don't care anymore. Dying will stop the pain in my head.

He opened his medical bag and asked me to remove the bedsheets from my legs. With a dull noise, he tapped repeatedly on my kneecaps with a petite rubber mallet—no knee-jerk. He asked me to rest my chin on my chest. I couldn't. He took my temperature. "One hundred and six degrees Fahrenheit," he muttered. I told him, again, that my head felt like it would explode.

Mum's eyes darkened with worry. Clearly, she was concerned about another possible prognosis. "Just like his uncle Patrick," Mum mumbled, shaking her head in despair.

Is she worried about me or her damned wallpaper being messed up with blood and brains?

I looked at the doctor. "My legs ache. I can't find a position where they will rest."

Dr Harris took my mum aside and whispered to her. Mum reacted angrily. "And you were mad at me for phoning you this morning?"

The doctor asked Mum if he could use the phone. He called for an ambulance. I heard him say that as his patient had suspected meningitis, the ambulance needed to attend urgently. Mum said later that I had yelled out, "No shit Sherlock. I'm a 17-year-old thicko, and you're a grown-arsed doctor."

Given his patient was delirious, and his mother was on the verge of murdering him for wanting to attend synagogue rather than save her son's life—Dr Harris ignored my outburst and paced up and down, waiting for the ambulance to arrive.

CHAPTER 34
M.I.A.
JUNE, 1978

I HEARD THE DOPPLER WAIL OF THE AMBULANCE'S SIREN GET louder and closer. Then it ceased. I was in a brain fog, but I remembered being put onto a gurney by ambulance personnel. A pretty, blonde, kind-faced female paramedic held my hand. "Hang in there, you'll be okay, sweetheart."

The siren began once again. Mum was left behind—she had the twins to care for and had to wait for Lone to come over to drive her and the boys over to the hospital. I remember the tears running down her face.

I love you, Mum.

I felt an immense relief—I'll be okay now that the medics were looking after me. It was as if I was in a race against time. I had vividly seen the distressing images in textbooks of meningitis complications: brain damage, hearing loss, septicaemia, organ failure, and even death. My insatiable curiosity about all things medical intensified my anxiety to a fever pitch. If my head hadn't been jackhammering so intensely, I would have been on the verge of a panic. I knew I'd soon receive medication and get much-needed antibiotics pumped into my blood.

I'm in the best possible hands.
The problem was, I wasn't. I arrived at the Sussex County Hospital, and the next thing I knew, a plastic bracelet was on my wrist. Hospital orderlies gently placed me on a different gurney; I was left in a corridor, drifting in and out of consciousness.

I wanted to cry as the pain was so merciless. I thought of my dad when he crawled up our stairs, face white as a sheet and groaning in agony. The hospital's ceiling lights were spinning round and round.

The following period was based on what Mum and the medical staff told me. After about six hours—yes, six long and painful hours—a nurse appeared, looked at my wrist bracelet, called for a hospital orderly, and wheeled me into an examination room. The bright lights in the room became unbearable. Meningitis, even suspected meningitis, makes the victim light intolerant. It was a shame that the trained medical staff didn't notice my discomfort and turn down the spotlight-esque lighting.

As my neck was totally rigid, I couldn't turn my head away from the lights; it was my own experience of torture, and I'd had enough. I wanted it to all be over and for me to slip away into the painless silence.

What kept me from giving up and drifting into la-la land was the "THUMP! THUMP! THUMP!" sounds in my head, syncing with each heartbeat.

I can't even die in peace.
Finally, a doctor entered the room, looked around, and disappeared.

Bastard. Are you kidding me?
I stared at the massive clock on the examination room's wall —it helped me not to gaze directly into the savage bright lights. TICK. TICK. TICK.

I remained focused on the second hand of the clock, witnessing the dimming light of life within me. It became clear that people do not yearn for death, but for an escape from their suffering.

The "ticks" became one with the "thumps." I was totally exhausted. The door opened again, and I saw my mum's beautiful face—a sight for sore eyes. "Ga! There you are, my boy," she burst into tears.

Mum had been working as a nursing auxiliary at the busy hospital and had been waiting for news since arriving. Finally, she was told they didn't know where I was. The hospital was huge, and due to a series of unfortunate events, I had been forgotten because of a colossal pile-up on the motorway. Injured people were being brought into the hospital *en masse*—they had overlooked me amidst the commotion.

Mum found me, held my hand, and reassured me that she'd return with the artillery. Naturally, Mum went ballistic. One doctor visited me, scribbled something on a clipboard at the bottom of my gurney and said he'd be back. He lied—I never saw him again.

Another doctor appeared and took my blood pressure and temperature. I was severely dehydrated. I hadn't had any liquids for hours, and he didn't offer me any. He asked how I felt, and I whispered to him to dim the lights. He did so. I told him I thought I'd got meningitis and shared my symptoms with him. The young doctor's chiselled jawline accentuated his steely gaze. He smirked, and a sense of unease washed over me. Even in my confused state, I detected a disturbing undertone behind his grin.

My mind is playing tricks.

He reminded me *he* was the doctor. I had no fight left and wanted the pain to stop. "Well, 'Dr' Gary," he said mockingly, "you'll be aware of what we must do to determine what is making you sick?"

Oh, no, it's Dr Satan. "A lumbar puncture," I muttered.

"Yes, a lumbar puncture, also known as a spinal tap."

Of all the doctors in this hospital, why must I deal with this guy?

On reflection, having recovered, I should have returned to the hospital, tracked this medic down and forced a sweetcorn and chicken Phall (the hottest and spiciest Indian curry) enema on him, then asked him, "Hey, Dr Chiselled Jaw, you *must* know what's going to happen next?"

The sarcastic medical professional left the room and returned with an enormous black orderly within a few minutes. The doctor informed me the orderly was going to turn me over and put all his weight on my upper body. "You need to stay still. You'll be paralysed if you move when I put the needle into your spine," he laughed under his breath. "This will not be pleasant."

Wrong profession. You should be a dentist. I was terrified.

He neither lied nor was competent. He took *three* attempts to draw fluid from my spinal column. I had my back turned to him. He told the orderly that he may have to do a fourth one, as the cerebrospinal fluid was cloudy. The orderly, with more compassion in his little finger than the oaf in the white coat, said, "I'm sorry. It will be over soon—try not to move; well done."

Dr. Mengele exited the room, carrying the vial containing my CSF sample, destined for the labs to undergo testing. Mum came back and sat with me, her presence providing comfort as I fixated on the rhythmic ticking of the wall clock until four o'clock in the morning. Finally, I was moved to the intensive care unit, where the staff took good care of me. The administration of IV drips lessened my pain and gave me the much-needed antibiotics; I drifted off to sleep.

Two days later, I was lying on a gurney, having regained consciousness as ceiling lights flashed by. I was moving. I was dozy, yet I recalled being wheeled into a ward.

My condition was stable enough to allow visitors. I had no idea where I was. Mum's smile greeted me at the end of the bed. She asked me how I was and told me about my drama at the hospital. "You're going to be okay. I've spoken with the consultant."

Lone, my nephews, and Kathy appeared over the next few days. I wasn't eating the hospital food. I used the bedpan and decided I wouldn't be using it again. My appetite gradually returned. Mum snuck fish and chips into the ward—the salt and vinegar tasted heavenly.

I felt discombobulated; something didn't feel right. I wanted to leave and asked Mum to take me home. She said the staff were not allowing me to be discharged. As a precaution, nurses removed my clothing and footwear in case I made a dash for freedom. The truth was that I couldn't stand up for more than a few seconds before being overcome with nausea.

CHAPTER 35
HONEY, WHO FRIED MY BRAIN?
1978-79

THE NEUROLOGIST TOLD MUM THAT MY FULL RECOVERY MAY TAKE some time. My cerebral spinal fluid extracted had been cloudy, and the gram-negative test was inconclusive. I believe one more mess-up occurred during the first 24 hours of my hospital experience. As viral and bacterial meningitis symptoms are very similar, doctors will err on the side of caution and give the patient an IV drip of antibiotics. That happened to me, but not until about 18 hours after my admission.

Nowadays, if viral meningitis is suspected, I may have been given a DNA-based test known as a polymerase chain reaction amplification to confirm the diagnosis. The disease always has the potential to cause severe, irreversible neurological damage. I really believe that I was lucky to be alive. The consultant warned Mum that victims of meningitis may acquire different types of brain injury. Changes may occur over time, leading to behaviour and memory issues. The good news was that the doctor said I was on the mend. The bad news was Dr Harris did not follow up after discharge. In Mum's tongue-in-cheek way, she passed on the doctor's prognosis.

Mum smiled a big smile. "Ga, they don't know how fried your brain is—if at all." I exchanged a bewildered look.

"Fried?"

"Yes, like an egg," she chuckled. "I'm not sure they believed you had a brain in your head," Mum playfully went cross-eyed, contorting her face. "So, it's difficult for them to know if there will be any long-term damage. With a bit of luck, you'll end up being as normal as I am!"

While I was at the hospital, I was irritable and difficult to deal with. My mum told me that I wasn't following the advice of the ward nurses. I really wanted to leave the hospital, but it was obvious that I wasn't ready to be discharged. I collapsed several times going to and from the toilet. On one occasion, I passed out while in the bathroom and slumped against the door. I caused a load of kerfuffle as staff tried to gain entry.

The most noticeable difference in my personality before and after meningitis was the lack of logic in my decision-making. I was filled with anger towards the world after my father's passing, but gradually, I found solace and happiness within. After the illness, I became prone to outbursts, aggression, and alcohol abuse. Moreover, I seemed to have lost my ability to empathise. I often gave in to fits of rage, experiencing flashes of blind anger when all I wanted to do was to hurt someone. As my physical strength improved, I became a guy that folk didn't want to pick on.

The "Doody" who had kissed Kathy goodnight under the bridge on Sackville Road wasn't the same person who met her following the illness. I left the hospital after ten days or so, and it took the entire summer to recover from constant headaches, back pain, brain fog, and balance issues. Although I couldn't play cricket that summer, I worked hard to get fit again before starting my A-Levels, using weights and bulking up. Back at BHASVIC in September of that year, I began to make some very reckless decisions.

CHAPTER 36
MEET THE PARENTS
1978-79

THE CHANGE IN MY PERSONALITY WENT UNNOTICED BY ME. I GUESS I was lucky in some respects; I did not suffer hearing or sight loss, lose limbs, or struggle with organ failure and the like. Unfortunately, my relationship with Kathy didn't last a month after we started back at BHASVIC for the Autumn term. I had quickly fallen out of love with her, and it would be years before I fell in love with anyone else. However, falling in lust was a different animal, and I was soon to experience the emptiness of letting no one share my heart.

At BHASVIC, I started to date Charlotte, a super bright Oxbridge candidate taking the more esoteric "Nuffield" route to university; these were more observation and experimentation-based sciences. Charlotte was blonde, had big blue eyes, was super-laid back, and came from a good, upper-middle-class family. Kathy had heard I had been flirting with Charlotte and gently broke off our relationship. I didn't feel sad; I just thought it was time to move on, which wasn't like me. I asked Charlotte to go out with me on a date, and she accepted.

We soon became an item. We saw each other most days, and we lost our virginity together. Charlotte was super confident, and I was proud that this kid from a rough school like the Knoll was dating a super-smart girl with a great self-image and an even greater tolerance for beer than I did. Charlotte knew where she was going and how to get there.

One day, we were hanging out together, and she felt it was time for us to have a serious conversation. Although I didn't use condoms, I wasn't worried about her getting pregnant because I couldn't have children due to Billy and Mum's mumps diagnosis. Charlotte seemed preoccupied and tense, with furrowed brows and fidgety hands.

As we walked together, she stopped abruptly and blurted, "My dad wants to meet you." I clearly remember Kathy saying the same thing to me in the past. Meeting her dad had been a very positive experience and had helped our relationship grow. However, Gary 2.0 (post-brain fry) took this news differently.

"Why?" I asked, my voice laced with defensiveness.

"Well, you've been seeing his daughter for a while now, and he's curious to get to know you in person."

"Do you need Daddy's permission to date someone?" I asked, mockingly.

"I need my father to approve our relationship; that's how my parents roll."

"I don't understand," I exclaimed, my voice filled with disbelief and bewilderment. I began jumping to all the wrong conclusions.

"My dad is a bit old-fashioned and wants to get to know you. He wants to know what your ambitions are and what university you want to go to. He wants to know a bit about your family, and I want him to give you the green light so we can move forward. He's heard lots about you; you're funny and intelligent, and you've gone through adversity and have become stronger because of it."

"You told him we shagged?"

"No! Don't be a jerk."

I remained silent for a few seconds, contemplating Charlotte's words, and the straightforward favour she had asked.

"No."

"What?"

"I won't meet him," I said, my voice dripping with anger.

"If you don't meet him," she pleaded, "we won't be able to continue seeing each other."

"Why didn't you just tell him, 'No!' Is he the Gestapo?"

"Duh. Perhaps it's because I'm his daughter. Look, both of my parents are in complete agreement. I am thankful to my parents for providing food and shelter and granting me the financial resources to pursue my education."

"Get a grant or a student loan; take back your freedom!"

"But 'no' is not the right answer. 'No' to meeting Dad means 'no' to having me as your girlfriend."

"So, I have an ultimatum."

"Just come over to the house one evening. It will be cool and nice for Mum and Dad to meet my boyfriend, whom I keep talking about."

"Charlotte . . . I don't do threats."

She started to get teary-eyed. "I don't want to break up with you. I really like you," she said.

"Meeting your dad would be awful."

"Why?"

"He'll ask me to talk about Schrodinger's equation and throw chalk at me when I screw it up!" *Just like "Mr Hippo" used to do. Or, he'll give me "the look" like Dad gave me when he disapproved or was irritated by me.*

"What are you talking about?"

"I hate being put on the spot. Your dad will write polynomials on his whiteboard and expect me to solve stuff."

Charlotte sighed and rolled her eyes. "Dad can be a bit serious sometimes, but if I'm a chip off the old block, he can't be *that* bad, eh? Gary, please come and meet him."

I sighed, smiled, and nodded. A broad grin spread across Charlotte's face.

"I'll come, but there's a caveat you should know about first."

"A caveat? What's the caveat?" she asked.

"I will come *if* I can bring Billy with me."

"Billy?"

"Yes, Billy. I won't feel isolated and anxious with Bill being there."

It was Charlotte's turn to ponder. Billy was my best friend—intelligent, clean-cut, and, most importantly, polite. Queen Mary College, London, had offered him a place to study chemistry and computer science.

"Okay, it's a deal. I'll ask Dad. It's a bit of a strange request, but I'll make a strong case if he's hesitant."

We both hugged, I wiped away the tears from her cheeks, and as we held hands, I skipped and danced like an eejit, singing ABBA's *Take a Chance on Me* and *Dancing Queen*.

CHARLOTTE'S DAD approved of my bizarre terms, and we were set to meet Charlotte's parents mid-week. Billy and I discussed the ultimatum. He was happy to support his pal and accompany me to meet Charlotte's family. We went to our go-to pub, laughed heartily, and devised a strategy to make an excellent first impression on her dad, who we suspected might be a tad pompous.

My wardrobe mainly comprised of casual wear, such as jeans, T-shirts, and a few loose-fitting tops. I informed Mum about my predicament and the plan Billy and I devised to impress Charlotte's father. Mum, sportingly, donated some extra clothes that would be useful for the task ahead.

Giggling nervously, Billy and I embarked on the seven-mile, 45-minute journey out of town towards Charlotte's home. Mum donated some alcohol to help give us some Dutch courage. Mum was a good egg like that. We arrived in Saltdene and walked up a steep hill. I was giddy with excitement.

We stopped close to Charlotte's address, opened a large plastic bag containing our "meet the parents" clothes, took further swigs from a small bottle of Canadian Club, changed, and helped each other look as impeccable as possible. This was a huge moment for me, and I wanted us to look our fabulous best.

A few steps later, we arrived at her home, and I pressed the doorbell, which chimed, "Ding, dong."

I took a step back and waited for the first interaction. Charlotte opened the door with a broad smile. She looked at me, then at Billy, then back at me. Her blue, almond-shaped eyes were wide open as I felt them bore into the depths of my soul. With a curled upper lip and fury etched on her face, Charlotte slammed the door in my face.

"Um. Good talk," sniggered Billy.

"Rude," I replied.

Once more, I pressed the bell. This time, her dad opened the door with a face like thunder.

"Hi, I'm Gary. You must be Charlotte's dad." I glanced at my best pal, dressed as a hospital nurse. "This is my friend, Billy."

"Actually, it's Staff Nurse Billy," Billy corrected, with a stern expression.

In collaboration with my mum, Billy and I borrowed her white nurse's uniform and added makeup and fishnet stockings. With Mum's skilful input, our makeup was flawlessly done to seal the deal. We looked stunning with bright red lipstick, eye liner, blue eye shadow, and scarlet blusher for our cheeks. Before reaching Charlotte's house, Billy and I commented on how comfortable fishnet stockings were. "I might start wearing a pair of these full-time," Billy said. We roared with laughter.

What wasn't a laughing matter was Charlotte's dad's expression. "What is the meaning of this?" he barked.

I felt deeply disappointed by my future father-in-law's reaction. "Billy and I—"

"Staff Nurse Billy," Billy added helpfully.

Without waiting for an explanation, Charlotte's dad shook his head, walked away, and left the door open. He called Charlotte, asking her to come to the door to talk with her friends. When Charlotte appeared, her pretty eyes were narrowed, and her lips were pressed into a thin line.

"Do we look pretty?" asked Billy.

"Both of you look absurd. I can't believe you both came here like this!"

"Is it possible for us to come inside your house and meet your famjam?" I asked optimistically, blinking rapidly to show off my greeny-blue eyes, which I thought looked stunning with mascara, eye shadow and liner.

"*That* —" pointing at my face, "needs to come off right now, then I'll let you in."

"The uniform as well?" asked a perplexed Billy.

"Yes!" and Charlotte walked away along her hallway, leaving us at the doorstep.

Billy and I removed our outfits just as she requested. We couldn't remove the makeup as well as we could have because we didn't take the right kit. Billy's appearance now closely resembled that of pop star Gary Numan, and I looked like Robert Smith, the lead singer of *The Cure.*

When we walked in, Charlotte's Mum, Dad, and brother were in the kitchen with her. I had to think quickly and come up with an explanation. I fibbed and informed her stunned family that Charlotte had invited us to a fancy-dress party and to meet her parents, who loved to dress up in costumes.

Billy quickly caught on. "Your daughter is such a prankster," he looked at my girlfriend. "Good one, Charlotte!" he nodded in a "you got us good" kind of way.

Charlotte's brother roared with laughter as her mother and

father smiled. Their daughter had pulled off a great prank—very unlike her, perhaps showing a different side of her. Meanwhile, Charlotte sported a fake smile and glared at me. My explanation seemed (almost) believable, and the tension in the kitchen lifted.

I took her dad aside and offered him a sincere apology. I asked him who in their right mind would be audacious enough to meet someone's parents dressed in such an inappropriate way. I told him I felt humiliated and asked for his forgiveness. It was a terrific prank, and I praised his daughter for her outrageous and off-the-wall sense of humour. The truth was I was totally out of my tiny mind.

Her dad "kind of" believed me. He soon got down to business and asked me about my academic aspirations and the career I was interested in pursuing. My nurse's outfit came to mind, and sharing my interest in a healthcare or medical career didn't seem appropriate. I told him I longed to fly fast jets, hear the engines' roar, and feel the g-forces pressing against me. As a cherry on the cake, I wanted to impress him with my knowledge of current affairs. I told Charlotte's dad I wanted to bomb the hell out of Iran, as their troops had recently opened fire on rioters in Tehran. He didn't appear swayed by my narrative.

Keeping a straight face throughout the evening was a challenge. While Charlotte's mum asked Billy about his academic future, I noticed his blackened eyes, blue eye shadow, and rouged cheeks as he answered her questions with sincerity. *I wonder if she thinks he's completely bonkers?*

I had a pleasant conversation with Charlotte's brother; his friendly, easy-going nature made me feel more at ease. Towards the end of the interrogation and parental interviews, I asked Charlotte to give us a 15-minute heads-up before the last bus departed to avoid a long, treacherous walk home. Her anger had melted away like a snow-capped mountain in summertime as she watched me and my future brother-in-law interact and laugh together. I was completely unaware of the time as I didn't have a

THE HATE GAME

wristwatch. Charlotte finally spoke up, interrupting us and indicating it was time to leave. Picking up our discarded nurses' clothing and paraphernalia, I gave her a peck on the cheek. With a broad grin, she said, "Whoopsie, it seems you missed the last bus!"

I was stunned, "Why didn't you tell us 15 minutes earlier?"

"Why did you bring your drag outfits instead of dressing *normally* and meeting my family like a *normal* boyfriend?" she snapped back. "Oh, and enjoy your walk home—" she added with a smirk, "too bad, so sad," and slammed the door in our faces.

"That went well," snickered Billy, rubbing the top of his head.

"Nailed it!" I replied.

"At least we have our fishnets to keep us warm," he said.

"You'll be wearing them in the summer," I teased.

As we contemplated our options, a chilly breeze stirred the surrounding leaves. We faced a grim decision: trudge home in the cold, risking hypothermia, or find shelter and wait for the early morning bus back into town. The walk from Charlotte's home to Livingstone Road was at least two and a half hours.

I swallowed my pride and rang the doorbell; Charlotte answered. I asked if staying overnight and catching the bus in the morning was possible. "I'm sorry—not an option," she replied firmly.

Billy shivered as he asked if she had a coat to spare for the three-hour walk along the blustery seafront.

Charlotte rummaged through the cupboard until she found a green combat jacket to toss to Bill.

"Is there one for me, too?" I asked, hopefully.

"Sorry, Nurse Ratched. Oh, and don't be late for class tomorrow." The door shut in our faces.

"Harsh," Billy chuckled, "but she's got a point. Gary, you look like the nurse in *One Flew Over the Cuckoo's Nest.*"

"I'm insulted by you both—I thought I was more like Nurse

Duckett from *Catch-22*. She was sweet; Nurse Ratched was a cow!"

As we started to walk home, we shivered like crazy. We rolled on our fishnets to keep us cosy. We were both fed up, but through our chattering teeth, we bellowed with laughter. However, Charlotte had the last laugh on us and deserved respect. In the freezing cold, we clenched our teeth and trembled while Bill searched through Charlotte's jacket pockets for a beanie or gloves. Out of nowhere, he burst into laughter and started dancing on the sidewalk. "What is it, you lunatic?"

"Thank you, God!" he cried out.

Billy found a 20-quid note inside a small pocket of Charlotte's oversized green combat coat. He held it up like he was holding the winning lottery ticket. The money had been left in Charlotte's coat by mistake.

We laughed heartily, spotted a telephone booth, and called for a taxi. As soon as the taxi arrived, we inquired with the driver about the cost of the cab fare. The charge, in his estimation, would come to about twelve pounds. We told him to take his time and that we would give him a hearty tip for his troubles. Upon arriving home, we gave him Charlotte's 20-pound note and told him to keep the change. His face lit up with joy. I asked for a receipt, drew a smiley face upon it, and placed it in the same pocket of Charlotte's coat where Billy had discovered the cash.

Surprisingly, when Billy returned her coat when back at the college, Charlotte never mentioned the evening or any missing money. Our relationship as boyfriend and girlfriend sadly ended a few weeks later. I thought she would definitely finish with me after the Nurse Ratched incident. However, she didn't. She was a genuinely lovely person. Then, out of the blue, I terminated the relationship by immaturely telling her she was "chucked!" In other words, we were finished. Charlotte looked shocked and broken-hearted.

"Why?" she asked.

"I don't know! I guess I just felt like I was in a chucking kind of mood," I said without a hint of emotion. She thought it was another sick prank. It wasn't.

I had a deep fondness for Charlotte and truly enjoyed her company. She was a total Rockstar. Unfortunately, due to my fried brain, my common-sense filter was no longer in play. Like Kathy before her, I made a rash, unemotional, and illogical decision and moved on as if nothing had happened. It was a gain for her and a loss for me.

CHAPTER 37
DACHAU
SUMMER, 1980

AFTER FINISHING EXAMS AT BHASVIC, I TRAVELLED WITH A couple of friends on a train around Europe. I visited Munich, stopping off at Dachau, a small town in Upper Bavaria, about 20 km northwest of Munich.

The town is infamous for its proximity to the Dachau concentration camp, operated by the Nazis between 1933 and 1945. Lieutenant Colonel Felix Sparks of the 157th Infantry Regiment, 45th Infantry Division of the US Army, was the first to liberate the camp over a side wall. Many Allied units have also been recognised as liberating Dachau, including the 101st Airbourne Division, 10th Armoured Division, and the 103rd Infantry, to name a few.*

Once inside the gates of Dachau, the experience was surreal, like stepping back in time. One of the first things you'll see is the gate with the inscription *"Arbeit Macht Frei,"* which translates to "Work Will Set You Free," the same greeting that welcomed the

---

* MarshallV. (2022, July 14). *The last days of the Dachau concentration camp*. The National WWII Museum | New Orleans. https://www.nationalww2museum.org/war/articles/last-days-dachau-concentration-camp

Auschwitz prisoners. The original gate and sign now rest in an on-site building, and a glass casing shields them. I recall seeing a glass case that held prisoners' uniforms, each adorned with a number and a triangle symbol on the sleeve. These symbols represented their identities - Jewish, gay, Jehovah's Witness, objector, or Gypsy.

One image I'll never forget was seeing the restored gas chamber. The Nazis disguised the execution room to look like shower stalls, duping prisoners into going inside without a fight. The ovens still contained the ash of its victims.

How can a person witness such barbarity without feeling a lump in their throat and a dagger in their heart? Although shocked and horrified, I made the odd wisecrack to mask my extreme discomfort and shame. I didn't know whether to cry, laugh or throw up.

Why, just why? All the lives lost? The barbarity? Women and children? Babies?

My stomach churned.

The thought of the kids at the Knoll School playing a game based on the Holocaust sickened me. I sent Mum a postcard from Dachau, a place that left me with a heavy heart and a newfound understanding.

Upon returning from the four-week Europe trip, Lone approached me, excited to talk. As he held the postcard in his hands, memories of being one of the camp's first liberators came flooding back, and he eagerly shared his experience with me.

My eyes widened, and my mouth hung open in astonishment and disbelief. Considering Dachau's inland location, the sight of a boat, let alone a frigate from the Royal Australian Navy, arriving at its gates would have been a miraculous event of biblical magnitude.

"Lone, I've seen hours and hours of TV, film, and footage of the liberation of Dachau and haunting images of survivors and the harrowing stories they shared. I never saw your Anzac class frigate at the camp's gates. The camp's museum did not feature movies showcasing your heroic deeds."

He looked at me without batting an eyelid, "It was deemed a matter of utmost secrecy at that time. Gary, the memory of me sailing down the Rhine, firing our five-inch guns with 20 rounds per minute, gave the Jerry's a warning that Captain Lone meant business!"

Yer, right.

"We sea captains had to retain high-level information; as years have passed, I can now share this highly classified information with you!"

I sighed, smiled, and hugged him. I'm sure that if Mum hadn't started to blast off his fibbing ears, he probably would have shared that he was in the thick of it at Stalingrad, Pearl Harbour, and the Norman invasion of England in 1066. That was Lone, the man, the myth, and the legend—a lovely guy who told tales that would make Geppetto's puppet's nose look short.

Gary's original postcard was sent to his mum in 1980 from Munich.

CHAPTER 38
HONEY, WHO REWIRED MY BRAIN? THE DREAM
1980-1990

TEN LONG YEARS HAD GONE BY SINCE BEING STRUCK BY meningitis. Despite having regular migraines, my muscle control was unaffected, and I didn't experience seizures. Physically, I was as fit as a fiddle. Despite graduating with a science degree from university, I grappled with cognitive challenges. It was as if my brain was wired differently, causing me to experience a dyslexia-like confusion with words. It was difficult for me to retain information and learn new things. To visualise DNA combinations and physical chemistry, I used coloured Legos to create intricate 3-D models, bringing the concepts to life. The things that I used to find easy to understand had suddenly become much more complex.

I battled the never-ending chorus of voices that taunted me, repeating over and over that I was unintelligent and dense. Relationship after relationship fizzled out. I met and dated some amazing women. I can't say that I didn't feel what love was like, but I never felt truly loved. I was always too scared to lose someone, so self-sabotage became a habit.

With a degree, I was thrilled to be accepted for officer flying training within the Royal Navy's Fleet Air Arm. Mum and one of my nephews witnessed my graduation from Britannia Royal Naval College; she said it was one of the proudest moments of her life. I set off on a football tour with the Royal Navy in Cyprus and then embarked on the dreaded aircrew survival school in the New Forest, Hampshire.

Just when everything seemed to be going smoothly, the sound of a crack echoed through the air as I suffered a debilitating back injury during the survival course. I felt a clicking sensation in my lower back when an instructor stepped on it while I passed under a fence in a boggy field. Years later, the same instructor supposedly caused brain damage to a young officer during another survival course. Dehydrated, the young man collapsed, and the instructor showed no empathy by urinating on him. A TV documentary aired, shedding light on the incident and the disturbing allegations of bullying and hazing.

I passed the course and went through helicopter underwater escape training, but reached a point where every step became unbearable, the pain shooting through my body with each movement—I could hardly walk. I formed amazing friendships, and we were "38 Flight," a tight bunch of pilots and navigators. I discharged myself impulsively because I didn't want to be held back (back squadded) from progressing with my flight training until I fully recovered.

After months of free physio treatments from the Navy, I visited an osteopath in Loughborough. I thought these bone-clickers were a tad sketchy. However, I had become desperate, and the osteopath had been highly recommended.

CLICK. CLICK. CLICK! I was amazed as the osteopath expertly adjusted my body with gentle yet firm movements, providing immense relief. It seemed as if I had never experienced any pain. I submitted an application as a graduate entrant to the police force. I transitioned into a different profession, trading my sub-lieutenant's navy-blue uniform for a police officer's blue-black one.

Essentially, I was behaving irresponsibly as a law enforcement officer and in my personal life. Many funny anecdotes and incidents occurred. However, I felt an overwhelming desire to take my own life. I had felt like this since my 14th birthday when I was given the news that Dad only had a few days left to live. In the Navy, the death wish was to navigate a helicopter into a cliff; as a cop, it was to get shot. It's hard to explain these desires as they were far from rational feelings. I told friends I'd be dead before I reached 30, so I didn't care what risks I took.

I drank heavily, was reckless in my relationships, and even received bravery commendations due to my wild "I don't give an eff" behaviours.

I remember going to bed one night, knowing I was due to work undercover the following day in a pub to observe drug dealing and the fencing of stolen property. That night, a vivid technicolour dream changed my life.

Standing on the ocean promenade, I heard the crashing waves and felt the salty breeze on my face. Everything was peaceful and serene. The air was filled with the cheerful chirping of birds, the loud squawking of seagulls, and the laughter of people enjoying a day at the seaside. My eyes fixated on the horizon, where a solitary wave began to form, gradually growing. This wave was small but still noticeable. I was captivated by the way this wave swelled and expanded.

Within a few seconds, the wave grew in size and strength, resembling a terrifying tsunami rapidly approaching my location. I was rooted to the concrete floor, unable to tear my eyes away from the colossal wave inching closer to me and the oblivious crowd. My scream pierced the silence, shattering the calm of the room. No sound escaped my lips as I tried to speak. I attempted to warn everyone, shouting out frantically to get their attention.

It was too late to react as the tidal wave engulfed me, its power overwhelming and terrifying.

On the verge of death, I cried out to God with desperate pleas for help. I felt remorse for my impulsive behaviour. I deeply regretted the harm I'd inflicted upon others throughout my path. I regretted both my self-hatred and the way I had mocked people for their religious convictions. It may sound crazy, but I saw the face of God. I woke in my bed, drenched in sweat, in my police flat above the station. I was completely soaked, along with my pillow and duvet. My body quivered uncontrollably.

Whether it was God (my own belief), a natural phenomenon, or too many takeaway curries, *something happened* that evening—*something* rewired my brain. It's as if my meningitis-ravaged brain underwent a complete reboot, correcting whatever had been malfunctioning. I believe I experienced a minor miracle. After unpacking the dream to Jo Taylor, someone I knew and respected, I gave my life to God. As I drifted to sleep the night before, I was still the familiar person I always was—Gary, known for his humour and lack of caution. When I opened my eyes the following day, it seemed as if I had magically returned to the young man who had said goodbye to Kathryn on Sackville Road. I no longer wished for death. My self-hatred disappeared, and I felt purified as if someone or something had cleansed my spirit. The most beautiful feeling that came back that season was the capacity for empathy.

I recall walking along a road in Loughborough, where I served as an officer. *What were those smells? Beautiful fragrances.* They were the lilacs, azaleas, and jasmines planted in the gardens as I walked past. I'd not noticed them before. Even the air smelt crisp and refreshing. The other transformation was that my heart began to beat. No, not my blood pump, but my feelings and emotions had awoken. It was overwhelming, in a beautiful kind of way.

My viewpoint as a police officer completely transformed

overnight. I had little mercy, and my reputation was solidified by a long list of arrests and convictions. As mentioned, I was honoured with a double (a Red Robe Judge's and Chief Constable's) commendation for bravely diving onto an enraged man in the middle of the street. Ready to strike, he held a samurai sword above his head, targeting his ex-wife. I ended up with deep lacerations to my hands and bruises to my face and body as I grappled with the enraged assailant. In all honesty, it was a completely reckless and devil-may-care act.

As I arrested drug users and dealers, I became more captivated by their personal stories, seeking to comprehend the reasons behind their choices. The more I thought about it, the more I realised the importance of finding accessible rehab options for the junkies. I discovered that those who are hurt often end up hurting others. While conducting an interview, I found myself sitting across from a drug dealer who shared the story of his tragic family life. As the arresting officer, tears welled up in my eyes. During the interview, my teammate and co-worker kicked me under the table in disbelief at my emotional reaction.

Other transformations occurred in my heart. These had a profound impact on other people's lives. I worked in an area with many social problems and issues. I was the point of contact with several community members, many of whom got in trouble with the law. One notorious family on the Hermitage Road estate regarded me with much caution. I was "the law," and their previous dealings with law enforcement hadn't been positive. The family matriarch had sent one of her many children to steal goods from a local store, knowing he was too young to be charged with shoplifting. As I sat in their home, my gaze shifted to the lounge floor, which moved with a sea of tiny silverfish. Of course, she denied sending her son anywhere.

I got to know the young boy, Chad, who was always in the thick of causing mischief. I felt for the lad as his siblings wore newish clothes, and he wore the same grubby blue coat daily. Chad's hair had been "touched by the flames" and was bright ginger. My heart ached for him and the other youth on the estate. My fellow police officers found Chad a pain in the arse; I became very fond of the lad. All he needed to help him was a decent role model who believed in him. I saw myself in Chad and many other youths living on the estate. If only someone would have believed in me?

I built trust with him and others in the community. Chad and I were often seen in the community holding hands and walking down the street with my oversized police helmet on his head. This new relationship with him and others in the community led to a strange phenomenon—the crime rate began falling throughout the area. I reached out to community players like Ro Riley, a local youth worker, and Keith and Denise Munro, a couple with a heart for youth in the community. This was unthinkable for me to do in the past, as my work was all about me and how I could arrest as many people as possible and solve crime. I became known as Gary the "Do-Gooder" amongst some colleagues who saw their role as purely law enforcement rather than taking a preventative approach and sowing goodwill into the community.

One colleague said, "Gary, you're in the wrong job, mate. You act like a social worker rather than a cop." It's funny that I took a leap of faith a few years later, returned to university, and became one! Of course, I can't attribute the falling crime rate to me alone. However, serving the community and building collaborative partnerships became a significant factor.

This was the new reality for me. Don't judge. Some people are dealt a crappy hand from birth. Boys like Chad need positive role models. This was all due to the transformation that began manifesting in my life. I not only began to feel alive—I could feel others' pain and trauma.

My decade of recklessness and the aftermath of the tidal wave dream was over, and many stories, adventures, and more trials and tribulations were to follow. However, this time, I could face them with God, as I, like Chad, walked with Him hand in hand, on my journey into a much more positive future where I could finally deal with many of the demons from my past.

CHAPTER 39
GWENDOLINE'S ASHES
APRIL, 2008

Mum struggled with rheumatoid arthritis when in her fifties, and Carole and her husband, Trevor, stepped up and took Mum under their wing, eventually converting part of their house to accommodate our ailing mother. Her two sons were unable to look after her. I lived in Canada, and Paul was involved with his large extended family in Gloucestershire. In the later stages of her life, Mum was very unwell and bedridden; Carole, Trevor, and my nephews cared for her with devotion. I will always be in awe of my big sister for doing so, as our elderly mother could be demanding and cranky. Carole was a rock to lean on when I went through several more trials and tribulations in Canada.

Mum died in 2008 when she was seventy-eight years old. Through complications associated with rheumatoid arthritis and being bed-bound, she was rushed to The Royal Sussex County Hospital. Carole and the family were informed she was dying from sepsis. I heard the awful news from Carole on a phone call in Canada. A week or so before I received the news, I had chatted and laughed with Mum on a call, and she appeared to be bright as a button.

On the night of her death, my mum had the chance to speak to me one last time on the phone. I felt a wave of dread as the conversation approached. Despite being heavily medicated with morphine, I expressed to her she had been a fantastic mother and nanna to my children and nephews. Recognising my voice, she spoke softly with a Welsh lilt, saying, "Ga, my son. It's so nice to hear your voice. I love you, too. I love you more than you'll ever know." She slipped away later in the night with one of her beloved nephews holding her hand.

William and Sue, my friends from Toronto, kindly paid for an air ticket for me to attend the funeral. Although the children also wanted to go, taking the family would have been far too expensive. Carole requested (or commanded) that I take charge of the crematorium service to celebrate her life: "Mum wouldn't want anyone else to take the service." I reluctantly accepted because I'd not attended my dad's funeral, which I still regret to this day. Maybe I could right some wrong karma.

Ultimately, Mum was such a ray of sunshine in everyone's lives; telling beautiful stories about her at a funeral wouldn't be difficult; on the other hand, keeping my composure would be. After I arrived at Carole's home, we went for a coffee together. We reminisced about our mum and giggled as we looked out at the busy Marks and Spencer car park in Shoreham. We told each other stories about Mum's aversion to all things driving. Our mum was one of the most nervous drivers in the history of mankind. After Dad died, she was persuaded to buy a car to give her more independence. She reluctantly bought one, but it quickly became a forgotten object, sitting idly outside our house for many months.

Eventually, after much nagging from her children, and despite her nervousness, we stood outside our house as if witnessing a ceremonial ship launch without the champagne. Mum took a deep breath, settled into her car's driver's seat, and readied herself for her maiden voyage. Holding onto the leather steering wheel for dear life, Mum sat like a statue for 10 minutes before turning on the ignition, followed by the car's indicator. We attempted to remain patient, but it was challenging for our family to abstain from sarcasm. She was super-vigilant, looking for non-existent traffic, waiting for an opportunity to turn onto the street as the blinker ticked away.

Eventually, Mum hesitantly pulled away from the kerb and stopped at every junction, even if no other cars were around and she had the right of way. "Better to be safe than sorry," she said in her softly spoken brogue. My dry irony and impatience were too much for her, and I was banned from travelling in a car with her. Mum decided there were too many insane drivers on the road and kamikaze pedestrians walking in front of her, so she forwent her new-found independence and sold the car.

Some years later, working as a police officer and having an excellent knowledge of the *British Highway Code*, I took her to the Marks & Spencer store in Shoreham. It was the first and last time I would ever drive Mum anywhere:

"Son, you're awful close to that blue car."

"Mum, it's a *parked* car, and unless I pass it, I'll have to wait until the driver returns, which may be two weeks as he may have travelled to Mallorca for his holidays."

"Don't be so stupid. I'm on the passenger's side. I'm the one who'd get injured if you crashed into it—Gary, be careful. STOP!"

"Mum, for goodness' sake, why?"

"A car might T-bone you at the junction."

"I have the right of way. There's a stop sign for oncoming traffic. Calm down."

"Don't you tell me to calm down! You calm down; you're going to cause an accident. You're driving like a crazy person! You're speeding!"

"Mum, I'm doing 30 mph in a 30-mph zone."

"Your speed dial might be out of whack. I'm not paying for your speeding ticket."

"Please let me drive."

"Then drive *properly* . . . you're too damned close to that car—stop tailgating."

I squinted and saw a vehicle in the distance. "What car?"

"The green car, the one in front . . . you're right up their arse."

"That's a red car, and it's over a hundred yards away from us."

"Bloody slow down, concentrate, and stop trying to show off. Carole's a far better driver than you."

"Carole hasn't got a driving licence, you numpty."

"Exactly. The meningitis must have eaten away half of your brain."

"Your nagging ate the other half—so you're travelling in a car with a man with no brain."

"Feels like it, too. Slow down. I'd be safer walking there."

"With sketchy knees and dodgy hips. I'd put money on Brian the Snail from *The Magic Roundabout* to get there before you do." I felt her green eyes burrowing into the side of my face.

"You aren't checking the rear-view mirror."

"I am."

"I'm looking at you, son; you're a liar. You know what happens to liars."

"Don't go there, Mum."

"Use your mirror—you're being bloody reckless."

"Mirror, indicate, manoeuvre. I've passed my advanced driving course, and I'm now a trained police driver. Mum, please stop nagging."

"Call yourself a police officer; you're breaking too many laws. If I didn't have all this arthritis going on, I'd arrest you myself."

"Do you want me to stop the car so we can exchange places?"

"I'd be much safer than travelling in this car with a show-off. You think you're a bloody Grand Prix driver. I'd feel safer if Stevie Wonder drove me to Marks and Sparks."

"Good one! You may be the world's worst back-seat passenger, but I love your wit—in that respect, we are two peas in a pod."

"Focus on the road, you maniac. Your wit? (Chuckles) If your wit was made of shit, you'd be constipated!"

"Hey! Watch your language, or you might get in trouble with the Big Guy upstairs!"

"If you keep driving like this, I'll join the angels sooner than I thought!"

"Yes, Mum."

"Gary! Watch the traffic light. Don't be an amber gambler. Slow down; slow down!"

"For goodness' sake, it's still on green."

"It will bloody change soon. You need to have your eyes tested for colour blindness. While you're at it—retake the driving test."

That was our mum; she was seldom lost for words and always had a comeback comment that made you laugh or pull out your hair. However, it was impossible to stay angry with her. Mum would chuckle and tease you like nothing had happened.

Before the funeral service, Carole made one more request to accompany her to the funeral home (parlour), where Mum's body was being "shown." I hated the idea of seeing my dead mum and resisted. Carole reminded me of all she had done for me these past years. The guilt pep-talk worked, and we arrived at the spooky funeral place with fear and trembling.

My four daughters, Nadia, Tasha, and twins Gina and Anja, had written their nanna goodbye notes and given me cuddly toys to put in her casket—they loved their nanna and were also heartbroken by her death. My eldest daughter, Nadia, wanted me to take one last picture of her as she was devastated that she couldn't come with me.

Carole and I arrived at the funeral home and were led into a room. Mum had been beautifully prepared, and it looked like she was deep asleep. My mouth was bone dry; my hands were shaking. However, Carole was white as a sheet and looked in acute distress. I did what I tended to do and brought dry humour into this awkward situation. Mum had always said her head was like a tough walnut and impossible to crack.

I pretended to knock on her head and slyly tapped the wooded casket, which was hard as a rock. "Hello, is anyone at home in there?" Ventriloquist Gary began to do a double act with his deceased mother. "Mum, it's Carole and your favourite child, Doody. We know you're in there!" I put on my best softly-spoken Welsh accent: "Eat your damn vegetables! If you don't, The Lord will strike you down with the Bell's Palsy!" Carole started to snigger. Mum's 'voice' said, "You don't want to end up looking like your ugly big brother, do you?"

Carole started to laugh, calling me "a silly sod" and "stupid balls," but it broke the ice. I solemnly put my children's letters on her body and their gifts by her folded hands.

I had one more task to perform and needed to take a photo of her for my kids. When she died, there was slight bruising on one side of her face from tubes going into her mouth. So, I decided to go to the other side of the casket and take a picture from her unbruised side. The only way to achieve this was to crawl under the coffin. I ducked down and went under, avoiding the table legs that supported the casket.

"For God's sake, Gary, if our mother could see you now—you flippin' idiot. She was right about Dad's lunacy genes being passed down to you." Carole held her hand to her mouth and sniggered. Unfortunately, I got up way too early in a hurry to complete the awkward task. As I got back to my feet, my back hit the casket, and Mum started tipping over to one side.

Carole reacted as quickly as a diamond rattlesnake striking its prey and caught the casket at a 45-degree tilt. We avoided the ignominy of Mum's body lying on the funeral home floor like a crime scene.

My eyes were wide open, and I held both hands to my face in

shock. We both started to laugh, which turned into tears of sadness and howls of laughter. We cried and snorted and cried again. We replaced the casket and moved the stuffed toys and letters to their rightful place. I snapped a few photos and squeezed around the end of the casket, avoiding further "upsetting of the apple cart" incidents.

At the best of times, I find funeral directors particularly creepy, and as we opened the door to leave Mum for the last time, the undertaker was lurking outside; he must have heard us both laughing and sobbing. I didn't care what he thought; it was Carole's and my last date with our mum.

Paul and his wife, Julia, joined us for the funeral, as did the Welsh contingent from Llanelli and one of Dad's nephews. When the time came to talk about her at the eulogy, I shared how Mum was a daddy's girl. William Green, the father of at least eleven children, dropped dead in the family home. Shortly afterwards, Mum and her siblings returned from school to find their mother had left her children a note on the dining table telling them she wanted to start a new life without them. My grandmother had abandoned them; this included Mum's brother, a mere toddler not yet out of nappies (diapers). Mum said they were all shocked and gripped by fear and loss. Sent away with two of the 11 siblings, she endured a life of servitude until she reached the legal adult age, and promptly left home to join the Women's Royal Naval Service. Mum met a dashing young RAF flyer and wed. Mum married Denis Trew and the RAF; she was proud as punch when her youngest son was commissioned to fly in the Navy.

The sombre atmosphere quickly lifted as stories about her were shared. I recalled attending the survival course in the New Forest in Hampshire—about an hour-and-a-half journey by car from Mum's home. The exact whereabouts of the survival course were unknown to us, as it was classified information. However, by scoping out the area on maps before the start of the course, I noticed a couple of key parking spots in the vicinity. The Seafield Park survival course would take up to a couple of weeks of living from the land, equipped with a parachute canopy, a flying suit, a knife, socks, and boots. At the end of the ordeal, there would be an "escape, evade, and interrogation" phase, which didn't sound like fun. We even had a body cavity inspection in case we hid food or money in our bums. I mean, who wants to eat a chocolate bar that's been shoved up someone's hairy arse? We had heard we would be forced to run and perform survival exercises, with the only food being the killing and skinning of a solitary bunny rabbit.

Mum was concerned about her 26-year-old son's wellbeing. She assured me she would do some reconnaissance beforehand. Lone, the twins, and herself would find potential drop-off locations and attempt to leave some food there for my colleagues and me, totally against the Fleet Air Arm's rules and regulations.

To cut a long story short, my pals and I pulled a fast one over the eagle-eyed instructors and legged it to a random location where we knew there was a car park. We arrived at the drop-off spot, and I saw an enormous blue, white and red Tesco bag. I grabbed the bag, opened it, and discovered a smorgasbord of food: sausage rolls, pies, peanuts, pop, chocolate, and crisps. She'd written on the plastic bag in humungous letters, "To G.T. Love from Mum!" We divvied up the contraband and smuggled it back into the camp. That was my mum to a tee. She would do anything for her children.

I shared many funny stories about her, but keeping my composure was tough. We played *Summer Breeze* by the Isley Brothers, as she loved that song—driving me up the wall with her constant singing. Mum had endured much suffering in her life. Not only did she have to tolerate poverty, the death of a parent, and the cruel abandonment by others, but she also put up with the pain and agony of rheumatoid arthritis, which literally ate away her bones. Despite all she had been through in the past and the present, I remember her always smiling, having a compassionate and kind heart, and laughing heartily.

Mum had a terrific sense of humour. How many parents would dress their son and his friend in nurses' outfits to formally meet their girlfriend's parents? She regularly dyed my hair in various colours when I went through the punk and New Romantic phases at university, and she never judged me, unlike so many others. I couldn't forget when she peed herself laughing as we watched the silly *Airplane* movie with Leslie Neilson. Mum also loved the film *Angela's Ashes*, which reminded her so much of what she had gone through. I also loved to make Mum laugh, and she accepted my whack-a-doodle antics with a grin, constantly referring to the fact I'd been "touched" with the "madness," like my Uncle Patrick.

Leaving Mum to return overseas to Canada was traumatic for both of us, as Mum hated any of her children or grandchildren leaving. I caught her crying a few hours after arriving at her home and asked her what the matter was? She said she had started to dread when we would leave again, even though we were due to stay there for three or four weeks. She struggled with abandonment issues for most of her life. Mum also dearly loved her grandchildren; she had nine of them at her death (four daughters of mine, including identical twins, a son and two daughters from Paul, and the identical twin boys from Carole).

Mum had a strong Christian faith. How ironic that after all the years we spent quarrelling about her mean and cold God, I took her service and shared about God's love.

As Gwendoline Lillian Trew was cremated, I played Johnny Nash's *I Can See Clearly Now*, because I knew she loved the song. It was fitting as the song talks about overcoming obstacles, rain, and dark clouds. But now that she was at peace and in the arms of Jesus, there was a silver lining for her. No more pain, no more bad memories, just sunlight and blue skies lined with her very own rainbow. Her casket rolled towards curtains, closing for Gwendoline Trew's final performance: "Earth to earth. Ashes to ashes. Dust to dust."

It's easy for me to imagine that in the presence of the Holy Trinity, she's making the Heavenly Hosts laugh as she reminds the Lord to eat his vegetables!

Gwendoline Lillian Trew (1930-2008)

EPILOGUE

I PENNED THIS MEMOIR AT THE BEHEST OF MY TWIN DAUGHTERS, Anja and Gina, who were adamant the stories I'd recounted to them should be passed down to their offspring and their progeny. Having a lovely yet reclusive father made it a challenge to get to know any of my extended family, never mind retrieve stories and anecdotes from them. I'm thankful to have reconnected with my cousins, the Brits in the UK and Australia, and the Germans who live in Germany and Morocco.

I felt a burning desire to share my Knoll experience. I am cognisant of the generational trauma that has occurred in my family. I'm sure almost every child (and teacher) attending the Knoll School grappled with trauma that had been passed down through the generations. I thoroughly recommend Mark Wolynn's book, *It Didn't Start With You* (How Inherited Family Trauma Shapes Who We Are and How to End the Cycle), Penguin Books, 2016. At the Knoll school, the trauma chickens came to roost for me.

This memoir is about my truth as I both experienced and saw it. I'm sure there have been many Knoll School for Boys attendees who loved their experience there and went on to live a happy and joyous life. Congratulations to you all for succeeding in your chosen life and career paths. I have seen several ex-pupil comments suggesting that experiencing the harshness of Knoll School was part of the "growing-up phase" in their lives and helped make them the people they are today. On the other hand, I spent much time collecting stories from ex-pupils. I decided to include some of their verbatim quotes in the memoir.

My time at The Knoll School was an incredibly challenging experience, and I'm aware that many others shared the same sentiment. Despite the difficulties, the support of my friends and acquaintances helped me find moments of laughter amidst the adversity. However, it's important to note my laughter served as a coping mechanism and shouldn't be mistaken for genuine enjoyment. A few years after my departure, The Knoll School permanently closed its doors, and I couldn't be more relieved.

Working in child protection investigations for several years has helped me to understand the nuances of abuse and neglect. Many staff members were complicit in paying no heed to what had happened, and several were downright wicked in the abuse handed out regularly. I have changed various characters' names, as we all do things when we are younger that we regret; survival of the fittest sometimes makes us engage in behaviours which, with hindsight, make us cringe. One friend, an ex-Knoll attendee, recently "bumped" into the character "Skinner" in a large store in Brighton. Skinner approached my friend and acted like they were old buddies. As Skinner looked dishevelled and rather unwell, the friend told him they were far from pals and was glad that life had not treated him well.

I forgave Skinner and his sidekick, Arnold Fickle, a youth with no moral compass; he was always willing to do Skinner's dirty work. I hope others will forgive me for not being present, turning a blind eye or standing up for them in their own hour of need. I made many poor decisions during my time at the Knoll.

Despite the passage of time, the memories still lingered,

making writing this book a cathartic experience. When my old friends and I reminisce, we tell stories that leave the younger generation in disbelief over how difficult it was. Schools in the UK have made successful strides since the '70s, and now there is an increased emphasis on promoting tolerance, diversity, and respect among students.

The Trew family was dysfunctional yet very loving during the 1960s and 1970s. I was a happy kid growing up—until the Knoll School era. My second memoir (the prequel) includes much of my journey leading up to attendance at the Knoll School, where our quirkiness and warmth are highlighted. Conversations with my mother and, much more recently, with Paul and, to a lesser extent, Carole helped me assemble much of the narrative.

Feel free to visit my website, **www.garytrew.net**. The website offers news, new releases, resources, and additional content for *The Hate Game*.

Gary Trew in 1976

RESOURCES
DON'T SCREAM IN THE SILENCE.

UNITED KINGDOM

Child Abuse

CHILDLINE: 0800 1111 Get help and advice about a wide range of issues, talk to a counsellor online. You can also send ChildLine an email or post on the message boards.

www.childline.org.uk

SURVIVORS UK: Helpline: 0845 1221201. Survivors UK provides information, support and counselling for men who have been raped or sexually abused. Thousands of men contact them each year.

www.survivor.org

HELP FOR ADULT VICTIMS OF CHILD ABUSE (HAVOCA): HAVOCA is run by survivors for adult survivors of child abuse. We provide support, friendship and advice for any adult whose life has been affected by childhood abuse.

www.havoc.org

Bullying

KIDSCAPE: Kidscape is an award-winning charity that offers practical help. Parent Advice Line: 07496 682785, WhatsApp: 07496 682785.

www.kidscape.org.uk

NATIONAL BULLYING HELPLINE: Information and advice for anyone dealing with bullying. Helpline: 0300 323 0169.

RESOURCES

www.nationalbullyinghelpline.co.uk

Mental Health

SAMARITANS (UK) 116123 Available 24/7. Suicide prevention. Depression and anxiety support

Eating disorders & negative body image helplines

BEAT (UK) 0808 801 0677. Provides support for anybody affected by eating disorders, anorexia, bulimia.

CANADA

Child Abuse

CANADIAN CENTRE FOR CHILD PROTECTION. All of Canada.

www.protectchildren.ca

REPORTING CHILD ABUSE in BC – 1-800-663-9122: Ministry of Children & Families.

www2gov.bc.ca/content/public-safety/protecting-children/reporting-child-abuse

VICTIM LINK BC is a support program for victims of crime and trauma across B.C. and Yukon. This service is toll-free, confidential, and available 24 hours a day, 7 days a week in different languages. Call Toll Free: 1-800-563-0808

CHILDREN'S AID SOCIETY: Various Child Protection Agencies in Ontario.

www.oacas.org/childrens-aid-child-protection

Bullying

BULLYING CANADA: Telephone(877) 352-4497 Prefer to text?

Text us anytime! Simply send an SMS message to: (877) 352-4497.

www.bullyingcanada.ca

Mental Health

MENTAL HEALTH CRISIS LINE: If you or someone you know is in immediate crisis or has suicide-related concerns: Call 1-833-456-4566 toll free (In QC: 1-866-277-3553)

For More Information - visit the Resources page on Gary's Website: www.garytrew.net

A PERCENTAGE OF ANY PROFITS MADE FROM THIS MEMOIR WILL BE DONATED TO VANCOUVER HOLOCAUST EDUCATION CENTRE.

ACKNOWLEDGEMENTS
A NOTE

I want to thank my daughters, Nadia, Natashja, Gina and Anja, who have shown me that life is one grand adventure. We have shared highs and lows, yet I am here today due to your incredible love for me. Despite my flaws, you have been by my side and helped me laugh at life's funny and sad occasions.

Nadia, you share Uncle Pat's looney-tune gene with me and are one of the funniest people I know. You're so brilliant, a go-getter who deserves the highest praise from your dad. Tasha, you've achieved so much in a few years, and I'm very proud of you. Although reserved, you shy away from drama and focus on the positives in life. Gina and Anja, my constant buddies and partners in crime, I owe my life to you. You pulled me out of the gloom and despair that I went through in the challenging years of living in Nova Scotia. I'm so proud of you both, and you still manage to fill your old man's heart with joy and laughter. Thanks to Hannah Smith for bringing so much joy to our hearts.

Shelley, my resplendent partner, you have reawakened my sense of being loved and cherished. Your acts of kindness and tender-heartedness will never fade from my memory. I believe God brought us together after our losses, and I'm so lucky to have you in my life.

My sister Carole, I know you didn't want to be mentioned in any capacity, so tough titties! You have been a rock to your boys and me, and I love you dearly. Your life of sacrifice and devotion is truly humbling.

My brother Paul, I'm glad we finally connected after all these years. You are so bright and witty, and I admire how you have been a wonderful husband to Julia and a fab dad to your children. Thank you for being so helpful in recounting memories and moments (especially) in the second memoir, which focuses on our family's early years together. Brother, I look forward to seeing you again when I return to Blighty!

I want to express my gratitude to my fantastic alpha and beta readers for their help in writing this memoir. Thanks to Ann O'Donnell, Ashy, and especially Shelley. I also want to acknowledge the Fiverr crew - Crystal R., Gloria M., Tiffany, and Maddy D. for their valuable and candid feedback, and Oskar Leonard for the proofreading.

A massive thank you to Kerryn Du Plessis for editing the initial draft and the amazing Sandra Cain for editing *The Hate Game*. I truly appreciate your outstanding editing and invaluable advice.

Shout out to old and new friends, Robert S., William S., Mervyn C., George B., Dave C., Billy S., Dave C., and Derek M., for sharing memories with me. Dez M., you have been an enormous help. Although in different years, we attended Middle Street Primary and Knoll School together. Up the Seagulls!

Finally, thank you, God, for giving me a new life.

Billy & Gary: Still pals after 50 years!

ABOUT THE AUTHOR

Close friends, family, and colleagues describe Gary Trew as a funny British guy living in Canada. His quick-witted humour has been perfected as a child protection social worker, minister of religion and police officer. Gary holds two university degrees: a B.Sc. (Biochemistry & Chemistry—Birmingham) and a BSW (Social Work—Victoria), overcoming brain trauma from meningitis and several beatings received at Knoll School.

Gary has written many plays and skits for non-profit groups and churches. He also writes humorous fiction under the pen name Denny Darke (his dad's first name and his grandma's maiden name). Gary can only blame his father, Denis, for passing the noir humour gene to him. Gary is thankful his dad brainwashed him with slapstick comedies like *Monty Python* and *The Goodies* and encouraged him to read books by Joseph Heller.

Despite Gary's "non-education" at the Knoll School, he devoured books like *Cancer Ward*, *First Circle*, and *The Gulag Archipelago*. His dyslexia didn't help him remember characters' names like "Oleg Filimonovich Kostoglotov" and "Ivan Denisovich Shukhov"—never mind spelling the likes of "Bolshevik" or the Russian author's last name. However, Gary read books because he missed so much schooling, and The Atari 2600 or Nintendo Entertainment System hadn't been invented. So, he liked to be reminded that although life was often miserable and gloomy, at least he wasn't *living the dream* in the Soviet Union.

Books have always been a source of solace for Gary, helping him to escape, appreciate, and dream. His work as an investigator with abused and neglected children and youth has taught him the value of laughter in the face of life's challenges. Gary attributes his ability to find humour in difficult situations to his long-suffering wife and his four spirited daughters, who have inherited his resilience and ability to laugh through their own struggles.

He may not have Prince Harry's popularity, but Gary has kept his English accent and has met Harry's dad and uncle. HRH, the King (then a lowly Prince), muttered a few words to Gary on his passing out parade as a Sub-lieutenant. Harry's uncle, HRH Prince Edward, used Gary's officer's mess, or dining area, when on secondment during Edward's brief service in the Royal Marines.

Gary Trew: 38 Flight, BRNC Dartmouth, UK

Gary Trew: 2024

ALSO BY GARY TREW
AKA DENNY DARKE

The Man With The Pink Sombrero by Denny Darke

"International Crime meets Dark Humorous Fiction"

Have you ever yearned for a much-needed escape to a distant, exotic getaway? Eager to escape the hullabaloo and drama occurring back home? What if, just as you settle into your tropical paradise, you uncover the shocking truth that your partner is being pursued by a merciless hitman from a ruthless cartel?

Welcome to Lucy Myers' world, as partner Jimmy experiences a series of unfortunate events that lead him to break a solemn promise to save himself, his new-found buddy, and his own family's lives.

This is **a zany tale** of a vacation gone very, very wrong...

A selection of Reviews:

"Dark, intelligent and laugh aloud funny."

"A laugh out loud story from start to finish!"

"This is genuinely funny. Think Joseph Heller meets Ricky Gervais meets John Cleese. A rip roaring tale in the vein of fear and loathing in Las Vegas but set in Mexico amongst crazy cops and murderous cartels. Look out for *los cocodrilos* and check your freezer!"

"This book was a giggle from start to finish. Denny Darke the author is refreshing and I look forward to his next book."

"Well worth a read unless you've had a sense of humour bypass."

www.darkematter.ca

www.ingramcontent.com/pod-product-compliance
Lightning Source LLC
Chambersburg PA
CBHW060553080526
44585CB00013B/543